Twayne's English Authors Series

EDITOR OF THIS VOLUME

Herbert Sussman

Northeastern University

Charles Dickens

TEAS 314

Charles Dickens

CHARLES DICKENS

By HARLAND S. NELSON

Luther College

TWAYNE PUBLISHERS

A DIVISION OF G. K. HALL & CO., BOSTON

Library of Congress Cataloging in Publication Data

Nelson, Harland S.
Charles Dickens.

(Twayne's English authors series ; TEAS 314)
Bibliography: pp. 249–256
Includes index.
1. Dickens, Charles, 1812–1870—Criticism and interpretation.
2. Dickens, Charles, 1812–1870—Authorship.
I. Title   II. Series.
PR4588.N36   823'.914   81–5050
ISBN 0–8057–6805–X   AACR2

PR
4588
N36

For my wife Corinne
and for our son and our daughters
Hilary, Sarah, and Catherine

Contents

About the Author

Harland S. Nelson is professor of English at Luther College, Decorah, Iowa, where he has taught freshman composition and literature, modern fiction, Victorian literature, and film since 1962. He has also taught at the University of Missouri and at the University of Connecticut, and as Fulbright professor of American literature at the University of Bergen in Norway and the University of Innsbruck in Austria. He has published articles on Dickens, Joseph Conrad, E. M. Forster, Stephen Crane, John Steinbeck, and John Updike, and several film critiques. His B.A. degree is from Concordia College, Moorhead, Minnesota, his M.A. from Washington State University, and his Ph.D. from the University of Minnesota.

Preface

This book is an approach to Dickens, not a survey, either of his work or of his critics. My main idea has been to send readers back to Dickens with a viewpoint from which they can survey him themselves, and with a chance to appreciate him as his contemporaries did. So I begin with three chapters, a third of the book, about Dickens and the way he did his writing and publishing, because the work was the expression of the man, and the qualities of the man and the way his work reached his readers had a lot to do with his popularity. In the rest of the book I turn directly to Dickens's fiction, discussing first the elements of a Dickens novel as a reader takes them in, then working through one novel according to what I develop in that discussion, and finally describing what I see emerging from such reading as Dickens's vision of things. (Along the way I do what I can to indicate what other writers on Dickens have said and are saying, drawing support from some of them and arguing with others.)

The book's general direction, then, is from form to idea, and I end with Dickens's ideas: both his conscious convictions, and what comes across as his unmeditated intuition—what seemed to him the given in human experience. This order of development makes a kind of parallel to Dickens's concerns, first with his art and craft as he practiced them in his long career, but finally and always with what life is about, and ought to be about.

HARLAND S. NELSON

Luther College

Acknowledgments

Acknowledging my debts, I begin with my gratitude for the permission I have received to use material from other published work.

To Harcourt Brace Jovanovich for permission to reprint passages from Virginia Woolf, *Moments of Being*, ed. Jeanne Schulkind (1976).

To W. W. Norton & Company, Inc., for permission to quote from the Norton Critical Editions of *Hard Times* (1966) and *Bleak House* (1977), ed. George Ford and Sylvère Monod.

To Oxford University Press for permission to quote from the following works: the Pilgrim Edition of *The Letters of Charles Dickens*, ed. Madeline House, Graham Storey, and Kathleen Tillotson (1965–); the Clarendon Editions of *Oliver Twist*, ed. Kathleen Tillotson (1966), *The Mystery of Edwin Drood* (Margaret Cardwell, 1972), and *Dombey and Son* (Alan Horsman, 1974); and Philip Collins's introduction to his edition of *Charles Dickens: The Public Readings* (1975).

To Penguin Books Ltd for permission to quote from the Penguin English Library editions of *Great Expectations*, ed. Angus Calder (1965), *David Copperfield* (Trevor Blount, 1966), *Little Dorrit* (John Holloway, 1967), *Martin Chuzzlewit* (P. N. Furbank, 1968), *A Christmas Carol* (Michael Slater, 1971), *Our Mutual Friend* (Stephen Gill, 1971), *The Pickwick Papers* (Robert L. Patten, 1972), *The Old Curiosity Shop* (Angus Easson, 1972), *Barnaby Rudge* (Gordon Spence, 1973), and *Nicholas Nickleby* (Michael Slater, 1978); and from Angus Calder's note on the text of *Great Expectations*, Raymond Williams's introduction to *Dombey and Son* (Peter Fairclough, 1970), and Angus Wilson's introduction to *The Mystery of Edwin Drood* (Arthur J. Cox, 1974).

To the Bodley Head for permission to quote from the Nonesuch Edition of *The Letters of Charles Dickens*, ed. Walter Dexter (1938).

I also thank the Huntington Library, San Marino, California, for permission to reproduce the portrait of Dickens appearing as the frontispiece.

I thank the Wilson Library of the University of Minnesota for permission to reproduce the monthly part cover design of *Bleak House*.

I have had the cooperation and assistance of many persons and institutions. My colleagues in the English department at Luther College have supported me in all ways, ranging from warm and continuous interest to relieving me of many chores so that I might get on with my book. Students in several seminars in recent years have given me ideas that I have used. Luther College awarded me the sabbatical leave in 1978 during which I did most of the work on the book, and a Faculty Growth Award from the American Lutheran Church helped me meet research expenses. The Graduate School of the University of Minnesota appointed me an Honorary Fellow of the University, which opened all university facilities to me during my leave, on the recommendation of Edward Griffin and J. Lawrence Mitchell of the English department at the University of Minnesota. The Wilson Library of the University of Minnesota provided me with a carrel all the while I read and wrote there, and among the library staff Anne Workman earned my special gratitude. Austin McLean, director of Special Collections at Wilson Library, and his assistants John Jenson and Kathy Tezla took an interest in my work going beyond the call of duty. I did final writing and revising at Luther College's Preus Library, where library director Leigh Jordahl made it possible for me to keep my own hours at a crucial stage, and where a superb interlibrary loan service operated by Ruth Reitan and the painstaking photographic services of Harlan Sanderson provided me with everything I needed to supplement the library's own resources.

Early in my Dickens studies the late Ford K. Brown kindly made the manuscript of his then unpublished *Fathers of the Victorians* (Cambridge, 1961) available to me, and his account of the Evangelical reformers of English life lies behind my view of the Victorian era. Over the years I have benefited in various

Acknowledgments

ways from the work of many other scholars and critics as well. Some of them I can specifically identify, and do, in my notes and bibliography. The work of others has so mingled with my own, either from long familiarity or from close harmony, that I cannot disentangle it from what I found out for myself. To all, my thanks.

My debts to two men go beyond these, and beyond specifying, except to say that I owe, and feel, the deepest gratitude for professional and personal enrichment and encouragement to G. Robert Stange, and to Samuel Holt Monk.

Finally, my longest debts of all.

To my parents Hartvig and Mabel Nelson, who always knew their eldest son would never make a farmer, and never thought him a failure on that account.

And to Corinne Rye Nelson, whose typing and indexing are the expression in this book of her love that has borne me up in writing it.

A Note on Texts and Conventions

For quotations from Dickens's novels, I use the Clarendon Edition texts of *Oliver Twist, Dombey and Son*, and *The Mystery of Edwin Drood*; the Norton Critical Editions of *Bleak House* and *Hard Times*; and for the rest, the Penguin English Library editions. To facilitate reference in any edition of Dickens's novels, I identify passages by chapter number using Arabic numerals, adding book numbers in Roman numerals where relevant (*Hard Times, Little Dorrit, A Tale of Two Cities, Our Mutual Friend*): thus *Bleak House* (36), *Our Mutual Friend* (II, 9).

For Dickens's letters I use the Pilgrim Edition as far as possible at this date (through 1846). Thereafter I quote from John Forster's text of them if his *Life of Charles Dickens* is the only authority, which according to the Pilgrim editors (I, xi) is the case for nearly all Dickens's letters to Forster after 1842, the date with which the first volume of his original three–volume edition ends. Otherwise I quote from the Nonesuch Edition if the letter appears there; if not, from the work I found it in. For both Pilgrim and Nonesuch I use Roman numerals for volume, Arabic for page.

For quotations from Forster's *Life* I use the version that is the basis for all reprinted editions: the 1876 two–volume revision of his original 1872–74 three–volume edition. I have modified the traditional practice of giving pagination in the *Life* according to J. W. T. Ley's 1928 annotated edition by also giving book and chapter, for example V, ii, 392; anyone lucky enough to have access to Ley is served thereby, and the rest of us can look up any edition of Forster. I cite Edgar Johnson's *Charles Dickens: His Tragedy and Triumph* by page number for specific borrowings, by book and chapter (III, i) for summaries.

For quotations from the Bible I use the version that runs in the veins of Dickens's style, the King James.

For brevity and convenience (both in my text and in my notes) I substitute parenthetical references wherever possible, using abbreviations: P for Pilgrim Edition, N for Nonesuch, F for Forster, J for Johnson, and for titles of Dickens's works the following:

AYR	*All the Year Round*	MC	*Martin Chuzzlewit*
BR	*Barnaby Rudge*	MED	*The Mystery of Edwin Drood*
BH	*Bleak House*	NN	*Nicholas Nickleby*
DC	*David Copperfield*	OCS	*The Old Curiosity Shop*
D&S	*Dombey and Son*	OT	*Oliver Twist*
GE	*Great Expectations*	OMF	*Our Mutual Friend*
HT	*Hard Times*	PP	*Pickwick Papers*
HW	*Household Words*	SB	*Sketches by Boz*
LD	*Little Dorrit*	TTC	*A Tale of Two Cities*
		UT	*The Uncommercial Traveller*

Chronology

1812 Charles John Huffam Dickens born 7 February at Land-
      port (Portsmouth). Father: John Dickens, clerk, Navy Pay
      Office, son of butler and housekeeper, Crewe Hall. Mother:
      Elizabeth Barrow, daughter of senior clerk, Navy Pay Of-
      fice. Brothers and sisters living to adulthood (two d. in
      infancy): Frances ("Fanny"), b. 1810; Letitia, b. 1816;
      Frederick, b. 1820; Alfred, b. 1822; Augustus, b. 1827.

1814–ᅠJohn Dickens transferred to London 1814, to Chatham
1822 (near Rochester) 1817, back to London late 1822. CD at
      school in Chatham 1821–22. Family settles winter 1822–23
      at Camden Town, northern suburb of London.

1824 Increasing financial difficulty; CD put to work at shoe-
      blacking warehouse February–June. John Dickens im-
      prisoned for debt during spring; family (except CD) joins
      him in Marshalsea Prison lodgings.

1824–ᅠDay pupil at Wellington House Academy, London.
1827

1827–ᅠSolicitor's clerk; studies shorthand.
1828

1829–ᅠFree-lance reporter at Doctors Commons courts. Regular
1831 reader at British Museum from eighteenth birthday for
      several years. Meets Maria Beadnell (1830). Studies act-
      ing.

1831–ᅠShorthand reporter of Parliamentary proceedings for *Mir-
1832 ror of Parliament* (from 1831 or early 1832). Reporter
      for evening newspaper *True Sun* March–July 1832. Bad
      cold prevents theater audition. Beadnells send Maria to
      finishing school in Paris 1832.

1833 Break with Maria Beadnell in May. First published story,
      "A Dinner at Poplar Walk," December (eight more publ.
      in *Monthly Magazine* January 1834–February 1835.)

1834   Reporter for *Morning Chronicle* from August; publishes there and elsewhere. Moves to Furnival's Inn, Holborn.

1835   Engaged to Catherine Hogarth, daughter of George Hogarth, editor of *Evening Chronicle.*

1836   *Sketches by Boz* (first series) publ. February. *Pickwick Papers* begins publication in monthly parts April (continues through November 1837). CD marries Catherine Hogarth 2 April; sixteen-year-old sister Mary Hogarth comes to stay with them at Furnival's Inn. Plays produced: *The Strange Gentleman* and *The Village Coquettes.* Leaves *Morning Chronicle* November, accepts editorship of new monthly *Bentley's Miscellany. Sketches by Boz* (second series) publ. December. First meeting with John Forster December.

1837   *PP* continues through November; publ. in 1 vol. November (CD's regular practice on completion of serial publication; mention omitted hereafter). Son Charles Culliford Boz born 6 January (other children and birthdates: Mary 1838, Kate Macready 1839, Walter Landor 1841, Francis Jeffrey 1844, Alfred Tennyson 1845, Sydney Smith 1847, Henry Fielding 1849, Dora Annie 1850 [d. 1851], Edward Bulwer Lytton 1852). *Oliver Twist* begins monthly in *Bentley's Miscellany* February (continues through April 1839). CD moves to house at 48 Doughty St. April (now Dickens House, home of Dickens Fellowship). Mary Hogarth dies 7 May; *PP* and *OT* suspended one month.

1838   *OT* continues in *BM.* CD travels in Yorkshire February. Mary (Mamie) born 6 March. *Nicholas Nickleby* begins in monthly parts April (continues through October 1839). *OT* publ. in 3 vols. November (before completion of serial publication).

1839   *OT* continues in *BM* through April. *NN* continues through October. CD resigns editorship of *BM* in January. Planning begins July for weekly periodical edited by CD. Kate born 29 October. CD moves to 1 Devonshire Terrace, York Gate, Regent's Park December (family home until 1851).

1840   First number of *Master Humphrey's Clock* 4 April. *The Old Curiosity Shop* begins in *MHC* 25 April (continuously from 16 May through 6 February 1841). *MHC*, vol. 1, publ. October.

1841   *OCS* continues through 6 February. Walter born 8 February. *Barnaby Rudge* begins in *MHC* 13 February (continuing weekly through final part 27 November). *MHC*, vol. 2, publ. April. CD travels in Scotland with Catherine June–July; decides (September) to visit United States. One-vol. editions of *OCS* and *BR* publ. December (also *MHC*, vol. 3).

1842   CD travels with Catherine in United States and Canada January–June. Catherine's fifteen-year-old sister Georgina becomes permanent member of CD household. *American Notes* publ. in 2 vols. October.

1843   *Martin Chuzzlewit* begins in monthly parts January (continues through July 1844). November CD tells Forster of intent to go abroad for extended period. *A Christmas Carol* publ. December.

1844   *MC* continues through July. Francis (Frank) born 15 January. Early discussions of a new periodical (spring). CD family to Italy July, settling in Genoa. CD travels in Italy November; in London December to read *The Chimes* to friends. *The Chimes* (Christmas book) publ. December. CD leaves publishers Chapman and Hall for Bradbury and Evans.

1845   CD travels with Catherine in Italy January–April; family returns to London July. Idea for weekly periodical (title *The Cricket*) July. Manages and performs in amateur production of Jonson's *Every Man in His Humour* September. Alfred born 28 October. CD agrees November to edit new daily newspaper. *The Cricket on the Hearth* (Christmas book) publ. December.

1846   First number of *Daily News*, edited by CD, publ. 21 January; CD resigns 9 February. *Pictures from Italy* publ. May. CD family goes abroad May, settling at Lausanne, Switzerland, moving to Paris November. CD begins writing *Dombey and Son* June. *D&S* begins in monthly parts October (continues through April 1848). *The Battle of Life* (Christmas book) publ. December.

1847   *D&S* continues. CD family returns to London February.

Sydney Smith born 18 April. CD provides active advice and superintendence for establishment by heiress Angela Burdett-Coutts of Urania Cottage, for helping prostitutes begin new lives abroad. (CD collaborates with Miss Coutts in this and many other welfare projects for the next dozen years.) Cheap Edition of CD's works begun (in weekly numbers and complete volumes).

1848 *D&S* continues through April. CD directs, acts in amateur theatricals May–July in London, Manchester, Birmingham, Edinburgh, Glasgow. Sister Fanny (Mrs. Henry Burnett) dies of TB September. *The Haunted Man* (last Christmas book) publ. December.

1849 Henry Fielding born 15 January. *David Copperfield* begins in monthly parts May (continues through November 1850). Letters to *Times* November protesting public hangings. *The Life of Our Lord* written for CD's children (unpubl. until 1934). Thinking again of weekly miscellany toward end of year.

1850 *DC* continues through November. First number of weekly *Household Words* 30 March. Heavy editorial work becomes part of CD's life from now on. (Subeditor W. H. Wills manages CD periodicals until ill health forces resignation 1868). Dora Annie born 16 August. Amateur theatricals November at home of novelist Bulwer-Lytton, with whom CD promotes Guild of Literature and Art.

1851 Amateur theatricals (benefits for Guild of Literature and Art) through August. Catherine in poor health from March. Father John Dickens dies March. Daughter Dora Annie dies April. CD moves to Tavistock House November (family home until 1860). Begins writing *Bleak House* November.

1852 *Bleak House* begins in monthly parts March (continues through September 1853). Edward Bulwer Lytton (Plorn) born 13 March. CD works with Miss Coutts on low-income housing. Amateur theatricals.

1853 *BH* continues through September. CD family in Boulogne summer. CD completes *A Child's History of England* September (running in *HW* since early 1851). Tours Italy with Augustus Egg and Wilkie Collins October–December. Gives first public reading (a benefit) from his novels December in Birmingham. *CHE* publ. complete December.

1854 *Hard Times* begins weekly publication in *HW* 1 April (to bolster slipping circulation); continues through 12 August. CD family in Boulogne summer and early fall.

1855 Maria Beadnell (now Mrs. Henry Winter) writes CD February; CD disillusioned when they meet. CD begins writing *Little Dorrit* May. Amateur theatrical production of Collins's *The Lighthouse* June. CD family to Paris October. *Little Dorrit* begins in monthly parts December (continues through June 1857).

1856 *LD* continues. John Forster marries. Negotiations concluded March for purchase of Gad's Hill Place near Rochester. CD returns to London April, family to Boulogne in June (until August). CD–Collins collaboration on play *The Frozen Deep* completed October.

1857 *LD* continues through June. Library Edition of CD's works begun. *The Frozen Deep* performed January in Tavistock House. Gad's Hill renovated; CD family to Gad's Hill for summer. Hans Christian Andersen visits CD June–July. Son Walter (age sixteen) to India as cadet in East India Co. regiment July. *The Frozen Deep* revived in July, special performance for queen; Ellen Ternan joins cast for August performance in Manchester. CD to Scotland with Collins September. Letter to Forster (August/September) discusses incompatibility of CD and Catherine. CD considers public readings for pay.

1858 First series of public readings by CD from his own works opens 29 April. Separation from Catherine, with considerable publicity and bitterness. Quarrel with Thackeray. First provincial readings August–November, more London readings begin 24 December.

1859 London readings continue to February. CD begins new weekly *All the Year Round* 30 April, closes *HW* down 28 May. Breaks with Bradbury and Evans, returns to Chapman and Hall. *A Tale of Two Cities* (begun in *AYR* opening number) continues weekly through 15 November. Public readings October and at Christmas.

1860   Essays (*The Uncommercial Traveller*) in *AYR* January–
        October. Son Sydney appointed naval cadet January.
        Daughter Kate marries Charles Collins (Wilkie's brother)
        17 July. Brother Alfred dies 27 July. September: CD sells
        Tavistock House, moves to Gad's Hill; burns quantities of
        personal letters; begins writing *Great Expectations*. Be-
        gins publishing *GE* in *AYR* 1 December to stem fading
        circulation.

1861   *GE* continues through 3 August. Public readings in Lon-
        don March–April. Sister Letitia's husband (Henry Austin)
        dies October. Public readings in provinces begin October
        (some readings canceled December on Prince Albert's
        death). Son Charles marries Bessie Evans (daughter of
        CD's former publisher) November.

1862   Public readings continue through January. Readings in
        London March–June. CD decides against Australian read-
        ing tour. To Paris October.

1863   Public readings in Paris January and London March–June.
        Mother Elizabeth Dickens dies 13 September. CD agrees
        late September to begin new novel in the spring. Recon-
        ciled with Thackeray a week before Thackeray's death
        December. Son Walter dies in India 31 December.

1864   Son Frank to India January to enter Bengal Mounted
        Police. *Our Mutual Friend* begins publishing in monthly
        parts May (continues through November 1865). CD's
        health poor; suffering from lameness (probably gout) at
        end of year.

1865   *OMF* continues through November. Son Alfred emigrates
        to Australia May. CD and Ellen Ternan, returning from
        Paris holiday, in train wreck 9 June; CD badly shaken up.

1866   Public readings in England and Scotland April–June; CD
        agrees to another series of fifty. Brother Augustus dies in
        Chicago October.

1867   Charles Dickens Edition begun. Public readings in En-
        gland and Ireland January–May; CD unwell but continues.
        Agrees September to American reading tour. Farewell
        dinner in London 2 November. CD sails 9 November.
        American tour opens in Boston December. CD's health
        worsens. Plans another tour in England for fall 1868.

1868 American readings continue through April in major east coast cities. CD's health very bad. Profits total nearly £19,000. CD returns to England April. Bad health forces subeditor Wills's retirement summer; CD takes over *AYR* duties. Son Edward emigrates to Australia September. Son Henry to Cambridge University October. New series of readings begins 6 October. Brother Frederick dies October. CD gives sensational new reading (death of Nancy in *OT*) to private audience 14 November.

1869 Readings continue in England, Scotland, and Ireland. CD shows symptoms of stroke; provincial series discontinued 20 April by doctor's orders. CD draws up will in May. Begins writing *Mystery of Edwin Drood* late summer–early fall.

1870 Final series of readings, all in London, 11 January–15 March. Private audience with queen mid-March. *Mystery of Edwin Drood* begins in monthly parts April (continuing as far as written through September). Work and social life as usual in May. CD directs private theatrical production late May–early June. Suffers stroke 8 June at Gad's Hill after full day's work. Dies 9 June. Buried Westminster Abbey 14 June.

CHAPTER 1

"Bound to Write Everything"

WHY did Dickens spend his entire life writing stories?"[1]
The question is Virginia Woolf's, but it could be anybody's at the moment of realizing just how much Dickens wrote.
The two volumes of the sketches that he broke into print with;
fourteen novels in thirty years (eight of them running to 875
pages or so in the Penguin English Library edition) and a fifteenth in progress when he died; five novelettes published for
the Christmas trade between 1843 and 1848; the stories for the
annual Christmas numbers of his magazines in the 1850s and
1860s, and other stories and articles he wrote for those magazines; not to speak of the composite writings—articles planned
as collaborations, and articles originally by other persons but
requiring substantial rewriting and editing before publication—
or the letters.[2] Letters and articles are not stories, but they show
that while he wrote stories all his life, the writing did not occupy his whole life, by far; and they show that the kind of
activity which went into writing the fiction characterized much
more of his intellectual life than just the part which he devoted
to his reading public. Dickens himself remarked in a relatively
early letter to his friend and biographer John Forster, "I write
because I can't help it," and to his first love Maria Beadnell a
dozen years later, "I hold my inventive capacity on the stern
condition that it must master my whole life, often have complete
possession of me, make its own demands upon me, and sometimes for months together put everything else away from me."[3]
Dickens of course was talking about his work to Forster (and to
Maria Beadnell covering his retreat), but what he said was true
in a wider sense than he knew, or at least than he meant in these
instances. His daughter Kate said he was "by nature bound to

25

write everything."[4] She was referring specifically to the unfortunate letter (unfortunate because so explicitly accusatory, and
because it got into print) which made for so much bitterness
in Dickens's separation from Catherine Hogarth after twenty-
two years of marriage. Gladys Storey, who recorded Kate's
opinion, was shrewd enough to see farther than Kate on this
point. Kate meant only that Dickens, in his passion for exactness,
always had to get things set down on paper. Storey did not believe Dickens's view of this particular affair, but she believed
"Dickens perpetrated the truth about the unreal . . .": she saw
that the letter expressed his construction of his and his wife's
relationship.

The word "construction" is the right one here because in that
letter Dickens gave objective shape to the reality he felt: that
is, in writing it he harmonized his experience and his belief.
That of course is what he did in his fiction, too, and Virginia
Woolf's question, following as it does a passage explaining why
she writes herself, shows she understands that Dickens's stories
meant for him what hers mean for her. Some experiences strike
her as "sudden shocks," and these "exceptional moments," she
feels, are valuable because they can become "a revelation of
some order" behind "the cotton wool of daily life," "a token of
some real thing behind appearances" to which she gives body
"by putting it into words." I quote the rest of the passage because (allowing for the difference in idiom) the part about pattern could be by Dickens himself.

Perhaps this is the strongest pleasure known to me. It is the rapture
I get when in writing I seem to be discovering what belongs to what;
making a scene come right; making a character come together. From
this I reach what I might call a philosophy; at any rate it is a constant idea of mine; that behind the cotton wool is hidden a pattern;
that we—I mean all human beings—are connected with this; that
the whole world is a work of art; that we are parts of the work of art.
Hamlet or a Beethoven quartet is the truth about this vast mass that
we call the world. But there is no Shakespeare, there is no Beethoven;
certainly and emphatically there is no God; we are the words; we are
the music; we are the thing itself. And I see this when I have a shock.
This intuition of mine—it is so instinctive that it seems given to me,
not made by me—has certainly given its scale to my life. . . . If I were
painting myself I should have to find some—rod, shall I say—something

that would stand for the conception. It proves that one's life is not confined to one's body and what one says and does; one is living all the time in relation to certain background rods or conceptions. Mine is that there is a pattern hid behind the cotton wool. (pp. 72–73)

Dickens certainly did not share the atheism expressed here, and I do not remember any place where he says so explicitly as Woolf that writing is how one comes to understand. But there is a passage from Forster, often quoted, that shows Dickens shares this sense of a pattern hidden in the "cotton wool" of daily life: "On the coincidences, resemblances, and surprises of life, Dickens liked especially to dwell, and few things moved his fancy so pleasantly. The world, he would say, was so much smaller than we thought it; we were all so connected by fate without knowing it; people supposed to be far apart were so constantly elbowing each other; and to-morrow bore so close a resemblance to nothing half so much as to yesterday."[5] Dickens was also fond of remarking how often important events in his life turned up on Fridays, and he had a lively interest in occurrences and phenomena that seem to show a web of connections among different minds of which we are largely unconscious.[6] And Woolf's idea that art is the way to find out pattern does appear in a letter of Dickens to Wilkie Collins, taking issue with Collins's way of handling plot:

I do not positively say that the point you put might not have been done in your manner; but I have a very strong conviction that it would have been overdone in that manner—too elaborately trapped, baited, and prepared—in the main anticipated, and its interest wasted. . . . I think the business of art is to lay all that ground carefully, not with the care that conceals itself—to show, by a backward light, what everything has been working to—but only to *suggest,* until the fulfillment comes. *These are the ways of Providence, of which ways all art is but a little imitation.*[7]

Take away Providence, and the idea could be Woolf's. To hear this resonance of Dickens in someone from a literary world seemingly so remote from his as Bloomsbury was, is to sense how widely Dickens's influence has been felt, and something of the reasons for it.

Writing, then, was surely more to Dickens than making a living. I return to this in my last chapter, where I describe the patterns he saw in the world. Here I want to go a little into the question of what made Dickens the kind of writer—inventive, various, copious, even obsessive—that he was. This will mean calling attention to some biographical matters, of course, but the works themselves are the best place to go for part of this inquiry, as I hope will be obvious when it becomes plain what sort of thing I am after.

Imagination, energy, will: without these Dickens would not have been Dickens, and his works would not have been at all. I hope no reader thinks that in saying this I am claiming to "account" for Dickens, or disclaiming some unpleasant undersides of those traits. Furthermore, the boyhood job in the shoeblacking warehouse, the inaccessible Maria Beadnell, the newspaper experience, his sister-in-law Mary Hogarth's early death, American response to the book on his travels in the United States—all these helped make Dickens what he was, as he himself knew.[8] But an impression of the man (so long as one avoids caricature—though a good caricature is convincing exactly because it calls attention to the features we recognize the person by) is more valuable for getting a view of the authentic Dickens in a study of this sort than a catalogue of his traits and shaping experiences, which is sure to be incomplete anyway, and which is likely to diffuse Dickens's image rather than sharpen it.

I   *Imagination*

First, then, Dickens's imagination, by which I mean the source of his creations: his consciousness, in its operations of taking in, digesting, and reforming experience (under the pressure of his enduring attitudes and beliefs as well as his preoccupations and anxieties of the moment), as we are able to describe it from the kinds of things Dickens made up again and again in creating his stories. It is particularizing, but not much like a camera. Dickens envisions people and the human world of the city more vividly and particularly than he does the world of nature, as Angus Wilson says.[9] But Dickens's city, as a physical place, is not usually imagined in much particularity either.

The human activity going on there is almost always the focus of interest, and we get just enough particularity to establish a setting for that. Apparent exceptions to Wilson's remark about nature in the Dickens world, like Dickens's description of the awesome Pass of the Great Saint Bernard where the Dorrits find themselves on their stately progress to Italy, turn out to have the same purpose. The rocky summit in the clouds, where "everything was seen through cloud, and seemed dissolving into cloud," gives moral proportion to the social gamesmanship that absorbs all the Dorrits but one, as in another way the outbuilding does where the dead travelers, casualties of the dangerous road, stand in frozen mockery of the living ones around the fire in the convent hall.[10] Nor are the buildings and streets of Dickens's cities more important for themselves than his Alps and his mountain road to Italy. They are there to enrich in some way the human story he is telling: to emphasize the neglect of "the ordinary home-made article" by those who can see no objects of need nearer than the tropics: "Jo comes out of Tom-all-Alone's, . . . and munches his dirty bit of bread as he comes along. . . . [H]e sits down to breakfast on the door-step of the Society for the Propagation of the Gospel in Foreign Parts. . . . He admires the size of the edifice, and wonders what it's all about. He has no idea, poor wretch, of the spiritual destitution of a coral reef in the Pacific, or what it costs to look up the precious souls among the cocoa-nuts and bread-fruit" (*BH* 16). Or to suggest the moral quality of the world that Pip is entering when he enters upon his expectations: "So, I came into Smithfield; and the shameful place, being all asmear with filth and fat and blood and foam, seemed to stick to me. So, I rubbed it off with all possible speed by turning into a street where I saw the great black dome of Saint Paul's bulging at me from behind a grim stone building which a bystander said was Newgate Prison" (*GE* 20). Or to provide an image of what worldly affairs amount to: "That mysterious paper currency which circulates in London when the wind blows, gyrated here and there and everywhere. Whence can it come, whither can it go? It hangs on every bush, flutters in every tree, is caught flying by the electric wires..." (*OMF* I, 12). Or to convey Arthur Clennam's state of mind: "Nothing to see but streets, streets, streets. Nothing to breathe but streets, streets, streets. Nothing to change the brooding mind, or raise it up" (*LD* I, 3). Or—and this is how the centrality of human beings in Dickens's fiction is most vividly demonstrated—to give the whole setting an emotional tone appropriate to the human action going forward at the moment, as when David Copperfield is about to hear news of Emily at the home of her betrayer's mother: "None of the best rooms abutted on the road; and the narrow, heavily-framed old-fashioned windows, never cheerful under any circumstances, looked very dismal, close shut, and with their blinds always drawn down. There was a covered way across a little paved court, to an entrance that was never used; and there was one round staircase window, at odds with all the rest, and the only one unshaded by a blind, which had the same unoccupied blank look" (*DC* 46).[11]

There is in *Great Expectations* a rare passage that expresses something like Hardy's steady sense of an infinite cosmos, infinitely uncaring for the tribulations of puny humanity: "And then I looked at the stars, and considered how awful it would be for a man to turn his face up to them as he froze to death, and see no help or pity in all the glittering multitude" (7). But here, too, the real contrast is a human one. The passage foreshadows Estella ("by name a star," as G. Robert Stange says),[12] whom Pip is about to meet, and whom he sees from the first as far above him (9), and pitiless; the remoteness and indifference of the stars is a metaphor for his relationship with Estella then.

There is a vividness about the people of Dickens's imagination that everyone feels and that critics struggle to account for. Angus Wilson says we see them "as it might be after three or four glasses of champagne" (p. 81). More characters have it in the early novels; in the later novels we see it mostly in the secondary characters, and hardly at all in the central ones. (Part of the reason for feeling a change in the later Dickens comes from perceiving a change in the distribution of this special quality.) "Exaggeration" is a word that comes to mind, but it is the wrong word, as Dickens always insisted, diplomatically in response to a friend like Bulwer-Lytton: "[I do not] for a moment question [your] criticism (if objection so generous and easy may be called by that hard name) otherwise than on this ground— that I work slowly and with great care, and never give way to my invention recklessly, but constantly restrain it . . ." (F IX, i, 721). He was more energetic in his public statements: in his preface to *Oliver Twist*, responding to opinion that Bill Sikes in his brutality and his mistress Nancy in her fidelity are both improbable, he wrote, "There is not one word exaggerated or over-wrought." He responded more fully in the preface to the Charles Dickens edition of *Martin Chuzzlewit*: "What is exaggeration to one class of minds and perceptions, is plain truth to another. That which is commonly called a long-sight, perceives in a prospect innumerable features and bearings non-existent to a short-sighted person. I sometimes ask myself whether there may occasionally be a difference of this kind between some writers and some readers; whether it is *always* the writer who colours highly, or whether it is now and then the reader whose eye for colour is a little dull?" What Dickens went on to say in this preface Forster echoed in writing about the character Pecksniff in that novel: "When people call the character exaggerated, and protest that the lines are too broad to deceive any one, they only refuse, naturally enough, to sanction in a book what half their lives is passed in tolerating if not in worshipping" (F IV, ii, 310). Dickens would have liked, too, what George Santayana wrote fifty years later in a passage often quoted since: "When people say Dickens exaggerates, it seems to me they can have no eyes and no ears. They probably have only *notions* of what things and people are; they accept them conventionally, at their diplomatic value. Their minds run on in the region of discourse, where there are masks only and no faces, ideas and no facts; they have little sense for those living grimaces that play from moment to moment upon the countenance of the world."[13]

William Axton and Robert Garis deal with this quality of Dickens's imagination as theater.[14] Axton believes that Dickens, deeply interested in the theater all his life, "sought to translate the frivolous idioms of the playhouse into imaginative prose fiction with a serious social purpose" (p. 139). Garis says that a Dickens novel *is* a theater: a verbal structure providing the reader with something like the experience of theater, "manoeuvring performing theatrical characters into various arrangements, in order to provide new and different occasions for thrilling or affecting performances" (p. 92). Of course Axton and Garis are not the first to connect Dickens to the theater; in fact, Axton's title comes from Dickens's younger contemporary John Ruskin.[15] One assents readily enough to this way of thinking about the form of Dickens's imaginings, especially considering what nineteenth-century English theater was: a "welter of forms," as Axton says, prominent among them pantomime, burlesque, and melodrama, and all of them more or less infused with the grotesque style, of which the tendency is—Axton again—"to estrange reality without dispensing with it" (p. 28).[16] But while the idea of nineteenth-century theatricality applies to many things in a Dickens novel, taken one by one—features of the plot, vividly drawn characters, the language of melodrama that some of them speak—stretched over the whole work, it comes apart. Displayed as a catalogue of types which "estrange reality without dispensing with it," nineteenth-century English theater takes on a cultural gloss that hides less imposing characteristics. It was also thin and superficial, with crudely drawn characters and flimsy artificial plots. It estranged reality, as Axton says, "by means of sudden, surprising transformations of its elements, so that the processes normally associated with the working of everyday life are undone, or the conventional relations between things are dislocated." Dickens's way was rather to leave everyday life and conventional relations in place, penetrating the surfaces of reality to show the strangeness within: what he was talking about in that letter to Collins about plot. Dickens certainly was influenced by the theater of his time. He was often thin and superficial, sometimes from failure of imagination or press of time or constrictions of space, but also from the effect of the theatrical mode upon his utterance: for it was Dickens's bad luck that theater, the art which came nearest meeting his need for imaginative expression, was far from adequate in his time to that need. Dramatic adaptations of his own books rarely pleased him (F IV, iii, 321). Dickens wanted to say more than the stage could carry, and he needed to say it *himself*: which the novel, as later the public readings that occupied more and more of his time in the last twelve years of his life, enabled him to do.

A better word than "theatricality" to describe the quality of Dickens's imagination is "intensity." It occurs often in Forster and others; Walter Allen speaks of the "quite abnormal clarity and intensity of vision" with which Dickens's characters are presented "in all their minute peculiarities of physiognomy, stance and gesture...."[17] Defining that intensity, Allen refers to the notion of a childlike vision, which occurred early to critics, and has been much favored by those who condescend to Dickens.[18] Allen takes this idea seriously (it "is still worth pursuing for the light it throws on the nature of his comedy"), but it takes us only so far, and, he says, we have to explain "the extraordinary intensity of his vision . . . if it can be explained at all, in other ways" (p. 11). He turns back to an 1872 essay where G. H. Lewes writes, "He was a seer of visions.... [I]n no other perfectly sane mind (Blake, I believe, was not perfectly sane) have I observed vividness of imagination approaching so closely to hallucination."[19]

We are trying to put a name to something no name will fully cover. Allen appears to resist "hallucination," as do I; the word carries connotations of mental trouble too strong for Lewes's insistence on Dickens's sanity. "Vividness" is better, but "intensity" seems better still to me, applying more to the source, the imagination, where "vividness" makes me think of the thing imagined, the image. But it is clear that we are considering the same thing from different angles, from another sentence of Lewes quoted by Allen: "When [Dickens] imagined a street, a house, a room, a figure, he saw it not in the vague schematic way of ordinary imagination, but in the sharp definition of actual perception, all the salient details obtruding themselves on his attention" (pp. 11–12). Galvanized by danger, the English marine who narrates Dickens's chapters of the 1857 *Household Words* Christmas story remembers how little escaped him: "I remarked to myself, even then, what a number of things I seemed to see at once."[20] It is as if Dickens's imagination, working as Lewes described it, was characteristically in that narrator's state of heightened awareness, taking in everything, whereas most of us are like Sam Weller: "Yes, I have a pair of eyes, and that's just it. If they wos a pair o' patent double million magnifyin' gas microscopes of hextra power, p'raps I might be able to see through a flight o' stairs and a deal door; but bein' only eyes, you see, my wision's limited."[21]

The metaphor of magnification fits here, because the intensity

of Dickens's observation *is* like a microscope, making visible
multitudes of "salient details." The effect of that imaginative
intensity is abundance, or copiousness, or plenitude, in the novels
and out of them. Lewes was speaking of local effects in Dickens,
but his point has broader significance too. Dickens imagined
profusely. Everyone with any reading experience of Dickens
carries around a general impression of that: shoals of characters,
acres of plots, geysers of language. Dickens felt cramped and
uncomfortable writing the weekly installments of *Hard Times*,
much shorter than the monthly parts in which he composed his
longer novels; the difficulty, he complained to Forster, was
"CRUSHING" (F VII, i, 565). He needed room. Trying to illustrate Dickens's luxuriance by quotation is no use unless one has
plenty of space to spend. But my point—that this is a general
quality of his sensibility, and not a special effect reserved for
his novels—is borne out by his letters. The life of Dickens's novels,
in this respect, is continuous with the life in his letters. He will
go to extraordinary lengths to describe a play he has seen, or
a magician's performance he has especially admired. He describes
his old friend the actor William Charles Macready (who had
just heard his reading of Nancy's murder) with the particularity
and the eye for significant detail that one finds in the novels, and
his negotiations for a house in Exeter for his parents make a vivid
and amusing little episode.[22]

To say much more about the profusion that is characteristic
of Dickens's imaginings—the variety, the way this plenitude is
disposed and organized—would be to anticipate a later section
on the shape of Dickens's visions. But there is one more thing
I want to point out about his imagination before moving on. The
intensity of focus that generates all that detail also detects like-
nesses that most of us would miss. In the same letter of 1865
to Bulwer-Lytton that I quoted from earlier Dickens wrote, "I
think it is my infirmity to fancy or perceive relations in things
which are not apparent generally" (F IX, i, 721). Any study of
his style will show evidence of that, in the high proportion of
metaphors and similes, those figures of speech that assert resemblances.[23] A great deal of Dickens's humor comes from metaphor and simile, as he yokes things together in ways that surprise
us. His use of the pathetic fallacy is another sign of this imagina-

tive discerning of resemblances. Of course it might be argued that this latter sort of evidence shows Dickens inventing resemblances, not just seeing them; when he writes about the close-packed houses in the working-class districts of Coketown that "the chimneys, for want of air to make a draught, were built in an immense variety of stunted and crooked shapes, as though every house put out a sign of the kind of people who might be expected to be born in it" (*HT* I, 10), he does it to make a point about the relation of character to environment, not to bring out some latent physical resemblance between people and buildings.

But granting this objection would not greatly change my main point. Whether Dickens was gifted beyond others at finding out resemblances in things (as he thought), or was instead capable of being so possessed by a conception that he could invent convincing data for it believing he was finding them, the instrument was the same: an imaginative intensity that proliferated details in which we have pointed out to us all sorts of resemblances and echoes. This is a pattern- and order-seeking kind of imagination; here, too, the train of thought leads to discussion of the shape of Dickens's visions, which I want to keep clear of now, concerned as I am to focus on the man who wrote them: a man possessed of (perhaps I should say "by") an intensely active imagination focused on the world of human beings, and not noticeably concerned with the questions of cosmic order that afflicted contemporaries like Tennyson; a proliferating imagination, calling up a densely detailed fictive world, and imposing (or finding) order and pattern in it. (Dickens would insist, "finding.")

II *Energy*

The public Dickens commonly surprised people by his "extraordinary composure." The phrase is from Dickens's letter to Forster from Philadelphia in January 1868, about American amazement at his stage presence (F III, viii, 287). English audiences experienced the same surprise.[24] What everybody expected was a figure pulsing with the energy that brought those dense, vibrant, luxuriant books into being. Their instinct was correct; Dickens certainly had, for much of his life, extraordinary energy.

He was working full time as a reporter of proceedings in Parliament for the *Morning Chronicle* when he began writing the monthly installments of *Pickwick Papers*, with no notion, it is true, what the scope of that work would turn out to be; but six months later, in October 1836, when it was clear that *Pickwick* would continue, he intended to stay with the *Chronicle*, and he only resigned that position to edit a new monthly magazine, *Bentley's Miscellany*—and help fill it with a new serial novel. So in February 1837, as Forster summarizes it, Dickens "was now writing, month by month, the first half of *Oliver Twist*, and . . . the last half of *Pickwick*, not even by a week in advance of the printer with either. . . ."[25] In April 1838, with *Pickwick Papers* less than five months behind him and only about halfway through *Oliver Twist*, he began his third novel, *Nicholas Nickleby*. Once again he had two monthly serials going at the same time, with heavy editorial duties for *Bentley's Miscellany* besides. He resigned those in January 1839, having finished *Oliver Twist* for publication in three volumes in November (though it continued to run serially in the *Miscellany* through April). *Nicholas Nickleby* ran through October 1839. But in 1839 Dickens was also planning another periodical, a weekly this time, which began publishing under the name *Master Humphrey's Clock* in April 1840, six months after the last number of *Nickleby* appeared. *The Old Curiosity Shop* was published there through 6 February 1841, and *Barnaby Rudge* began in the next week's number and ran through 27 November: with editorial duties, of course, continuing all the while. Five novels in five and a half years, besides what else he wrote as editor, and the dozen or more letters every day (P III, 548).

Domestic life in these years was full, exciting, and demanding, too: marriage to Catherine Hogarth in April 1836, almost the same moment the first installment of *Pickwick* appeared; children one after another, four of the ten eventually born to them; the summer sojourns out of London, most regularly at Broadstairs on the Kentish seashore, Dickens going back and forth to London as necessary; house-hunting and moving, from the first home, the rooms in Furnival's Inn, to a house in Doughty Street a year later, and from there in December 1839 to a much larger and more imposing house at No. 1 Devonshire Terrace near Regent's Park, the Dickens home for twelve years. The joys of a young family at

48 Doughty Street were checked sharply almost on moving in:
Catherine's sixteen-year-old sister Mary, who was living with
them, died suddenly in May 1837, and Dickens was so shaken
that there were no numbers of *Pickwick* and *Oliver* in June.[26]
All the writing went on at home then, in a spacious library at
Devonshire Terrace, but in a little back room in the Doughty
Street house, and even, on at least one occasion there, literally in
the midst of the family, when he joined Catherine and his sister
and future brother-in-law Henry Burnett one evening and wrote
away at *Oliver*. "We, at his bidding, went on talking our 'little
nothings,'" Burnett wrote years later, "—he, every now and then
(the feather of his pen still moving rapidly from side to side),
put in a cheerful interlude. It was interesting to watch, upon the
sly, the mind and the muscles working (or, if you please, *playing*)
in company, as new thoughts were being dropped upon the paper.
And to note the working brow, the set of mouth, with the tongue
tightly pressed against the closed lips, as was his habit."[27] Others
too were struck by the liveliness of that face. Forster remembered
the "eyes wonderfully beaming with intellect and running over
with humour and cheerfulness" (F II, i, 84). Thomas Carlyle
noticed his eyes too—"clear blue, intelligent eyes"—and the anima-
tion of his features: "eyebrows that he arches amazingly, large
protrusive rather loose mouth, a face of most extreme *mobility*,
which he shuttles about—eyebrows, eyes, mouth and all—in a very
singular manner while speaking."[28] In America the younger Richard Henry Dana thought he never saw a face "fuller of light,"
and his father observed that Dickens's "whole countenance speaks
life and *action*—the face seems to flicker with the *heart's* and
mind's activity. You cannot tell how dead the faces near him
seemed."[29]

Nor did desk and family use up all his energies. For a dozen
years, from 1845 through 1857, he was the leading spirit in a series
of amateur theatrical productions. Many of them were staged
to raise funds for literary people and their families in need of
help, but clearly Dickens loved them for their own sake, not only
acting leading roles but managing and directing the productions
as well. These interludes provided change from the private labors
of his writing. In earlier years his idea of resting from mental
exertion was to counterbalance it with physical, and Forster,

summoned again and again, answered the call "oftener than I could well afford the time for, the distances being great and nothing else to be done for the day": a fifteen-mile horseback ride, lunch on the road, and back again; or a long fast walk (though not so long as Dickens took alone in later years). Dickens would send him a note: "Is it possible that you can't, oughtn't, shouldn't, mustn't, *won't* be tempted, this gorgeous day!" Or "Come, come, *come*," he would write, "and walk in the green lanes. You will work the better for it all the week. COME! I shall expect you." Or he would propose a ride: "A hard trot of three hours?" or more urgently, "Where shall it be—*oh where*—Hampstead, Greenwich, Windsor? WHERE?????? while the day is bright, not when it has dwindled away to nothing! For who can be of any use whatsomdever such a day as this, excepting out of doors?"[30] But indoors, too, Dickens liked company. Forster and other friends dined with him often, at home and out, and Dickens loved to mark special occasions with such gatherings: a birthday or other anniversary; or the launching of a new work; or a return from travels, like the return from the United States in June 1842, celebrated by a dinner at Greenwich with a number of close friends—followed by another celebration in the shape of another trip, with Forster and two others, into Cornwall (F III, viii, 278).

In fact, Dickens traveled a great deal, to Scotland in 1841 and America in 1842 and 1867–68, and to the Continent repeatedly in the 1850s and occasionally later. He lived abroad with his family for extended periods in 1844–45 (Italy), 1846–47 (Switzerland and France), and 1855–56 (France); and he took his family to Boulogne for their summer holidays from 1853 through 1856. Dickens's energies demanded motion as well as society. In the last decade of his life he remembered with pleasure the rush and stress of his work as a reporter. He took pleasure, and pride, in astonishing the Americans by footing it on the towpath instead of huddling with them around the cabin stove in the canal boat he and Catherine took from Harrisburg, Pennsylvania, to Pittsburgh, just as he exulted in the rigors of a coach trip through terrible rains on dangerous roads in the Highlands.[31] Forster should have shouted with laughter to read, in a letter ticking off a long list of social activities in Edinburgh, "The moral of all this is, that there is no place like home; and that I thank God most heartily *for having given me a quiet spirit,* and a heart that won't hold many people" (P II, 317; my italics).

But perhaps that makes sense after all. From America Dickens wrote to Forster about Niagara, how in great excitement he "hurried to the Horse-shoe-fall" and went down alone "into the very basin," to look up at *"what* a fall of bright green water! The broad, deep, mighty stream seems to die in the act of falling. . . ." And the effect on him of this "tremendous spectacle," he says, "was peace of mind—tranquillity—great thoughts of eternal rest and happiness—nothing of terror" (P III, 210–11). In saying "nothing of terror," Dickens was underscoring that he had *not* felt the conventional thrill of delicious fear at the sublime power of nature. He had felt tranquillity: what he desired, writing Forster from Edinburgh about his "quiet spirit." Ordinary natures, going well insulated by dullness through life, are opened by the shock of terror to something like ecstasy in a heightened sense of being alive. Dickens, like the English marine in his story, lives in something like ecstasy, and takes the threat of extinction that administers a shock of terror to others as a promise of peace. It is an unexpected consequence to hear of, but it suggests another dimension of the glittering life, and another perspective on the energy that drove it.

III   *Will*

The energy diminished, of course, in time. From 1842 through 1850 Dickens held the pace, though with increasing strain, writing two works on his travels in America and Italy, three long novels, and five novelettes (his Christmas books); after that the novels came slower, and harder. But all things taken into account, he was doing even more after 1850 than he had before, editing and writing for his weekly journals from 1850 until his death, personally overseeing the home founded (with his advice) by the Baroness Burdett-Coutts to help fallen women rise, traveling and engaging in theatricals as I noted earlier, remodeling and developing Gad's Hill Place (his last home), managing his increasingly complex and difficult domestic and family affairs, and (from 1858) devoting more and more time to enormously popular public readings from his works. His letters give evidence of all this activity—in fact are themselves part of it. Until recently the largest single collection was published in three volumes in 1938 as part of the Nonesuch Edition of Dickens's works. The Pilgrim Edition in progress since 1965 under the Clarendon imprint of the Oxford University Press will be much larger, incorporating the 5,811 letters of the Nonesuch Edition, letters omitted from that collection, and letters discovered since. They keep turning up. The editors knew of 11,956 letters in 1965; by 1981, when the fifth volume was published (letters from 1847–49), they knew of 13,452. Many of course are about matters that would be handled by telephone now, but for that very reason we know things about Dickens's ordinary activities which we could not know about the routines of somebody like him today—the immense pains he took as an editor, in particular. And the time and thought he devoted to correspondence with friends and acquaintances is awesome.

How did he manage all this? By force of will, more and more. As energy failed will supplanted it; more and more the image of energy, and of vigor and high spirits too, was sustained by Dickens's unyielding will. At a time when he was trying to override the deepening misery he felt in his marriage by furious theatrical activity and as furious walks, he projected in a letter to the old actor William Charles Macready this image of a day in the Dickens life:

I saw the chance [of answering a criticism of *Little Dorrit* published in the *Edinburgh Review*] last Friday week, as I was going down to read the Carol in St. Martin's Hall. Instantly turned to, then and there, and wrote half the article. Flew out of bed early next morning, and finished it by noon. Went down to the Gallery of Illustration (we acted that night), did the day's business, corrected the proofs in Polar costume in dressing-room, broke up two numbers of Household Words to get it out directly, played in Frozen Deep and Uncle John, presided at supper of company, made no end of speeches, went home and gave in completely for four hours, then got sound asleep, and next day was as fresh as you used to be in the far-off days of your lusty youth.[32]

He always insisted on his health and physical vigor, and would attribute attacks of headaches or giddiness to not having walked as usual (F V, i, 386; v, 430); the paralysis that began to affect his left side during his last readings, he was sure, was due to the medicine he was taking (F XII, i, 848); and so on.

But his will had always been strong. It took determination (and gall) to insist as Dickens did that his narrative should determine the course of *Pickwick*, when he had been brought in originally only to write the continuity for a series of illustrations. It took even more to break the control of his first publishers over him (and over the profits from his work), with both tradition and his own contracts on the publishers' side. Edgar Johnson's account makes that clearer than Forster's, and Johnson entitles his next chapter "The Will in Command." But by then Dickens had the prospect of great rewards, if he prevailed, to sustain him. Earlier in life there was no such support from circumstances, when he taught himself shorthand to get a job as parliamentary reporter for a newspaper, or when a bit later, as he told Forster, he thought seriously of becoming an actor: "I went to some theatre every night, with a very few exceptions, for at least three years: really studying the bills first, and going to where there was the best acting. . . . I practised immensely (even such things as walking in and out, and sitting down in a chair): often four, five, six hours a day: shut up in my own room, or walking about in the fields. I prescribed to myself, too, a sort of Hamiltonian system for learning parts; and learnt a great number" (F V, i, 380).

The common element in all this is the aim to control. Mere self-gratification was surely not Dickens's purpose—except of course as having one's own way is pleasure—for the things he determined upon usually meant great exertions on his part. But not to be under the control of others, to be the director in the things that concerned him: that was it. Dickens's own "explanation of himself" (F I, iii, 38), which Forster and many critics since have found persuasive, was rooted in the scarifying episode of the shoeblacking warehouse, when Dickens felt abandoned to a life without hope, a life of absolute powerlessness. Another such experience of powerlessness was the brief love affair with Maria Beadnell, when Dickens's frustration in the face of her coyness and her parents' disapproval was intense and total. It is surely too simple to find the explanation of Dickens's lifelong determination in one or two episodes, but certainly these were quintessential. Dickens's tone to Catherine in a letter during their engagement, in which he tells her firmly that he will not submit to capriciousness, shows what he thought he had learned from his relations with Maria (P I, 61–62); and his life is full of such domestic management, usually not so adamantine in its style, but then his authority as paterfamilias was usually unquestioned. On the business side, there are the conflicts with publishers that I have already mentioned, and indeed over later publishing agreements too—though Dickens's value to a publisher (and no doubt his formidable reputation for asserting his rights) made it unnecessary for him in his late negotiations to blaze as he did earlier.

Not to be under the control of others in the things that concerned him: and what concerned him in all things was order. I have touched on this earlier, and most of what I mean to say about it belongs in another chapter, but the way this concern, even compulsion, showed in his personal life belongs here. From the family's summer quarters at Broadstairs in June 1840 he writes Forster: "Before I tasted bit or drop yesterday, I set out my writing-table with extreme taste and neatness, and improved the disposition of the furniture generally" (P II, 78). This, Forster says, was "his invariable habit upon entering any new abode, whether to stay in it for days or for years" (F II, viii, 159). Another time, on the 1842 trip to America, from an Ohio River steamboat: "I have smuggled two chairs into our crib; and write this on a book upon my knee. Everything is in the neatest order, of course; and my shaving tackle, dressing case, brushes, books, and papers, are arranged with as much precision as if we were going to remain here a month" (P III, 181). There is perhaps a note of amusement at his own expense in that: there surely is when he writes Forster wryly from Paris in 1846, in a letter about his troubles getting at *Dombey,* "You know what arrangements are necessary with the chairs and tables" (P IV, 675). But he needs a certain arrangement of his desk, too; earlier, in Switzerland, he is held up because a box has not arrived from home, "containing not his proper writing materials only, but certain quaint little bronze figures that thus early stood upon his desk, and were as much needed for the easy flow of his writing as blue ink or quill pens" (F V, ii, 400). (He always used the blue ink and quill pens, too.)

These quirks are common enough in writers, but they are of a piece with other things in Dickens's life. His children remembered how he used to hate the wind mussing his hair, and would run upstairs to get a hairbrush when it happened. Less comical to them was his discipline: Kate and Mamie had to endure notes pinned to their pillows about any disorders their father found in his daily inspections of their rooms, and Harry and his brothers (each with his own peg to hang coats and hats on, and responsible in turn for putting away games and toys at end of day, and all of them subject to weekly clothing inspection) dared only to mutter among themselves "slavery" and "degradation" and the like.[33] The same love of order shows in more public activity too. About the first of the theatrical productions Forster writes, "Such a chaos of dirt, confusion, and noise, as the little theatre was the day we entered it, and such a cosmos as he made it of cleanliness, order, and silence, before the rehearsals were over!" Dickens's management of those productions was admirable, not to say awesome. His letters to friends about texts, rehearsals, theaters, properties, casts, costumes—everything—show him taking all kinds of time and going into the most minute details. Forster ticks off the list of his involvements in that first one: "He was stage-director, very often stage-carpenter, scene-arranger, property-man, prompter, and bandmaster. Without offending any one he kept every one in order. . . . He adjusted scenes, assisted carpenters, invented costumes, devised playbills, wrote out calls, and enforced as well as exhibited in his proper person everything of which he urged the necessity on others." In fact, Forster sums up, "He was the life and soul of the entire affair" (F V, i, 383). It was not the least attraction of these amateur dramatics for Dickens that they were exercises in organization, in making order out of chaos (furnishing pleasure perhaps like Virginia Woolf's in making things come right); and that the scale and scope were such that it could really be done. To direct a great theater, he said late in life, would be supremely satisfying: "The pieces acted should be dealt with according to my pleasure, and touched up here and there in obedience to my own judgment; the players as well as the plays being absolutely under my command."[34]

To order *all* things after his heart's desire: that was the will of Dickens, which he pursued farther and more strenuously than most of us can. Forster, his oldest and most loyal friend, saw that, in its various colors; the "fixed and eager determination, the restless and resistless energy" took him to great heights, but "a sense that everything was possible to the will that would make it so" led him to assume burdens beyond even his strength, and sometimes sunk the kind and gentle in him in the hard, aggressive, and fierce (F I, iii, 38–39). He knew it himself sometimes. The separation from his wife laid heavy stresses on his children, and Mamie found him on his knees weeping in Katie's room after her wedding, his face buried in her wedding dress; when at last he got up and saw Mamie, he said in a broken voice, "But for me, Katie would not have left home."[35] Angus Wilson thinks that in *Great Expectations,* his last complete novel but one, "in the fierce attack upon those who make puppets of others or mould them into idols (Jaggers, Magwitch, Miss Havisham, Pip's own treatment of Estella) there is surely some doubt about that exercise of will which Dickens must have come with all his family trouble to question in himself; with that egoistic will that wore down his wife and children he may surely have come to associate the whole power of shaping real life into fictions."[36]

But it will not do to close this chapter on the image of Dickens as a worn-out, tragic, and embittered husk of the man he once was, still obsessed with power and control, and driven to an early grave by the undying will. Johnson's account of his last few weeks of life shows him in bad health but good spirits, still working with great power, dining out, going to the theater, keeping his friends in stitches, taking charge of some private theatricals in his old way, loving his family (J 1146–53). And even in the days when his marriage was close to breaking up, when he plunged into theatrical productions as into oblivion, he could play the Inimitable (his self-chosen half-mocking nickname) to his old actor friend Macready in a letter describing how he managed the varied tumult of his days: editing as usual, getting the annual Christmas number ready, keeping at the novel then publishing (*Little Dorrit*), and getting up a play for presentation at his own house (given over to all manner of production activities): "Calm amidst the wreck, your aged friend glides away on the Dorrit stream, forgetting the uproar for a stretch of hours, refreshing himself with a ten or twelve miles' walk, pitches headforemost into foaming rehearsals, placidly emerges for editorial purposes, smokes over buckets of distemper with Mr. Stanfield aforesaid, again calmly floats upon the Dorrit waters."[37] Dickens regularly took this hearty tone with Macready; it was part of cheering an old friend in retirement, I think. But there is more to it than that. Dickens had no "city of the mind," Forster says, no "inner consolation and shelter" against distressing realities (F VIII, ii, 641): his only remedy was to bend reality to his will, as his early, sudden, and complete success seemed to show him that energetic action could do. It was what he had been doing ever since, harmonizing his experience and his belief in the imagined world of his novels, and in the personal world that his letters show us. He was indeed *bound* to write everything—determined, and compelled. His voice in that letter to Macready, like the narratorial voice of the novels, is making a world. Dickens was *writing* to conquer the chaos of his life just here, asserting his control by projecting the image of his energy and will serenely topping the storm—and keeping it all real by the note of self-ribbing humor that one hears there, the voice of the comic vision.

The truth must be that imagination, energy, will all belonged to him all his days. They are all one really: Dickens seen from different perspectives. Forster says, "[T]here was that in the face as I first recollect it which no time could change, and which remained implanted on it unalterably to the last.... [There was] the restless and resistless vivacity and force of which I have spoken, but that also which lay beneath them of steadiness and hard endurance." Turning to imagery, he says, "Light and motion flashed from every part of it"; but the best image, carrying all that, comes from Mrs. Carlyle: "It was as if made of steel" (F II, i, 84–85).

CHAPTER 2

"That Particular Relation":
Dickens and His Audience

SURVEYING the range of Dickens's work, one needs some
other principle of order than chronology, which ceases to be
helpful almost immediately; from early in his career Dickens was
doing everything at once. My order of treatment is generic; but
a theme running through everything Dickens did in whatever
genre, and accounting to a large degree for everything he did,
is his consciousness of audience. So my survey of Dickens's fiction
in whatever kind, and his journalism, and his other work, is
really a profile as well of his career-long mode of regular and
intimate connection to his public.

I   *Fiction: Novels, Christmas Books, Christmas Stories*

The shape of the early years was not what Dickens could have
expected his career to take in 1836. *The Pickwick Papers* was a
sideline at first, undertaken because he needed money to marry
on. It was not even his idea, but the idea of a well-known comic
artist, Robert Seymour, for a series of captioned drawings about
the whimsical adventures of some Cockney sportsmen; Dickens
turned it around. Seymour committed suicide before the second
number was published; certainly his disappointment and anger
at the way his idea was reshaped had something to do with that,
but there must have been deeper causes too, as his own suicide
note suggested. He was replaced by a young man named Hablot
K. Browne, who as "Phiz" was to illustrate more of Dickens's
novels than any other artist. (Dickens considered the illustrations

important enough to give his illustrators detailed instructions and exacting criticism; see below, p. 53.)

Dickens declared "PICKWICK, TRIUMPHANT" after the first number, but his readers were not many at first, nor did they all respond favorably.[1] Interest quickened, however, with the fourth number, in which Dickens introduced Sam Weller (who became Sancho Panza to Pickwick's Quixote), and from then on Pickwick triumphed indeed. But the success of *Pickwick* "cut across the planned career at an unexpected and slightly disturbing angle," as John Butt and Kathleen Tillotson put it.[2] Dickens moved quickly to get back on course, eagerly accepting publishing commitments that his exploding reputation opened to him. He was, as Butt and Tillotson say, "working his way out of journalism" (p. 63) toward the kind of work that novelists of reputation were doing: publishing their novels entire in three volumes. According to Johnson, it was the publisher Hall who proposed publication in twenty monthly parts at a shilling a part, to tap a wider market than the circulating libraries like Mudie's and the relatively few people who could afford to lay out thirty-one shillings sixpence all at once for a three-volume novel. The convention of the "three-decker" at a guinea and a half had been established by Scott; serial publication was chiefly a mode of "bringing out cheap reprints of works like the Bible, the *Pilgrim's Progress,* and the *Book of Martyrs*" (J 117). Pierce Egan's *Tom and Jerry* had come out that way, but that would not have been a favorable precedent for a young writer aspiring to reputation: a writer in the *Edinburgh Review* found it curious in 1838 that such a book as *Pickwick* should appear in the format of "literary *ephemerae* . . . the lightest kind of light reading."[3] Dickens himself, in the preface to the first cheap edition of *Pickwick,* said the monthly number selling for a shilling was known to him at the time only "by a dim recollection of certain interminable novels in that form, which used, some five-and-twenty years ago, to be carried about the country by pedlars. . . ." Some of his friends, he said, were sure he would damage his prospects by that "low, cheap form of publication . . .; and how right my friends turned out to be, everybody now knows." Dickens's tone is cocky, but that preface is dated 1847, and by then he knew where he was. He never did publish a full-length novel in the traditional three-volume format without serializing it first. (He regularly published his novels in complete form at the time that the final part appeared, and some years later would issue cheap editions in volume form.) In all, he published nine of his novels in monthly parts and was at work on a tenth when he died (counting *Oliver Twist,* which must be thought of as structurally different from the others, having been composed in substantially shorter installments). The success of the monthly number for him must have been why he stayed with the mode. Dickens liked what worked; and by 1846, when he was gestating *Dombey and Son,* he would have been risking his niche in the public consciousness if he had gone to the three-decker that had been conventional when he began (and still was).

I suspect there are reasons deeper than this. The monthly number turned out to be a format that, in spite of Dickens's recurrent cries of anguish at having to work against a deadline, suited his temperament. It included regular "appearances" before the public. Dickens disciplined himself unfailingly to the solitary labor of literary conception, but he had to have an audience: it refreshed him and stimulated him to new exertions. He gathered a group of friends to hear the first number of *Dombey* whene he had finished it (F V, iv, 417). During his earlier trip abroad he traveled all the way to London from Italy for some prepublication readings of his second Christmas book, *The Chimes,* to his friends. What he wrote to Catherine about reading it to the Macreadys is as clear a clue as possible to the fulfillment he found in an audience: "P.S. If you had seen Macready last night—undisguisedly sobbing, and crying on the sofa, as I read— you would have felt (as I did) what a thing it is to have Power" (P IV, 235, 2 December 1844). Forster, however, was his main hearer over the years; Forster wrote that in the long term of their friendship there was scarcely anything Dickens produced which he did not show to Forster before it appeared in print (F II, i, 89). It is as if he could not wait for publication to his entire readership: or rather, as if he needed an immediate personal presence as an audience. Even self-confidence like his must have thinned at the prospect of weaving such dense fabrics as his imaginings, all in one piece; it was enough to do to hold the overall plan in mind and develop its full texture a twentieth at a time. Nor did he have the patience for the long haul. Forster noted that about him in another connection: "The interval between the accomplishment of anything, and 'its first motion,' Dickens never could endure . . ." (F II, i, 87). He fed on the stimulation of constant activity; the comic account he gave Macready of his own rushing life quoted earlier gets at a deep truth about him.

The size of the monthly installment also suited Dickens's style. Working out to thirty-two printed pages, it gave him room to advance his story significantly each time, and yet provided space for the copiousness of his style—the narrative detail, the exuberant dialogue. When he had to publish in weekly installments he felt hemmed in: he wrote Forster in 1840, about an early installment of *The Old Curiosity Shop*, "I was obliged to cramp most dreadfully what I thought a pretty idea in the last chapter. I hadn't room to turn" (P II, 80). Since each part of *The Old Curiosity Shop* (and *Barnaby Rudge*) ran to about 7,000 words instead of the 16,000 he was used to from writing *Nicholas Nickleby*, his feeling is understandable. It was worse still when he returned to writing weekly installments in 1854. An installment of *Hard Times* was only about 5,000 words long, and the monthly parts of *Bleak House*, his most recent novel, seldom were as short as those of *Nicholas Nickleby* had been, averaging 18,000 words and sometimes rising to 20,000. "The difficulty of the space is CRUSHING," he wrote Forster. "Nobody can have any idea of it who has not had an experience of patient fiction-writing with some elbow-room always, and open places in perspective" (F VII, i, 565). Five years later, it was the same story with *A Tale of Two Cities*: "The small portions thereof, drive me frantic . . ." (F IX, ii, 730). In fact, the weekly installments of *A Tale of Two Cities*, while running about 5,000 words like *Hard Times* before and *Great Expectations* later, vary greatly in length, from about 4,000 to 5,500; Dickens seems to have found himself unequal to the task he set himself in this interval of his life, strenuous even measured on the scale of his exertions.[4]

For all these reasons, the rhythm of publication in monthly parts was right for Dickens, and it must have fit with his sense of the design in human life that he came to it as it were by accident. The weekly publication he resorted to for five of his novels, however, offers further evidence how important in Dickens's career the pressure of immediate need was. Only one of them, *A Tale of Two Cities,* was undertaken in that format from the outset (to get his periodical *All the Year Round* off to a flying start in 1859). *The Old Curiosity Shop* developed in flight, so to speak; it was to have been "a tale of a few chapters" (F II, vii, 145) instead of the novel that kept *Master Humphrey's Clock* running.[5] *Barnaby Rudge* was originally conceived as a three-decker, and *Hard Times* went into *Household Words* to restore its circulation. *Great Expectations* went into *All the Year Round* in 1860–61 for the same reason, instead of into twenty monthly parts as Dickens originally intended.[6]

Thus, while Dickens clearly found monthly publication to suit him best, he was always able, and willing, to set aside this preference when he had to. In this as in other matters he acted as the excellent man of business that he was, moving promptly to head off losses and restore profits. This is not to suggest that Dickens was ready to sacrifice his art for gain, but rather to emphasize that he understood the priorities. His career as a man of letters was bound up with his periodicals (and in another way so were his responsibilities as a family man); *Master Humphrey's Clock, Household Words, All the Year Round*—each in its turn had to maintain its success. Dickens's immediate relationship to the marketplace, then, often decided important questions of form and content. Whether it worked against his art is less easy to say. His readiness to "come in" when needed shows again his own confidence in his craftsmanship: he *could* write something of merit even in a space he found intensely frustrating. Was he wrong? The novels written in weekly installments do not please every critic, but their faults are not usually attributed solely to the format. Many people feel that *Hard Times* does suffer from being "crushed." But on the other hand a significant number, led by F. R. Leavis, think its brevity is the conciseness of poetry. And *Great Expectations* is by general consent one of Dickens's best, a fusion of his craft and his art.

It is arguable, I suppose, whether all five of Dickens's Christmas books are properly seen as an expression of his intimacy with his readers. The first one, *A Christmas Carol,* is. The inspiration for it came from the glow Dickens felt in October 1843 growing out of a meeting he addressed in Manchester on behalf of the Athanaeum, an institution established to help working people educate themselves. The happy result he saw in it—sturdy spirit among the humbler classes, coming together with intelligent warmheartedness of the well-to-do in supporting the institution—inspired him to write a story that would cheer readers by showing the riches in human happiness available to all from the exercise of good will toward others. The writing of *A Christmas Carol* cheered him, too; he finished it in little more than a month, Forster says, "wept over it, and laughed, and wept again, and excited himself to an extraordinary degree, and . . . walked thinking of it fifteen and twenty miles about the black streets of London, many and many a night after all sober folks had gone to bed" (F IV, i, 299).

The other Christmas books (see the chronology for titles) came harder and harder; there was none in 1847, and the series ended in 1848. One feels that Dickens kept writing them because he hated to give up on anything, and that he came to think of the market more than the message. The later ones are not much good, but they all sold well, each better than the last. Ironically, *A Christmas Carol*, the one that still lives, was at first a bad financial disappointment to Dickens. Relations with Chapman and Hall had been deteriorating in 1843, and he blamed them for poor management of the *Carol*, although it was he who had insisted on a low selling price and expensive colored plates and other luxuries of format (J 496). In the end *A Christmas Carol*, the breathing image of Dickensian uncommercial good feeling and cheer, decided Dickens to seek wider profits with other publishers.

Carrying on in a different form the seasonal observance he began with *A Christmas Carol*, Dickens published a special Christmas number every year in *Household Words,* and in *All the Year Round* through 1867. Instead of writing everything himself, he used contributions by others as well, to lighten his own writing load. (This in fact is more evidence of Dickens's abiding motive. His various proposals for periodicals using writings by others aimed at providing for regular appearances to his audience that would be less demanding than his solo appearances as a novelist.) The first Christmas number contained stories, essays, and poems appropriate to the season, but Dickens did not keep to this; in October 1852 he wrote to a potential contributor, "I propose to give the number some fireside name, and to make it consist entirely of short stories supposed to be told by a family sitting round the fire. *I don't care about their referring to Christmas at all.*"[7] In 1854 Dickens began trying to make the number more unified by providing a narrative framework for all the contributions. He usually wrote this himself, including the links or bridges between parts, and he wrote one, two, or three of the segments. His last Christmas number, however, was *No Thoroughfare,* written with Wilkie Collins, and consequently without any narrative frame. Before that his tendency had been to give the framework more structural importance in the number each year. This may have been an effect of his disappointment with the results earlier; he complained to Wills in 1855 that the offerings of other writers were distinguished mainly by "the way they *don't* fit. . . ."[8] He apparently never found the attempt wholly satisfactory; in 1868, though "very unwilling to abandon the Xmas No.," he could conceive nothing "which would do otherwise than reproduce the old string of old stories in the old inappropriate bungling way."[9] So the last Christmas number turned out to be the 1867 *No Thoroughfare.* But as in 1849, when it was decided to attempt no Christmas book, the inciting circumstance in 1868 was most likely the press of work. His subeditor Wills, who had done most of the day-to-day work of running *All the Year Round,* had to retire that year for reasons of health. Dickens, whose own health was breaking down, had to take over much of Wills's work, and there was simply too much to do, especially since Dickens was still giving much time to his public readings.

II   *The Illustrations and Monthly Part Cover Designs*

Dickens told Forster that he really "saw" what he was writing about (just as George Lewes claimed Dickens once told him "that every word said by his characters was distinctly *heard* by him").[10] The illustrations of his novels and Christmas books thus were another mode of intimacy with his readers: a way to bring their perception of the characters and the story into close alignment with his, providing images for them to connect to the narrative rather than leaving them to make their own.

Other Victorian novelists who published in monthly parts followed Dickens's lead—J. R. Harvey says that *Pickwick* introduced illustrations, and that the traditional three-decker novel then usually had none—but nobody else made as much of the convention.[11] The importance of the illustrations to Dickens's effects, however, is clear to anyone who has read Dickens in editions which (unlike most modern paperbacks) include some of the original illustrations, especially Cruikshank's and Browne's. Dickens would specify the scenes to be illustrated, and often give detailed instructions about what he wanted. For an illustration he considered especially important he would not only specify setting and offer concrete images but also characterize the principals and glance at coming action to help the artist conceive what he wanted. One example will have to do. The first illustration for VII of *Dombey and Son*, according to Dickens's letter of instructions to Browne, was to include Major Bagstock, "the incarnation of selfishness and small revenge, a kind of comic Mephistophelean power in the book." The major is attended by a "Native," to be shown *"bearing a camp-stool and the Major's greatcoat.* Native evidently afraid of the Major and his thick cane." The major goes with Dombey on holiday to Leamington, where he introduces him "to a certain lady, whom, as I wish to foreshadow dimly, said Dombey may come to marry in due season." Dickens gives only general suggestions about her appearance, but explains that she has "something of a proud indifference about her, suggestive of a spark of the Devil within." Her mother ("who rouges") is "usually shoved about in a Bath chair by a Page who has rather *outgrown and outshoved his strength,* and who *butts at it* behind, like a ram, while his mistress *steers herself languidly* by a handle in front. *Nothing the matter with her to prevent her walking,* only was once *sketched (when a Beauty) reclining in a Barouche,* and having *outlived the beauty and the barouche* too, still *holds on to the attitude,* as becoming her uncommonly. Mother is in this machine, in the sketch. Daughter has a *parasol.*" The meeting was to be at the Leamington library, but Dickens allowed Browne to set it "in the street or in a green lane" if he preferred; apparently he did, for in chapter 21 Major Bagstock and Mr. Dombey

meet Edith and Mrs. Skewton in the street. Five days after sending Browne these directions Dickens wrote again to compliment
him in general, but also to specify two changes: the Native, good
as he was, had to be in European costume, and the Major had to
be older, and have a bigger face.[12]

Dickens also gave much thought to the design for the green
cover of the monthly parts (blue for *Bleak House*, *Little Dorrit*,
and *A Tale of Two Cities*), which was naturally repeated from
number to number. The usual design was a pictorial border
worked up with scenes, figures, and images related in some way
to the novel, "shadowing out its drift and bearing": as Dickens
wrote Forster (P IV, 648). The *Dombey* cover design suggests
the narrative line of the novel; other designs glanced at central
themes, as for example the *Little Dorrit* cover. The usefulness of
these designs in setting his reader on the right road is not so
sure, but the interest of the cover, with its network of pictorial
detail, is undeniable: something like the interest of a puzzle.[13]
(See the cover for *Bleak House* facing chapter 5.)

These are rather general significances, bearing on a story as
a whole. Dickens used illustrations to good effect in local ways,
too. The two illustrations in each monthly part stand at the beginning of the number, ahead of the text, in the six sets I have
seen (*Martin Chuzzlewit, David Copperfield, Bleak House, Little
Dorrit, Our Mutual Friend*, and *The Mystery of Edwin Drood*);
the reader gets some idea from them what is coming this time.
Sometimes this helped point a meaning not made explicit in the
text, as where the illustrations of Turveydrop and Chadband,
heading the same number of *Bleak House* cheek by jowl, and
showing them in strikingly similar poses, suggest a parallel between them.[14] But the placement of the illustrations in the monthly numbers was a printing convenience; only when all the monthly parts were in hand ready for binding (the title page and introductory matter supplied with the final double number) could the
illustrations be placed more precisely in relation to the narrative.
There is a more direct relationship between story and picture in
The Old Curiosity Shop and *Barnaby Rudge*, where the illustrations (each occupying a fourth to a half of a page) are placed
within the text. The general principle of placement is to put the

illustration as close as possible to the passage illustrated, and following it. Except for the very occasional use of an illustration at the head of the part, it will be placed below the passage, or, if the passage is on the lefthand side but too far down to leave room for the illustration, on the facing page. (When, as sometimes happens, the passage as printed turns out to fall too far down the righthand page, the illustration has to go on the next page. This would seem to be a defect intrinsic to the system.) The same principle governs in the two Christmas books I have seen, *A Christmas Carol* and *The Battle of Life*, except that in *The Battle of Life* some ingenuity is occasionally attempted in the placement of text: the cut is irregularly shaped instead of rectangular, so that some lines of text may appear in what amounts on the page to an open space in the illustration. Because the eccentricity makes the reader attend to the physical location of words on the page, a little uncertain where to go next, this innovation works against the main effect achieved by the general principle—which principle is more evidence of Dickens's determination that his readers should know what he meant—the nearly simultaneous taking in of text and illustration (and nearly unconscious fusion of verbal and visual images).

III   *Journalism*

Dickens's novels made him famous in his own time and keep his name familiar today, but the way he kept in continuous touch with his audience, through most of his career, was through his journalism. A good deal of it is still of interest, both for what it tells of Dickens's activities and interests apart from his novels, and for the light it casts on his novels. He worked briefly in 1832 as a reporter for a struggling new evening paper, the *True Sun*, and from 1832 to 1834 he worked for the *Mirror of Parliament*, which his uncle John Henry Barrow had founded in 1828 to publish reports of Parliamentary proceedings. The reputation he made there for speed and accuracy repaid the trials he had undergone to learn shorthand on his own; he became Parliamentary reporter for the daily *Morning Chronicle* in 1834, employed the year around instead of during Parliamentary sessions only. A dozen years later, in January 1846, he was the founding editor of the *Daily News*, resigning, however, after only seventeen numbers (J 583). He edited the monthly *Bentley's Miscellany* for its first two years, from January 1837 through the March number in 1839. A few months later he disclosed to Chapman and Hall his ideas for a weekly periodical. They liked his plan, and *Master Humphrey's Clock*, edited by Dickens, began publishing in April 1840 and continued through November 1841. As early as July 1845 Dickens was already thinking of another weekly (P IV, 327–28). But the *Daily News* venture and other things interposed, and not until 30 March 1850 did *Household Words* appear. Dickens closed *Household Words* in 1859 in a dispute with his then publishers Bradbury and Evans, having begun another weekly on the same plan, *All the Year Round*, which he edited until his death.[15]

He not only edited these periodicals, he wrote for them as well (apart from the novels he serialized in them). Nearly all contributions were published anonymously, but the *Household Words* office record of the contributors identifies a great many articles by Dickens on a variety of themes and subjects. These articles have been generally available since B. W. Matz first published them in Chapman and Hall's National Edition (1906–1908). Using the same contributors' record, together with evidence of proofs and manuscripts, Harry Stone has identified (though of course not with absolute certainty, as he is careful to say) Dickens's contributions to pieces that he collaborated with others in for *Household Words* (see ch. 1, n. 2). No corresponding records for *All the Year Round* have come to light; it seems unlikely, however, given Dickens's increasing involvement in public readings in the 1860s, that he did then as much of the sort of work identified by Stone as he had done in the 1850s. But he did write nearly forty essays on various topics, seventeen of them in the first two years of the new journal. He published these in 1861, adding eleven more in a new edition in 1866; the rest were added in editions published after his death, carrying like the earlier ones his title *The Uncommercial Traveller*. The essays were unsigned, but the essayist was clearly enough Charles Dickens himself, pursuing (sometimes in a reminiscent mood) topics of general interest and concern, the stock in trade of this traveling salesman for "the great house of Human Interest Brothers," with "rather a large connection in the fancy goods way," as he wrote in the first one.

Dickens wrote sketches and fiction, in fact, for almost all of the newspapers he worked for and the periodicals he edited.[16] Indeed, it was his rapidly growing reputation as a writer that opened the early jobs as editor to him; his various contracts specified that he was to write something regularly himself besides doing the editing. Publishers clearly expected his writing to be the mainstay of success, and the fortunes of *Master Humphrey's Clock* showed they were right. Sales dropped steeply when early numbers made clear to readers that the magazine was a miscellany, not another serial novel by Dickens. Dickens's subsequent development of *The Old Curiosity Shop* as a novel was what saved the magazine. By the time the *Shop* closed, *Master Humphrey's Clock* was selling 100,000 copies.[17]

Part of the explanation for Dickens's troubles with Bentley in particular, it seems to me, is to be found here. Dickens thought of himself as editor of the *Miscellany*, which indeed he was, under his contract. But the contract did not give him the final absolute authority he felt he should have, while Bentley saw himself as the ultimate editor of the *Miscellany*, and Dickens as its chief property. It was for his market value as a writer that Bentley had engaged him in the first place; while he performed valuable labors as editor (which Bentley recognized), those labors could have been done by someone else, and Bentley, as the owner, saw it as his own right to step into the management of the *Miscellany* when he saw fit. This is not to absolve Bentley from blame, but only to explain how, given Dickens's hatred of being under someone else's control, the arrangement Dickens had gladly entered into could turn out so sour. It was that, as he wrote in the last number he had anything to do with, the magazine had "always been literally 'Bentley's' *Miscellany*," and never his.[18]

But the experience taught him much. Thereafter his agreements to edit periodicals stipulated that besides drawing a salary he would be part owner himself, and would have full authority to hire and fire the other contributors and to determine rates of pay. His contract as editor of *Master Humphrey's Clock* gave him half the profits. He also had half the profits of *Household Words*, but his assistant editor W. H. Wills had one-eighth, and so did

Forster, so that Bradbury and Evans's share was reduced to one-fourth; and Chapman and Hall were paid strictly for printing *All the Year Round*—Dickens and Wills divided the profits between them, three-fourths and one-fourth.[19] Both *Household Words* and *All the Year Round* turned out to be very good properties. After Dickens reversed the decline in *Household Words* sales by going in with *Hard Times*, circulation during the best years was around 40,000. *All the Year Round* did even better, trebling the *Household Words* circulation by its fifth number and climbing to a circulation of 300,000 by the time of Dickens's death (J 946–47). These circulation figures assured Dickens of a steady and considerable income, what with his salary as editor and his share of the profits. But he earned his pay, not because his name insured a good sale—it did not, in fact, unless it was accompanied by his own fiction, as various episodes in the history of both periodicals show—but because he put a great deal of time and thought, especially during the early years of *Household Words*, into designing them.

Both *Household Words* and *All the Year Round* were, according to their title pages, "conducted" by Dickens, not "edited": a choice of words that made clear he had to answer to no one. He aimed *Household Words*, Stone says, primarily at the middle class; but "it was cheap enough and popular enough to be read by the literate lower classes, and it was interesting enough and diversified enough to attract the leisured as well. Dickens' influence, therefore, could be exerted immediately and widely. *Household Words* became a force to reckon with; its imaginative blend of knowledge and entertainment (combined with humanitarianism and a feeling radicalism) procured it a hearing, especially amongst the moderate and the uncommitted, that more doctrinaire journals rarely received" (p. 21). So, by his weekly periodicals, Dickens became a powerful force in mid-nineteenth-century England, even among people who did not read his novels, and even among those who expressed little regard for those novels, like the man G. H. Lewes referred to in an article shortly after Dickens died: "It is not long since I heard a very distinguished man express measureless contempt for Dickens, and a few minutes afterwards, in reply to some representations on the other side, admit that Dickens had 'entered into his life.'"[20]

IV *Poems and Plays*

Strictly speaking, an account of Dickens's poems and plays does not belong in this chapter, but it belongs nowhere else either, and some mention should be made. Mention is all the poems deserve. They include a few complimentary verses written in young women's albums (four of them in Maria Beadnell's), four songs in *Pickwick Papers*, songs from his own play *The Village Coquettes*, a few poems published here and there, and some verse he "dropped into" when writing friends. The poems appearing in *Pickwick Papers* and *The Village Coquettes* would probably have been assumed to be his; very few published elsewhere were signed. Most of the poems were searched out and published by Frederick G. Kitton in 1903 and included in the National Edition; a few more (including the album verses) had been discovered by the time the Nonesuch Edition came out in 1937–38. That Dickens never collected them himself is probably a fair indication how he valued them, and if so, a modest tribute to his critical perceptions. The poems to Maria Beadnell have some interest as coming from an important episode in his life, and they show Dickens trying hard to scintillate; mostly, though, Dickens's verse is poor stuff, metrically galloping and relying heavily on poetic diction that sounds like the eighteenth century.

His plays are a little more significant. Two of them belong to the *Pickwick* year and no doubt helped, and were helped by, the explosion of Boz's fame. *The Strange Gentleman* was funny enough, and done well enough, to have a run of nearly two months in the fall of 1836 and to be put on again after the new year. *The Village Coquettes*, a comic opera, opened in December, and while audiences enjoyed it critics found less to admire (liking John Hullah's music better than Dickens's play). His one-act comedy *Is She His Wife?* was produced in March 1837, but was not nearly as successful as *The Strange Gentleman* had been; and *The Lamplighter*, a farce Dickens wrote for Macready in 1838, never made it into production (Dickens later turned it into a story).[21] In later years Dickens collaborated with Mark Lemon in a farce, *Mr. Nightingale's Diary* (1851), and with Wilkie Collins in *No Thoroughfare* (1867), a five-act dramatic version of their Christmas story of the same title for *All the Year Round*.

Dickens's name does not appear as coauthor of *The Frozen Deep,* which was first produced in January 1857, but Johnson says he had almost as much to do with its ultimate shape as its ostensible author Collins.[22] *Mr. Nightingale's Diary* and *The Frozen Deep* were staged by Dickens's amateur troupe and were extremely successful, owing probably more to Dickens's energizing presence in the management and performance than to merits of the works themselves. *No Thoroughfare* had successful runs at theaters in both London and Paris.[23]

All these plays, according to the National Edition headnote, were published in pamphlet form shortly after they were produced. As with his poems, Dickens himself never gathered them for republication; in fact, he is supposed to have said he would not have *The Village Coquettes* republished for £1,000. Still, these works lay nearer his heart than the poems. He was intensely engaged with the earlier ones, had high hopes of their success, and haunted the theater during production. The later plays engaged him just as intensely, though not from the same motives; at that stage of his life his career was already made, in another direction. But the theatrical activity satisfied his drive to shape and control, as well as providing the satisfaction of appreciative audiences, and the chance to divert himself from the circumstances in his life that he found increasingly burdensome.

I turn now from the works of Dickens in which he met his audience in print, to those works in which he met them face to face—surely the most satisfying relationship to him, the one he envisioned himself in first of all when he thought of a career in theater.

V *Speeches*

Dickens was in great demand as a speaker throughout his career; the 115 speeches recorded by K. J. Fielding extend from 1837 to less than two months before his death in 1870.[24] The record shows him speaking on a variety of public forums: testimonial dinners, anniversary dinners, and other such public occasions conventional in Victorian society. The speeches are significant and interesting because in them we have Dickens mak-

ing public his personal views on a variety of issues, often issues
that he is dealing with at the time in a novel, and so we may
learn something by comparison of the two treatments. We will
never know, however, exactly what Dickens said in any of the
speeches he gave. He never read from a prepared text and he
never used notes except for facts, figures, and quotations. The
nearest we have to exact texts are for a speech he made to the
Metropolitan Sanitary Association on 10 May 1851, and for his
last speech, at the Royal Academy banquet on 30 April 1870.
Dickens wrote out texts of these two afterwards, the first one
for his brother-in-law Henry Austin, the last for *The Times*. For
some few other speeches he corrected proofs of what reporters
had taken down. For all the rest, the texts must come from reports printed at the time. The importance of comparing as many
reports as possible, for this majority of cases, is obvious; and
yet, K. J. Fielding says, as far as he has been able to tell, the
earliest edition of Dickens's speeches, and the reprints of other
speeches that have turned up over the years, were always taken
from a single source (pp. xvi, xxi). For his 1960 edition of the
speeches Fielding started over; apart from the speeches where
the authority of the text comes from Dickens himself, Fielding
consulted "all the better reports of any speech that could be
found." There is no way to settle the texts finally, considering
how widely the printed reports of speeches vary; "any one of
them by itself might be accepted as reasonably accurate," Fielding says, "if the others were not completely different" (p. xvii).
In some cases the reports are so fragmentary that about all
Fielding can do is to say Dickens did give a speech. But Fielding's edition, considering his methods, his knowledge of Dickens's
style and substance, and the state of the records, is as close to
what Dickens must have said as we are likely to get.

Dickens may not have written his speeches out beforehand,
but he certainly did prepare them nonetheless. He told George
Dolby (his manager for the reading tours from 1866 on) what
he did to get ready for a speech: he would take a long walk,
during which he would decide what ought to go into the speech,
and what order to take up the various subtopics in. He must
have worked it all out in considerable detail, for his delivery,

according to the Duke of Argyll, "was the very perfection of neatness and precision in language—the speaking of a man who knew exactly what he was going to say, and how best to say it."[25]

VI *Public Readings*

However, the duke felt the same surprise that many did at Dickens's manner—"without fire or tones of enthusiasm, or flights of fancy; there was nothing that makes the orator." But as a reader of his own works, the duke wrote, Dickens was a wonderful actor. Macready, who *was* an actor, was absolutely done up, as Dickens wrote to an American friend, by the reading from *Oliver Twist* (the murder of Nancy): " 'In my—er—best times—er—you remember them, my dear boy—er—gone, gone!—no,'—with great emphasis again,—'it comes to this—er—TWO MACBETHS!' with extraordinary energy. After which he stood (with his glass in his hand and his old square jaw of its old fierce form) looking defiantly at Dolby as if Dolby had contradicted him; and then trailed off into a weak pale likeness of himself as if his whole appearance had been some clever optical illusion."[26] There is plenty of other testimony to Dickens's power as a reader in the biographies, in reminiscences of people who heard him, and in his own letters, where he tells his correspondents—and it does not read like boasting, but like satisfaction, even joy—how overwhelming this or that reception by an audience was. The best place to read about this is in Philip Collins's introduction to his edition of Dickens's readings, where he quotes Carlyle (among others)—"I had no conception, before hearing Dickens read, of what capacities lie in the human face and voice. No theatre-stage could have had more players than seemed to flit about his face, and all tones were present"—and goes into the question whether the tradition of Dickens's power as a reader has been exaggerated, and concludes on the whole not.[27]

The public readings were just as significant in Dickens's career as his novels and his magazines were. For one thing, he made a great deal of money by them. His first series of readings for pay in effect bought Gad's Hill Place. From his American tour in 1867–68 Dickens took home nearly £19,000. In all, he earned about £45,000 from his public readings—nearly half, according to his tour manager Dolby, of the £93,000 estate that he left.[28] Still, only to summarize Dickens's profits over the whole run of his public readings—about 472 in all, Collins says, twenty-seven of them for charity (p. xxv)—is to give the financial motive an importance it did not have, certainly not when he undertook the first paid readings, and I think not later either. Of course Dickens had a pretty shrewd idea that such a venture could be profitable; as early as 1846, the success of that private reading at Lausanne of the opening number of *Dombey and Son* led him to suggest to Forster that "readings of one's own books . . . would take immensely" (P IV, 631). Forster was against it then, and always, for the reason that weighed decisively with Dickens then—it would not suit his dignity as a professional writer. Readings for charitable purposes were another matter, of course, and Dickens did several readings of *A Christmas Carol* for charity from 1853 on.

Two other attractions of the idea finally changed his mind. One of them arose from the deterioration of his marriage; things were at a crisis between him and Catherine when he undertook the first paid series of readings beginning 29 April 1858. Dickens's spirits had plunged from the exhilaration he felt during the final production of Collins's play *The Frozen Deep* in August 1857, in the course of which he had become interested in the young actress Ellen Ternan (J 910–11). Early in 1858, by a jeweler's mistake Catherine received a bracelet meant for Ellen, and the open quarrel that followed led to a separation in May (J 916–19). Dickens's usual response to stress was restlessness, and his antidote was motion. So it is not surprising that he should see a series of public readings, something new, a distraction, as worth trying now: "The domestic unhappiness," he wrote Collins, "remains so strong upon me that I can't write, and (waking) can't rest, one minute. I have never known a moment's peace or content, since the last night of The Frozen Deep. . . . In this condition though nothing can alter or soften it, I have a turning notion that the mere physical effort and change of the Readings would be good, as another means of bearing it" (N III, 14). This was in March, when he was also writing Forster, "It is all despairingly over" (F VIII, ii, 646), and going on to describe the tour he proposed; and his publisher Evans, asking his opinion on various

points of the proposal (N III, 11–12). Philip Collins suggests
that the marital crash may have come when it did partly because
"spring and early summer were the traditional season for many
kinds of platform events" (p. xxiii). The suggestion is persuasive:
a dreary joyless relationship from which as Dickens saw it there
was no escape—"a dismal failure has to be borne" (F VIII, ii,
646)—but from which he craved distraction; a plan he had been
turning over for years, offering the sort of remedy in action that
he always took; the relationship coming to a crisis at a moment
when putting the plan into effect was most favored by external
circumstances.

But if the marital breakdown was important for deciding
Dickens to launch the readings when he did, their main and enduring appeal for him was that they promised to put him in the
closest possible relation with his public. In later years he
would consider more and more the money he could get from them.
The reason he urged in that letter to Forster, however (and in
almost the same words to his publisher)—"that particular relation
(personally affectionate and like no other man's) which subsists
between me and the public"—was powerful with him throughout
his career.[29] His sense of that relationship, and his desire for it,
appears in his prefaces to his novels, where he acknowledges
the "unbounded warmth and earnestness of [my readers'] sympathy in every stage of the journey" (*Dombey and Son*), or looks
forward "with a hopeful glance towards the time when I shall
again put forth my two green leaves once a month . . ." (*David
Copperfield*). He expresses himself to this effect most completely
in the preface to *Little Dorrit*: "In the Preface to *Bleak House*
I remarked that I had never had so many readers. In the Preface
to its next successor, *Little Dorrit*, I have still to repeat the same
words. Deeply sensible of the affection and confidence that have
grown up between us, I add to this Preface, as I added to that,
May we meet again!" The importance he attached to this relationship was also evident in his early speculations to Forster
about a weekly magazine in 1845: "I would at once . . . take a
personal and confidential position with them which should separate me, instantly, from all other periodicals . . ." (P IV, 328).
And it appears in the opening number of *Household Words* five
years later: "We aspire to live in the Household affections, and

to be numbered among the Household thoughts, of our readers. We hope to be the comrade and friend of many thousands of people, of both sexes, and of all ages and conditions, on whose faces we may never look."

So when Dickens reminded Forster of "that particular relation" between him and his public, he was surely deeply in earnest. And if the money he could earn came to weigh more and more with him, the attractions of the audience did not grow less. He persisted in the readings against the advice of friends, business associates, and physicians, and gave them up only when his symptoms were too grave even for him to discount. Johnson suggests that this reckless persistence may have been unconsciously suicidal—"he had ceased to care what happened" (J 1104)— and goes on to specify the disappointments Dickens experienced in his latter years that robbed life of meaning for him. One meaning, it seems to me, life had for Dickens to the end: something to which he opposed his will daily, and opposing, subdued, and so affirmed his own being. So it is misleading to suggest that he sought death. Rather, he would risk death to keep on being himself. It is also too simple to conclude that he "killed himself for money."[30] His profits, Dolby wrote, "were purchased at the dear cost of the sacrifice of his health"; on the other hand, "the pleasure he derived from [this career] is not to be told in words."[31] Pleasure, yes, and something more than pleasure, to account for how the deep cold that never left him on his American tour, reducing his voice to a whisper, would somehow recede during performances so that, as he wrote Forster, "I was not (for the time) even hoarse" (F X, ii, 786). Dickens drew something more vital than pleasure from the contact with his public, from "that particular relation." Applause and affection confirmed his imaginings to him, authenticated the realities he had made of his beliefs and desires: assured him that he was, in some ultimate sense, *right*. Collins quotes from a report of his farewell performance in Dublin in January 1869: "The people stood up and cheered him lustily. It is not that the world knows Mr. Dickens to be merely a great man; but we all know him to be a good man. And, therefore, his reading is not looked upon as a performance, but as a friendly meeting longed for by people to whom he has been kind" (p. liii). A *New York Tribune* reviewer wrote, "An immense chord of feeling has been touched and sounded by Charles Dickens. . . . Something of this affectionate feeling was heartily expressed by his audience last night; nor in all that great throng was there a single mind unconscious of the privilege it enjoyed in being able, even so partially, to thank Charles Dickens for all the happiness he has given to the world." Collins quotes another remark of this reviewer, too, with which it seems appropriate to close this chapter: ". . . what he is doing now [i.e., reading his works in public] is only the natural outgrowth of what he has been doing all the days of his life." Collins's excellent edition of Dickens's texts for his readings gives us all that we can have of this climax; what Dickens's audiences received, we must infer from what scholars and critics recover.

CHAPTER 3

"A Low, Cheap Form of Publication": Dickens's Serial Composition

A S I NOTED earlier, Dickens could afford by 1847—eleven years into his fame—to poke fun at the friends who had been afraid publishing in monthly parts would damage his literary stock. K. J. Fielding, one of the critics who have helped to turn attention to Dickens's methods as a serial novelist, thinks that Victorian readers had no trouble accepting monthly serialization (no doubt in good part because of Dickens's successful performance). The reservations about that method developed later, as critical concern for structural unity in the novel grew stronger.[1] The conventional wisdom about Dickens's failings which developed out of that concern lasted a long time, although it is just a bit surprising to find it all offered so patly as late as this introduction to a 1964 edition of *Great Expectations*: "For a writer like Dickens, who often began the issue of serial novels before he had fully worked out a plan for them, the result was too often a temptation to tailor his work to public response as the parts appeared, to introduce sensational climaxes to keep the parts selling, and to resort to arbitrary measures to unravel the plot complications."[2] Such a judgment misrepresents seriously how Dickens's serial composition did affect the way he laid out his narrative, which my purpose is in this chapter to explain. Something else, implicit in that judgment, is misleading too, and needs setting in perspective if Dickens's work as a serial novelist is to be rightly appreciated: the image of Dickens as an inexhaustible fictive flowing well. I will take that up first.

This longstanding view of Dickens is an inference from his vivacious personality and the copiousness of his novels. Henry

Burnett's anecdote about Dickens writing *Oliver Twist* in the midst of his family (above, p. 37) comes from the early days. More typically, in December 1846 (working on *Dombey*) Dickens "sat six hours at a stretch, and wrote as many lines..." (P IV, 675). But that was often the case even early: during *Nickleby* (F II, iv, 124), and during *Oliver Twist*, too—he described himself one day to Forster as "sitting patiently at home waiting for Oliver Twist who has not yet arrived" (P I, 387). That was not unusual, for as he wrote Forster later about *Barnaby Rudge*, "The contents of one number usually require a day's thought at the very least..." (P II, 218–19). The gestation periods stretched out longer as the years went by, and brought more intense discomfort. Such stoppages were especially acute when he was getting underway with a new book. "The first shadows of a new story" (*Bleak House*, in this case) were likely, he wrote Mary Boyle in February 1851, to begin "hovering in a ghostly way about me...when I have finished an old one" (N II, 274); nearer the moment of actually sitting down to his writing table with its neat arrangement of knicknacks, he would be struck with "violent restlessness, and vague ideas of going I don't know where, I don't know why...," as he wrote Miss Coutts in August 1851 (N II, 338). The agonies continued into the actual writing. Trying to get started on the first number of *Little Dorrit* meant "walking about the country by day—prowling about into the strangest places in London by night—sitting down to do an immensity—getting up after doing nothing—walking about my room on particular bits of all the flowers in the carpet—tearing my hair (which I can't afford to do)—and on the whole astonished at my own condition, though I am used to it...."[3]

Such distress led Dickens from January 1855, before he began writing *Little Dorrit*, through the period when he was writing *Our Mutual Friend*, to keep a "Book of Memoranda" (now in the Berg Collection of the New York Public Library) in which he jotted down anything that struck him as possibly coming in handy someday—phrases, sketches for stories or characters, notes about things seen, bits of dialogue, lists of possible titles and of names for characters. Some of these ideas found their way into later works unconceived at the time; others never did get worked up. (It is interesting to speculate what Dickens might have done with such notes as "Bright-eyed creature selling jewels. The stones and the eyes" [F IX, vii, 753].) The strain of generating material also shows in Dickens's increasing concern to have a good running start before he began publishing. He usually began with fewer numbers finished than he had hoped, though, and lost ground along the way, and he would end up writing with the printer at his heels as in the early days. He hoped to start *Our Mutual Friend* with five numbers in hand (significant of his estimate of his own diminished energy in 1864: he had started publishing *Dombey* with two). He did get four ready, if I interpret Forster's account correctly, but within two months he lost half his margin (F IX, v, 740–43; V, vi, 441).

So the image of the Dickensian flowing well is a false one, which may hearten—or perhaps discourage—students, and professors, trying to condense the cloudy intimations hovering above their own arid paper plains. Filling those weekly and monthly pages was very much more than a matter of channeling the flow of invention. The reason for Dickens's difficulty, however, was not so much a drought-stricken imagination as something else. Of course he got older, and what Forster calls his "astonishing animal spirits" (F II, iv, 124) flowed with less force; his marriage got older, too; his family larger; his distractions greater—worries about the disappointing sales of *Chuzzlewit* dogged him as he began *Dombey*. But he also reached farther. His early manuscripts show him writing more and blotting less, which no doubt indicates as Butt and Tillotson say "a hand racing to keep pace with the mind's conceptions" (p. 20). The erasures and interlineations that are characteristic from *Dombey and Son* on, however, signify more than lessening force: they mean that Dickens had more in mind to do than he did earlier. He grew, as he said while writing *Our Mutual Friend*, "hard to satisfy" (F IX, v, 741).[4]

It is not coincidence, then, that from *Dombey and Son* on, with only two exceptions, Dickens worked from the number plans I shall turn to shortly. "Method in everything was Dickens's peculiarity," wrote Forster (F XI, iii, 836). I have already mentioned what Dickens's children remembered about his tidiness and about the orderliness he tried to instill in them. His habits of work too were orderly: "[He] passed his life from day to day, divided for the most part between working and walking, the same wherever he was."[5] The last working day of his life, "much against his usual custom," he spent the whole day writing; normally, Forster says, he worked from breakfast until luncheon (F XII, i, 851; XI, iii, 836). It was not always that neat, however. In the early years of his career, Dickens might be found writing almost any time from morning to midnight, trying to stay on top of all he had undertaken, as his brother-in-law wrote and on the evidence of letters Forster himself quotes (F II, iii, 111).[6] So in saying Dickens usually wrote only until luncheon, Forster probably meant that was his custom after those frenetic years of his rise. But his daughter Mamie wrote that at Gad's Hill, where Dickens moved his family after separating from Catherine in 1858, he would often return to his study after lunch, having been so absorbed in his work during the meal as scarcely to have spoken; and Dickens's niece said the same.[7]

So most likely it was not just at first that the working hours were extended. Nor was Dickens what Butt and Tillotson call a "clockwork performer like Trollope" (p. 19); the words did not flow on command from nine o'clock to one, even at the beginning. Hence the elaborate rituals of prewriting familiar to all writers facing jobs they know to be formidable: part evasion and postponement, part clearing the mind of dragging distraction (at the cost, unluckily, of dissipating some energy)—letters, of course (as instanced above), and walks, and arrangings. In the years at Gad's Hill Place, the final phase of Dickens's life and career, the arrangement of objects and writing materials on his desk, and chairs and tables in the room, would be preceded "(such was his love of order in everything around him) by seeing that all was in its place in the several rooms, visiting also the dogs, stables, and kitchen garden, and closing, unless the weather was very bad indeed, with a turn or two round the meadow before settling to his desk" (F VIII, iii, 657).

No wonder that Dickens still had writing to do often after lunch; that morning reserved to himself every day for work had to accommodate much else—or more precisely, the "work" of writing was very much wider than putting words to paper. It also went on nearly until the parts appeared at the booksellers'. His regular practice was to write as he composed and to correct and revise as he went. What the printer got was these first drafts, much or little written over as might be, since interlineations and strikeouts had to be pretty thick for Dickens to decide he needed to provide a clean copy for the printers (who assigned his manuscripts to picked compositors, presumably experienced at dealing with Dickens's hand).[8] Dickens corrected printed text on galley proofs if there was time, but usually there was not; most of the corrected proofs in existence are page proofs. These pages will show additions if Dickens found that he had underwritten the number, and deletions if he had overwritten. Thirty of his manuscript pages would come to about the required thirty-two pages of print, but minor adjustments were often necessary to make the text fit the space. This was regularly enough the case so that Dickens, writing someone on 28 January 1848, said he had to keep his time free of engagements about this time of month, "being always liable, if *my proofs are late, to have to revise them at the printers*, and if there is too much matter (as is the case this month) to take it out, and put them all to rights and leave them on the press" (N II, 70). To cut, Dickens would trim dialogue, usually comic scenes; sometimes space was saved by typesetting devices, or if Dickens felt the "over-matter" simply had to stay in, by adding a line to the page. More drastic change might involve switching chapters about, as Dickens considered doing when the first number of *Dombey and Son* turned out six pages too long; Forster persuaded him to cut instead (J 601). Coming up short, especially as much as two pages or more (as in *Dombey and Son* VI, *Bleak House* XVI, and *Our Mutual Friend* XVI) could be more trouble still: there was no time to fill out the sixth number of *Dombey* any other way than by going to London to write the necessary—and Dickens was in Paris when he found out he was short (F VI, ii, 482; N II, 16).

I *The Number Plans*

But if the achievement fell short of the purpose to do all the writing from nine o'clock to one every day, the pattern of working by "rule and order," essential as Forster said "to all men who do much" (F XI, iii, 836), is clear. The primary evidence of that is the thirty-five-year-long train of monthly and weekly parts, from the second installment of *The Old Curiosity Shop* never broken once set in motion, and only three times before that.[9] Not even Dickens could have sustained that output, however, or kept his readers by mere repetition of the loose discursive style he began. Dickens met the challenge of maintaining his hold on readers by learning to plan an action larger than the action of the individual number, which the number advanced and which the reader could see promised to be more than a chain of similar links. This involved more than mere outlines, too, such as Butt and Tillotson are sure Dickens had, though "in all probability they were never written down" (p. 28). But a merely general idea where he was going would have been useless to Dickens, considering the circumstances in which he wrote. Since composing these monthly (or weekly) parts was only one phase of a cycle of varied, voluminous, and demanding work and play every month (or week), how to keep track of where he was, and how to keep generating the story, were critical.

Dickens's basic resource as usual was method, in this case the practice he followed from *Dombey and Son* on (except for *A Tale of Two Cities* and *Great Expectations*) of beginning the composition of each part by making a plan of the number. (Notes for earlier novels exist, but not very systematic ones, except for numbers IV and VI of *Martin Chuzzlewit.*) He would fold a single sheet of paper across the middle, head the right-hand half-sheet with the title of the novel and the number of the part, and space down the sheet the numbers of the chapters to be included. On the left-hand page he would write down his ideas for what was to go into the number as a whole; notes of particular developments would be distributed into the appropriate chapter sections of the right-hand page. (Sometimes these latter notes seem to have been written in after the installment was written, which suggests Dickens also used these plans to refresh his memory as he was about to move into the next installment.)

Described as baldly as this, these plans seem more finished and orderly than they really are. Close study of the kind Butt and Tillotson did reveals how a monthly number plan records the process by which the number took shape in Dickens's mind. Often the notes on the right-hand pages would be as specific as bits of dialogue. Or Dickens may be seen debating which story development to carry out this time. Since I have more to say about this further on, I will leave it for the present, only remarking that from evidence of the different inks Dickens used, his underlining, and the like (even the placement and density of the notes, and the heaviness or faintness of the writing), Butt and Tillotson make Dickens's study live again. Anybody interested in Dickens's creative process will find their chapter on *David Copperfield* especially interesting, where they reprint all the monthly plans and show the story taking shape, and Dickens debating alternative developments with himself, perhaps not seeing some possibilities until actually involved in planning.[10]

But this brings me back to what I called at the beginning of the chapter "the conventional wisdom about Dickens's failings": that he improvised story material to suit immediate reader response, and to make sensational part endings, and to resolve his plots. Most of the passage I quoted will surely draw strong dissent today, from anyone appreciative of the sort of work done by Butt and Tillotson in particular. Angus Wilson, however—an accomplished novelist himself—agrees that Dickens was not strong on plotting: "In fact he was a very clumsy contriver of plots, and often, as in *Little Dorrit*, the 'mysteries' are only unravelled in the last chapters in a mass of complicated and suddenly revealed events that have taken place before the action of the novel began." Wilson (like G. K. Chesterton earlier in this century, who Fielding says fixed the image of Dickens as a hapless plotter) thinks this is relatively unimportant, because the plots "are only the mechanism by which the great imaginative magic lantern works; the total significance of what Dickens shows us in his novels is a hundred times greater than his plots."[11]

But this qualification shows Wilson would not agree that Dickens was tempted into irrelevancies by the method of serial publication. If he is right about that, two of the charges are wrong. In fact, these charges look like deductive exercises—descriptions of abuses that serial publication is hypothetically open to, which Fielding (writing in 1958) says critics until recently took for granted that Dickens committed. Let us look at some evidence: the texts of the novels, and Dickens's plans for the individual installments.

II   *The Influence of Readers' Response*

Dickens did of course care about ending an installment in a
way to bring his readers back next month, a matter I will return
to shortly. I will take up the other allegation first, about tailoring
his work to public response. That Dickens was keenly interested
in the reception of his work is surely true; his letters show that
he got the sales figures from his publishers as soon as he could,
and I have discussed in chapter 2 his need for a sense of close
contact with his readers. The point of the charge, however, is the
implication that he allowed public response to shape what he
wrote without regard to his artistic judgment: to go to examples,
that he changed his plan for *The Old Curiosity Shop* when it became apparent that *Master Humphrey's Clock* would stop unless
some change was made in its works; that he sent young Martin
to America in an effort to boost sales of *Martin Chuzzlewit*; and
that he materially altered the character of the dwarf Miss Mowcher in *David Copperfield* in response to the protest of the character's original in life.[12] Only one of these particular assertions
is untrue, but it is too simple to conclude therefore that Dickens
pandered to his audience. According to Forster he "had intended
to employ the character [Miss Mowcher] in an unpleasant way,"
but agreed to transform her "whatever the risk or inconvenience,"
and did, ten chapters and three monthly parts later (VI, vii, 548).
The change, however, does not affect the story line at all, and only
jars to the degree that the name "Mowcher" does not chime with
the transformed character; so Dickens did not change anything
significant in his plan.[13] Sending Martin to America was possible
to him because while he undertook in *Martin Chuzzlewit* to "resist the temptation of the current Monthly Number, and to keep a
steadier eye upon the general purpose and design" (as he says
in his 1844 preface), he was still writing enough in the style of
his first fame that to make room for an episode not originally envisioned was not to disturb the aesthetic shape of the work. This
sounds like a legalist's defense—it amounts to saying that he did
not alter his plan because there was no plan to alter. But there was
a plan by the time he had Martin announce his intention (at the
end of the fifth number), if not so complete a one as he developed for later novels (F IV, i, 290). And if one motive was to

appeal to readers with an appetite for caustic opinions about the United States, another (and a more important one, Forster says) was his desire to do combat: to reiterate the points he had made in his travel book *American Notes*, in the face of the clamor that that book had raised, especially in America (IV, ii, 302).

Finally, the instance of *The Old Curiosity Shop*, while often cited to show that Dickens improvised freely and without compunction, looks considerably different since Robert Patten studied that episode closely.[14] It is true that Dickens transformed *Master Humphrey's Clock* from the miscellany he had originally intended it to be, with contributions by others besides himself, into a twelve-page weekly pamphlet wholly given over to *The Old Curiosity Shop*. But it is not true that this change was entirely the upshot of an emergency conference called because of the disastrous fall in sales of the third number, as Edgar Johnson says (J 298). Without going into Patten's careful reconstruction of the sequence of events, I will simply summarize his case: that the decision to turn *Master Humphrey's Clock* into *The Old Curiosity Shop* was not a sudden expedient owing to the collapse of sales; Dickens made no drastic shift of plans for the next numbers; and Dickens's expansion of *The Old Curiosity Shop* was consistent with the rapid growth of the idea in his imagination, a development that began well before anybody knew of a crisis in sales—before, in fact, *Master Humphrey's Clock* began publishing at all.

There is far more evidence against the notion that Dickens improvised in tune to his public's reactions than there is for it. In the case of later novels, the number plans show that Dickens had many particulars in mind early; in *David Copperfield* Agnes Wickfield is identified as "the real heroine" in the plan for the fifth number, where she is introduced, and the admonition to himself to "carry the thread of Agnes through it all" appears during David's headlong infatuation with Dora in XII, as well as later. And on the other side, Dickens did not cancel any important move once he decided on it, whether his readers approved or not. Paul Dombey's death in the fifth number was not commuted, though there was great risk in cutting off a character so strongly developed as Paul. In the more famous earlier case of Little Nell, once Forster had suggested to Dickens that Nell's death was necessary to complete the effects he had developed, the reasons of aesthetic consistency prevailed over the protests and pleas of readers who saw where Nell's story was tending.[15] Dickens did write a new and happier ending for *Great Expectations* on the advice of his fellow novelist Bulwer-Lytton, to make the novel "more acceptable," as he told Forster (IX, iii, 737). While this change of plan was made possible by serial publication, it can hardly be a change made to keep sales up, since it comes at the end. And Dickens did not blithely change the whole tone of the novel with this ending; in fact, some critics think the second ending is at least as consistent with the story as the first.[16]

The case that used to be made against Dickens, then—that he used the chances serial publication offered to assure popularity at the expense of artistic intent—at the very least loses its clear-cut outlines when one considers circumstances in detail. And while I must disagree with Coolidge's view that serial publication generated Dickens's style, I certainly agree that it affected the arrangement Dickens gave to his material, and accounts thereby for a lot of the texture of his work.

To keep his readers' interest alive required that Dickens recognize clearly how different the relation was between readers and a novel published in its entirety, from the relation between readers and a novel published a piece at a time. In the former case, readers can deal with a relatively dull or heavy part by skipping, or if more conscientious, hearten themselves by glancing ahead to see if anything worthwhile lies at the end of the trip through the woods. But an uncongenial tract of a monthly installment cannot be redeemed that way. For one thing, a serial novelist "cannot afford," as Anthony Trollope saw, "to have many pages skipped out of the few which are to meet the reader's eye at the same time." To invite skipping is to risk creating the impression that one's novel has little substance: "who can imagine," Trollope continues, "the first half of the first volume of Scott's *Waverley* coming out in shilling numbers?"[17] And secondly, if readers find no relief this month they are less likely to be back the next. The lesson in both cases is that the action must be distributed; things have to keep happening at a pace which will bring some interesting "move" (as Dickens called it) along regularly, at least as often as once per part.

(His move in *Dombey and Son* V was the death of Paul, in VI the bringing forward of Florence, in VII the introduction of Edith, and so on. He wrote Forster in June 1849 that he had "a move in [*David Copperfield*] ready for this month; another for next; and another for the next," and so felt "quite confident in the story" [VI, vi, 536].)

Also, the serial novelist must remember that his readers have other things to do than concern themselves with his story; their recollection of any installment will be painted over daily. Dickens conceded (in his "Postscript" to *Our Mutual Friend*) that this was a disadvantage to periodical publication: "[I]t would be very unreasonable to expect that many readers, pursuing a story in portions from month to month through nineteen months, will, until they have it before them complete, perceive the relation of its finer threads to the whole pattern which is always before the eyes of the story weaver at his loom." He had made the same point to Forster about *Great Expectations*: "It is a pity that the third portion cannot be read all at once, because its purpose would be much more apparent..." (IX, iii, 737). So it will not do to let any character or plot line disappear from the story too long. Thus the importance of arrangement, as Coolidge says: all of the story elements have to be distributed into this pattern of regularly paced action to insure that they keep the prominence they should have.

The number plans show Dickens attending to these various needs as he thought the installment out.[18] As the novel lengthened in print, and the plot lines and characters multiplied, they would appear in notes on the left-hand page of later number plans, often with question marks following, and with the answers written down and underlined to indicate decision. Thus for *David Copperfield* VI, "Uriah Heep?" and "Mr. Micawber?" were decided "yes" ("and Mrs." added for the latter); presumably Dickens wanted to lay the groundwork for Micawber's later employment by Heep, which is to prove Heep's undoing. In VII, knowing the novel, one can see what Dickens has in mind when "Litttle Em'ly?" follows "Steerforth?" with both moves decided for; Steerforth has been absent since III and Emily since IV, and her seduction is to be started. "The two partners?" however are decided against. They stand over until VIII, where they appear, after some indecision, as "Spenlow and Jorkins," and

David's professional career and his romance with Dora Spenlow
are laid down there. It would have been extravagant of plot
material to cram two such important lines of action as Emily's
seduction and David's romance into one part, and also each
deserves undivided attention. In IX Steerforth's appearance
seems to have been decided against from the start—"No Steerforth this time. Keep him out"—while David's romance with
Dora is given full play. Some of the notes show how Dickens
contrived to keep a character before his readers without bringing him onstage: "Carry through, the unravelling of Uriah Heep,
always by Mr. Micawber" in XVI, for example. After Steerforth
has disappeared with Emily, he too must be brought back that
way: the note for XV about his mother and her companion Rosa
Dartle adds, "Carry Steerforth through by means of them." (The
double underlining looks like Dickens worrying a little that he
might forget, in the course of writing up the part.)

III   *Dickens's Part Endings*

The number plans show Dickens working out the pace and
distribution of his action, but they reveal less about how he
solved the problem of ending a number. It is necessary to look at
the text itself for that, because an ending is a question of tone
and intensity, or pitch, as well as incident. Many critics have
assumed sensational climaxes are the regular thing. But if parts
end at the cliff's edge as often as has regularly been claimed,
it is odd that recent editors of text editions have thought it
useful to indicate where the breaks between installments come:
one would think those places would be obvious. However,
Kathleen Tillotson says, not so: "It goes without saying that the
[part] endings do not deal in the grosser kinds of suspense,
familiar in the old film serials."[19]

So we are not to look for cliff-hanging. And this is sensible
of Dickens, given the basic condition of periodical publication,
which is interruption. Readers are engaged with the novel only
a very short time each month; most of the interval they are
occupied with other things. To leave readers at a high pitch
of suspense intensifies their frustration and risks making them

feel manipulated. But it also puts the next part under disadvantage, because while the narrative logic requires the story to move on at the same intensity at which it left off, to the readers, whose feelings have had a month to modulate, the pitch of this "grosser kind of suspense" will now seem decidedly artificial.

Dickens's practice was generally to leave off, as Coolidge says, with "events which the readers will see must have interesting consequences or which are left incomplete in some way" (p. 56). It might be done sometimes by juggling chapter order. We would need external evidence of some kind—in a letter, or a number plan—to be sure of Dickens's motives for changes, and there is none that I know of. Dickens did want to use the fourth chapter of *Dombey and Son* I in the the second number instead, but Forster persuaded him not to (VI, ii, 473). And in *Edwin Drood* he did shift chapter 5 from the second number to the first, providing a somewhat more ominous ending than chapter 4 would have done. But that cannot have been the main intent, because Dickens's motive was the length of the part: he had underwritten the first number by twelve printed pages (F XI, ii, 810). The problem in *Dombey and Son* I was space too, not the kind of part ending to be crafted; Dickens had overwritten the first number by nearly a fifth.

Coolidge sees seven patternings of incident by which Dickens contrived his "curtain" (borrowing a term from drama).[20] I will only characterize the range of part ending effects I see in Dickens, indicating how the ordering of incidents contributes. The simplest kind, nearest to the crude cliff-hanger, consists of an action underway as the part ends. Such a close gives the least sense of a pause, or of the identity of the part, and focuses reader interest on a point ahead. The suspense here seems more likely to survive a weekly interval than a monthly one. Dickens must have thought so, too, for he ends a part this way much more often in his five novels published in weekly parts than he does in the others. For instance, no more than three installments of *Nicholas Nickleby*, three of *David Copperfield*, and three of *Bleak House* are likely to strike a reader as belonging to this kind. But perhaps nearly a third of the weekly installments seem to end this way, and nearly a fourth even in *Great Expectations*, the last one. (The exception is *Hard Times*, where only four installments appear to the reader to end in midaction. — I explain why I say "seem" and "appear" at the end of this section.) Usually the tension of the narrative is not screwed tighter at the very end of the part, except in *Barnaby Rudge*, where part endings come close to cliff-hanging pretty often—oddly enough, considering that this is the only novel Dickens ever thought of publishing in entirety.

But even the relatively simple form of interest drawing the reader on in this kind of ending varies considerably. The first installment of *Great Expectations* ended with Pip heading for the marshes carrying food for the convict escaped from the prison ship. The coming encounter is one of the potential consequences of narrative material in the installment, and so reinforces the momentum of the narrative rather than braking it. The thirty-first installment (chs. 51–52) also ended with Pip heading for the marshes, this time in response to an anonymous letter calling for a rendezvous out there. It is a packed number: in chapter 51 Pip tells Jaggers he knows Estella's parentage and Jaggers explains why he has concealed it, and in chapter 52 Pip and Herbert Pocket have been planning how they will smuggle Pip's benefactor Magwitch out of England when the letter arrives. These events are dense with accumulated narrative meaning, for the thirty-first number comes far out in the story. So the episode introduced by the anonymous letter in a sense checks the narrative, interrupting the reader's expectations as it interrupts Pip's plans. Curiosity and dread mingle with something like worry about the matters Pip has to leave unresolved: an altogether richer mixture of responses than one feels at the end of chapter 2.

The most common kind of part ending, in fact, both in the weekly and in the monthly serials, checked the momentum of the narrative to some degree. Part of the time (more often in the weekly than in the monthly serials) this check would be fairly strong, sometimes strong enough to leave a sense of a full stop, as when Pip wakes to his ruined expectations on a morning when "the clocks of the Eastward churches were striking five, the candles were wasted out, the fire was dead, and the wind and rain intensified the thick black darkness"; or as when Louisa Gradgrind saves herself from the seducer Harthouse in *Hard*

Times by committing the lesser social sin of leaving her husband, Bounderby, to return to her father's barren house:

> "This night, my husband being away, he has been with me, declaring himself my lover. This minute he expects me, for I could release myself of his presence by no other means. I do not know that I am sorry, I do not know that I am ashamed, I do not know that I am degraded in my own esteem. All that I know is, your philosophy and your teaching will not save me. Now, father, you have brought me to this. Save me by some other means!"
>
> He tightened his hold in time to prevent her sinking on the floor, but she cried out in a terrible voice, "I shall die if you hold me! Let me fall upon the ground!" And he laid her down there, and saw the pride of his heart and the triumph of his system, lying, an insensible heap, at his feet.[21]

The sense of climax at these moments is like the intensity of the cliff-hanger ending, with one great difference: continuing the action will unwind that, but further action seems the last thing possible, for the moment, in Pip's story and Louisa's. As Dickens's friend Lord Jeffrey wrote him, much moved by the death of little Paul in *Dombey and Son,* "After reaching this climax in the fifth number, what are you to do with the fifteen that are to follow?"[22] Dickens's resource then was, as he noted in his number plan for VI, "to throw the interest of Paul, at once on Florence." In other words, he began immediately to work out the potential of another part of the story that held promise of interesting consequences: in this case, the real center, the heroine whose selfless love is to save Dombey from the ruin that his pride brings him to. Both *Hard Times* and *Great Expectations* have fictive complexities still to be worked out at these moments when the train of narrative smashes up. The wreck, in fact, is a way to reorient the readers' attention to central thematic issues.

But as Lord Jeffrey's question makes clear, this sort of part ending, powerful in itself, also makes powerful problems. That may be why Dickens more often slowed the narrative instead of bringing it to a halt, creating a sense of pause at the end of a part instead of a stop. The monthly parts usually closed this way, the weekly parts more often this way than any other. With no sensational development at the end to absorb all attention into itself, the potential for interesting consequences in the events of the installment was more in the foreground to the reader, and the pause had the effect of making time for considering possible developments to come. Thus *Nicholas Nickleby* X ended with Nicholas's villainous Uncle Ralph reading the letter in which Nicholas denounces him, having learned how Ralph has tried to use Nicholas's sister Kate as a lure to snare Lord Verisopht. The part had told of Nicholas's last day with the Crummle traveling theatrical company and his abrupt departure for London in response to a letter from Newman Noggs, Noggs's fears about Nicholas's likely impetuous reaction to finding out his uncle's baseness, Nicholas's encounter with Sir Mulberry Hawk where he learns all by chance, his fight with Hawk, and his taking charge of Kate and his mother and moving them back to live with Miss La Creevy. There was plenty here to think about while waiting for XI: possible consequences to Nicholas from the fight with Hawk; the question how he will support his sister and mother now that he has cast off Ralph's grudging assistance and is himself jobless, having left the Crummle company; whether the Crummles will show up again; what Ralph may do, out of his implacable hostility to Nicholas, and in reaction to his letter.

Sometimes Dickens intensified the draw of the next installment by explicitly promising a significant development to come. He did this four times in *Great Expectations,* at the ends of the tenth, twenty-second, twenty-third, and thirty-fifth installments (chs. 17, 37, 38, and 57). The first of these simply announces a coming change in Pip's life, the last indicates the approaching end of the story: having explained how he plans to go back to Biddy, Pip says, "I went down to the old place, to put [my plan] in execution; and how I sped in it, is all I have left to tell." The end of chapter 37 announces two things to come, specifying one but not the other: "A great event in my life, the turning point of my life, now opens on my view. But, before I proceed to narrate it, and before I pass on to all the changes it involved, I must give one chapter to Estella. It is not much to give to the theme that so long filled my heart." Dickens magnifies this "coming event" in two ways: directly, by labeling it explicitly, and indirectly, by making clear that it does not concern Estella. Considering how important she has been to him, this coming event must have a quite unlooked-for gravity. He enhances its importance another way in the fourth anticipatory passage, at the end of chapter 38. I must quote it in full.

And now that I have given the one chapter to the theme that so filled my heart, and so often made it ache and ache again, I pass on, unhindered, to the event that had impended over me longer yet; the event that had begun to be prepared for, before I knew that the world held Estella, and in the days when her baby intelligence was receiving its first distortions from Miss Havisham's wasting hands.

In the Eastern story, the heavy slab that was to fall on the bed of state in the flush of conquest was slowly wrought out of the quarry, the tunnel for the rope to hold it in its place was slowly carried through the leagues of rock, the slab was slowly raised and fitted in the roof, the rope was rove to it and slowly taken through the miles of hollow to the great iron ring. All being made ready with much labour, and the hour come, the sultan was aroused in the dead of the night, and the sharpened axe that was to sever the rope from the great iron ring was put into his hand, and he struck with it, and the rope parted and rushed away, and the ceiling fell. So, in my case; all the work, near and afar, that tended to the end, had been accomplished; and in an instant the blow was struck, and the roof of my stronghold dropped upon me.

Here Dickens deepened the gravity, and the mystery, of what was to come both by the allusion and by the rhetoric of his narrative. The effect, as in the other instances, was to tauten the pull of the next part.

His devices here, though, blur the neat distinctions I have drawn between kinds of endings. He blurred them other ways, too. He sometimes modulated a possible full stop to a pause by his placement of a highly charged event. Jo's mystification at the closely veiled figure of a woman whom Inspector Bucket asks him to identify is an instance, and so is Mr. Peggotty's announcement to David that he has had word from the fallen Emily; both occur in the chapter ending the number but are followed by further developments that lower the tension (*BH* VII, *DC* XIII). Earlier I implied another blur when I said that there

"seem" or "appear" to be so and so many endings that interrupt
an ongoing action. It is hard to tell about the end of *David
Copperfield* XI (ch. 34), for example, where David's aunt announces she has lost all her money. It could be a pause, or a
full stop, since two paragraphs from the end she says, "We'll
talk about this, more, tomorrow," and the last paragraphs concern
her stout courage. It is easy now to verify the type of ending by
glancing at the next chapter, and so settle the exact number that
fall in the class. But Dickens's first readers could not, and accuracy about how much he counted on this simplest kind of
suspense requires that we not settle this question any more
conclusively than they could.

IV *The Importance of Part Beginnings*

Similarly, the way Dickens opened a part could modify the
reader's hold on the story so far. Pip's description of his state
of mind at the beginning of *Great Expectations* IV (ch. 6)
recalls the events so far, but it also makes Pip seem less a victim,
and more guilty in his own sight. The little essay on the power
of rumor at the beginning of *Barnaby Rudge* XX (chs. 37–38)
more than offsets the triviality and apparent futility of Lord
Gordon's political movement at the end of XIX. A change of
focus—in time, as in the last installment of *David Copperfield*,
or space, as in *Barnaby Rudge* XXVI (chs. 49–50)—changes the
perspective on the preceding installment. David's narrative lifts
from a close reporting of his trials to a general account of his
recovery abroad; in *Barnaby Rudge* the focus shifts from a
closeup of the street where Barnaby is swept into the mob to a
panorama, the deployment of all the rioting mobs in London.

A change of plot line, however, would seem likely to have the
more drastic effect of making the novel less cohesive than if such
changes take place within the number. But I am not sure of this.
Nicholas Nickleby X (discussed in the preceding section), where
the plot is continuous throughout, accumulates narrative momentum toward XI. But in IX (chs. 27–29) the first two chapters
have to do with Kate's victimization by Ralph for the benefit
of his business schemes, while the last chapter turns to Nicholas's
adventures among the Crummle troupe. The shift in the last

chapter may dissipate the momentum of the first two. I offer this tentatively, conscious that it looks somewhat naively quantitative. My example may not be the best possible one, either, for Dickens's plot in *Nicholas Nickleby* is not nearly so complex a one as he builds in later novels, and the last chapter in IX is in fact sprinkled with details that recall to mind Kate and her predicament in the first chapters. A number like *David Copperfield* XIII (chs. 38–40) might be a better test of this idea. Developments in three distinct plot elements occur here: Dora Spenlow's father dies, with improving effect on David's courtship; Uriah Heep demonstrates his increasing dominance over Agnes Wickfield's father, and reveals his intentions toward Agnes; and Mr. Peggotty turns up, en route to Germany following the latest clue to Emily's whereabouts. The first-person point of view covers all with a kind of unity, but not enough, it seems to me, to keep the part from scattering. Moving to *Bleak House*, we have a more complex plot still, and a double point of view besides. We have shifts of plot necessarily whenever the point of view shifts, since Esther Summerson reports only those events she takes part in (or, rarely, those reported to her). But there are more shifts than are implied by two points of view, because the anonymous narrator reports more than one plot line. Nine parts begin with a different plot line than the preceding part ends with, and all except two parts have at least one internal shift of plot line. This sounds like trouble. But *Bleak House* holds together very well, and interest draws us on continuously. Perhaps the reasons belong to other considerations than the arrangements of material following from serial publication. In fact I think they do: to the density of this most completely imagined of all Dickens's novels, and to the connecting force of Dickens's rhetoric. But that is a matter for the next chapters.

As to the concerns of this one, I think that while Dickens built his installments toward recognizably different kinds of endings, there are many things about those endings that cancel most shades of "the grosser kind of suspense." The main effect serial publication had on Dickens's structure was not to make him organize tense part endings, but to distribute the action evenly throughout the narrative. Dickens's first readers were not racked by contrived suspense nearly so often as has been alleged.

Modern readers can test this for themselves by trying to locate
the breaks between installments without the help of editors'
asterisks (or page-counting). What Dickens depended on to
bring his audience back next time was their generalized engagement with a broad range of potentially interesting developments.

V Shape and Substance

All this stakes out the boundaries of Dickens's creative activity,
but of course it does not show us the workings of his imagination
or take us far into the enclosure where the work went on.
Dickens's speculations about titles offer glimpses of his shaping
imagination at work; in fact, the alternatives he considered are
often revealing of his specific concerns. Other proposed titles
for *Hard Times* show that the Utilitarian ideas of the character
Gradgrind are of central importance. *Little Dorrit* was *Nobody's
Fault* nearly until publication. *Buried Alive, The Thread of Gold,*
and *The Doctor of Beauvais* were possibilities Dickens considered for *A Tale of Two Cities.* For *Bleak House* Dickens
tried out a dozen titles, even arranging them on sheets of paper
to see how they would look on a title page.[23]
  Yet, it seems to me that Dickens usually decided on titles
that did not commit him excessively. *David Copperfield* certainly
leaves the field open, though I have heard an ingenious proposal
(which I am utterly unable to convey) involving the implications
of copper, considering both David's and Dickens's connection to
printing. *Bleak House* too retreats: the title in manuscript for
the two parts Dickens completed before beginning publication
was *Bleak House and the East Wind.*[24] The discarded part plainly
means trouble—an east wind brings bad weather (and if one
lives in the western part of a city, noxious air from the works and
slums to the east). *Little Dorrit, A Tale of Two Cities,* and
Our Mutual Friend are certainly noncommittal in Dickens's earliest fashion; *Little Dorrit,* in fact, retreats from the explicitness of
Nobody's Fault. (Perhaps as Dickens got into his story, the
intended irony of that title seemed less appropriate than it had
in prospect. But also, the change to *Little Dorrit* shifts the
emphasis from despair at the societal condition to the hope
embodied in the character Amy Dorrit; see below, pp. 184–85.)

Bleak House is suggestive but ambiguous, with both straight-forward and ironic meanings appropriate to the novel. *Hard Times* has at least two metaphorical meanings: the more specific one, of the times dominated by "hard fact" philosophy, must surely have been what appealed to Dickens (and Forster), but the more general meaning of economic distress is immediately evident, and safe. *Great Expectations* is a splendid title, ringing with ironies, and not one that Dickens worried over to Forster, but simply announced: "The name is GREAT EXPECTATIONS. I think a good name?" (F IX, iii, 733)—a question one feels he was confident he knew the answer to.

As for the man himself at work, his daughter Mamie may have been the only one who saw that, and she quite by chance, while they lived at Tavistock House (where they moved in 1851). She nearly died of cholera in September 1854, and during her convalescence Dickens wanted her in his study with him.

On one of these mornings, I was lying on the sofa endeavouring to keep perfectly quiet, while my father wrote busily and rapidly at his desk, when he suddenly jumped from his chair and rushed to a mirror which hung near, and in which I could see the reflection of some extraordinary facial contortions which he was making. He returned rapidly to his desk, wrote furiously for a few moments, and then went again to the mirror. The facial pantomime was resumed, and then turning toward, but evidently not seeing, me, he began talking rapidly in a low voice. Ceasing this soon, however, he returned once more to his desk, where he remained silently writing until luncheon time. . . . [W]ith his natural intensity he had thrown himself completely into the character that he was creating, and . . . for the time being he had not only lost sight of his surroundings, but had actually become in action, as in imagination, the creature of his pen.[25]

This sounds grotesque, but it confirms what Forster says in explaining why Dickens's illustrators "certainly had not an easy time with him; . . . that he was apt, as he has said himself, to build up temples in his mind not always makeable with hands . . ." (F VI, ii, 475). But Dickens really did not talk about the private act of creation, even with Forster. Forster was his confidant on nearly everything, he helped him with business, he read proof for him and even did considerable editing for him, he suggested a few story developments to him, he served as a sounding board for Dickens's fictive plans; but Dickens invented alone. He certainly found much grist for his mill in the events of the day. One of the younger men he moved with in later years, Augustus Sala, wrote after Dickens's death how he was always interested in the latest thing.[26] John Butt's chapter "The Topicality of *Bleak House*" in *Dickens at Work* demonstrates convincingly how Dickens's fictional concerns in *Bleak House* gathered up current topics of general concern dealt with in the daily press, and some special topics developed in his own *Household Words*.[27] Yet he denied any such connection in a couple of matters where it is quite clear that his denial was disingenuous, to say the very least.[28] Perhaps he had an uncomfortable sense of being caught out in an apparently unflattering attitude, in the case of the Niger River project that he was accused of ridiculing (and pretty certainly was) in Mrs. Jellyby's project to establish a colony in the African kingdom of Borrioboola-Gha. But there was surely nothing to his discredit in fictionalizing some ideas about London detectives, whom he had written of himself in *Household Words*. It is as if he resented any intimation that the world of his novels was not entirely of his own making, independent of realities not subject to his will and control. Perhaps his reaction had something to do with his state of mind, growing on him these years and self-diagnosed with a quotation from *David Copperfield* in a letter to Forster in 1854: "the so happy and yet so unhappy existence which seeks its realities in unrealities, and finds its dangerous comfort in a perpetual escape from the disappointment of heart around it" (F VIII, ii, 638).

CHAPTER 4

Rhetoric, Structure, and Mode

SO FAR I have discussed Dickens's technique as a question of arranging blocks of story-stuff. The implied principle of structure has been that narrative order creates meaning; particular narrative effects come from particular narrative orders. There are other principles, too. Harvey Sucksmith distinguishes a writer's "texture," or linguistic surface, from "structure," which he says is "the principle, idea, or design which organizes, or tries to organize, texture into a pattern that has more meaning, power, or effect than the texture by itself would possess; structure," he says, "would therefore range in my view from syntax to plot and form."[1] I extend that idea, to say structure is anything which generates meaning from the stuff of a novel. Plot, of course, but character too; narrative order, as I said (but including order of statement as well as order of story parts); imagery, as well as syntax; linguistic choices as to specificity, concreteness, and level of discourse; humor, as it qualifies the meaning of the narrative in which it occurs; and in the case of Dickens, first of all, and more than anything else (because it is what one meets first, and because it pervades every novel, creating and sustaining the fictive world of the novel), the narratorial voice.

I *Voice*

That voice, except in the novels where a character tells (or helps tell) the story, is the voice of an omniscient narrator, who tells us whatever needs telling, including what goes on in a character's head, if and when it suits the narratorial strategy. This convention for getting a story before the reader fell out of favor among twentieth-century critics making room in the world for the kind of novel written by Henry James, where the author, as Joyce's literary aesthetician Stephen Dedalus has worked it out in chapter 5 of *A Portrait of the Artist as a Young Man*, is "within or behind or beyond or above his handiwork, invisible, refined out of existence...." We have more lately discovered that narratorial omniscience is not such a crude method after all, is in fact capable of great flexibility and variety, and the surge of critical interest in Dickens has had much to do with that.

Most readers of Dickens will have some notion of this narratorial voice of his, probably from *A Christmas Carol*—

Oh! but he was a tight-fisted hand at the grindstone, Scrooge! a squeezing, wrenching, grasping, scraping, clutching, covetous old sinner! Hard and sharp as flint, from which no steel had ever struck out generous fire; secret, and self-contained, and solitary as an oyster. The cold within him froze his old features, nipped his pointed nose, shrivelled his cheek, stiffened his gait; made his eyes red, his thin lips blue; and spoke out shrewdly in his grating voice. A frosty rime was on his head, and on his eyebrows, and his wiry chin. He carried his own low temperature always about with him; he iced his office in the dog-days; and didn't thaw it one degree at Christmas.   (Stave One)

—an exuberant voice, exclaiming, asserting, restating, dramatizing, erupting metaphors and superlatives and vivid details. That exuberance sounds often too in *Martin Chuzzlewit*, the full-length novel Dickens was writing when he published the *Carol*: as here, characterizing the moral Pecksniff's daughters.

Mr. Pecksniff was a moral man: a grave man, a man of noble sentiments and speech: and he had had her christened Mercy. Mercy! oh, what a charming name for such a pure-souled being as the youngest Miss Pecksniff! Her sister's name was Charity. There was a good thing! Mercy and Charity! And Charity, with her fine strong sense, and her mild, yet not reproachful gravity, was so well named, and did so well set off and illustrate her sister! What a pleasant sight was that, the contrast they presented: to see each loved and loving one sympathising with, and devoted to, and leaning on, and yet correcting and counter-checking, and, as it were, antidoting, the other! To behold each damsel, in her very admiration of her sister, setting up in business for herself on an entirely different principle, and announcing no connexion with over-the-way, and if the quality of goods at that establishment don't please you, you are respectfully invited to favour ME with a call! And the crowning circumstance of the whole delightful catalogue was, that both the fair creatures were so utterly unconscious of all this! They had no idea of it. They no more thought or dreamed of it than Mr. Pecksniff did. Nature played them off against each other: *they* had no hand in it, the two Miss Pecksniffs.   (2)

There is a difference here from the *Carol* voice, consistent with the subject: a bright malicious irony, pointing the Pecksniff sham. But the relish in the *Carol* voice is there, the delight the voice takes in creation. The irony of the anonymous narrator in *Bleak House* is different, just as strong but more somber:

My Lady Dedlock has returned to her house in town for a few days previous to her departure for Paris, where her ladyship intends to stay some weeks; after which her movements are uncertain. The fashionable intelligence says so, for the comfort of the Parisians, and it knows all fashionable things. To know things otherwise, were to be unfashionable. My Lady Dedlock has been down at what she calls, in familiar conversation, her "place" in Lincolnshire. The waters are out in Lincolnshire. An arch of the bridge in the park has been sapped and sopped away. The adjacent low-lying ground, for half a mile in breadth, is a stagnant river, with melancholy trees for islands in it, and a surface punctured all over, all day long, with falling rain. My Lady Dedlock's "place" has been extremely dreary. The weather, for many a day and night, has been so wet that the trees seem wet through, and the soft loppings and prunings of the woodman's axe can make no crash or crackle as they fall. The deer, looking soaked, leave quagmires, where they pass. The shot of a rifle loses its sharpness in the moist air, and its smoke moves in a tardy little cloud towards the green rise, coppice-topped, that makes a background for the falling rain. The view from my Lady Dedlock's own windows is alternately a lead-coloured view, and a view in Indian ink. The vases on the stone terrace in the foreground catch the rain all day; and the heavy drops fall, drip, drip, drip, upon the broad flagged pavement, called, from old time, the Ghost's Walk, all night. On Sundays, the little church in the park is mouldy; the oaken pulpit breaks out into a cold sweat; and there is a general smell and taste as of the ancient Dedlocks in their graves. My Lady Dedlock (who is childless), looking out in the early twilight from her boudoir at a keeper's lodge, and seeing the light of a fire upon the latticed panes, and smoke rising from the chimney, and a child, chased by a woman, running out into the rain to meet the shining figure of a wrapped-up man coming through the gate, has been put quite out of temper. My Lady Dedlock says she has been "bored to death."   (2)

This is different too from the style of Esther Summerson in the other strand of narrative, and from the narrators in *David Copperfield* and *Great Expectations*, where the narratorial voice is that of a character in the story who asserts no more than is appropriate to that stage of the story, except insofar as the character's afterknowledge of the event is allowed. But the anonymous narrator in *Bleak House* is also different from the narrators in *Little Dorrit* and in *Our Mutual Friend*, though they are relatives of his. They state the fact and dramatize it by accumulating tonally appropriate details, building in the same way the fictive worlds that their readers are entering. In *Little Dorrit* Arthur Clennam's "Sunday evening in London, gloomy, close, and stale" (I, 3), in *Our Mutual Friend* Lizzie Hexam and her father on the river and the Veneerings in their dining room (I, 1–2), come before us like Lady Dedlock at the place in Lincolnshire. We hear various tones of irony in the narratorial voices of these later novels, authoritative and generally somber, and demanding less room in the spotlight for themselves than is the case in *Martin Chuzzlewit*. But even in *Dombey and Son*, the next novel after *Martin Chuzzlewit*, the comic joy has modulated to another note.

Those three words conveyed the one idea of Mr. Dombey's life. The earth was made for Dombey and Son to trade in, and the sun and moon were made to give them light. Rivers and seas were formed to float their ships; rainbows gave them promise of fair weather; winds blew for or against their enterprises; stars and planets circled in their orbits, to preserve inviolate a system of which they were the centre. Common abbreviations took new meanings in his eyes, and had sole reference to them. A.D. had no concern with anno Domini, but stood for anno Dombei—and Son.   (1)

It is the disappearance of that comic glare which Dickens's reviewers complained of about the later novels, and hailed the reappearance of when they thought they saw flashes of "the true Dickens."[2] But there is more to the true Dickens than that. (The few quotations I have collected here cannot of course represent the full variety of Dickens's voices, and I offer them only to jog the memory.)

Given Dickens's temperament the prominence of the narrator is not surprising—as Raymond Williams says, "[I]n Dickens's way of seeing his world, direct address and presentation are radically necessary"—and given the serial mode of publication, the narratorial voice provides important continuity. There is some irony in this fact, considering how Dickens advised contributors to his periodicals to let the characters carry the action.[3] The dreary places in *Dombey and Son*, the first novel of his to be conceived entirely in the more ambitious mode of his later career, are where his narrator is telling what his characters do and feel, without an adequate vehicle of incident for them to do and feel in. Dickens did learn to let his people do the business, of course. But he did "make" the people, and a good deal more; in sum, his narratorial voice creates and controls the world of the Dickens novel.

Critical modes for describing the Dickens world vary. Earlier in this century Percy Lubbock talked about "picture" and "scenic action" in Dickens, how in *Bleak House*, for example, Dickens "render[s] as incident, as a succession of particular occasions," the whole broad world, or picture, "out of which the intrigue of the book is to emerge."[4] But this takes no account of the voice of the teller, and contemporary critics do. Sucksmith's book is really about this voice, and so are Garis's *The Dickens Theatre*, and Axton's *Circle of Fire*, which I have mentioned before, as well as James R. Kincaid's *Dickens and the Rhetoric of Laughter* and Garrett Stewart's *Dickens and the Trials of Imagination*: at least, and to varying degree, in what they start with.[5] As Kincaid's title indicates (like Sucksmith's subtitle, *The Rhetoric of Sympathy and Irony in the Novels*), they are therefore all about Dickens's rhetoric as well: how he persuades by his choice of language.

That is my subject, too. But the rhetoric of fiction goes beyond the matter of the narrator's language, of course, as Wayne

Booth has taught us.[6] It includes plot and character, the primary forms that Dickens gave to his imaginings, and much else. So I deal first with Dickens's language and his rhetoric, as well as his symbolism and imagery—taken together, the medium in which his novels exist. Then I take up some patterns (including plot) according to which Dickens deploys the parts of his story; then his characters; then the question of realism in Dickens; then his humor; and finally something about the mode in which Dickens's fiction exists. A reader encounters all these elements of a text more or less simultaneously, but analysis has to proceed sequentially; the order I have chosen is not the order of importance, for these matters are all equally important, but an order of convenience. (I have provided, in an appendix, plot summaries of the novels that I draw on for illustrative examples.)

II *Language and Rhetoric*

This section is mainly about the language of the omniscient narrator from whose point of view most of Dickens's stories get told, but first some general remarks about the language Dickens gives his characters. A scholar in these matters, which I am not, can distinguish a variety of class and regional dialects in Dickens's characters.[7] The differences, however, go beyond class for many characters, in fact for many of the more memorable characters—probably, indeed, their language is what makes them memorable. It is sometimes a matter of syntax, sometimes of characteristic phrases. Mrs. Micawber's "I never will desert Mr. Micawber" (and its variants) is an example of the latter kind; it is a mark we recognize her by, but it is also a sign of her character. In *Little Dorrit* young Mr. Sparkler's mental capacities are sufficiently indicated by his conviction that every woman he finds desirable is "a doosed fine gal—well educated too—with no biggodd nonsense about her" (I, 21). Cousin Feenix in *Dombey and Son* shores up his insubstantial assertions by prefacing them "in fact" (31; or for special force, "in point of fact"). Mr. Snagsby the stationer in *Bleak House* is a good-hearted man, but inclined from his dependence on the favor of lawyers (and from his subordination to a sharp-tempered wife) to be deferential, and "not to put too fine a point on it" (11), will lead up with that phrase to any assertion he finds it necessary to make. He wants no trouble, and his statements are intended not to stab. Mrs. Plornish of Bleeding Heart Yard in *Little Dorrit* is modest and well-meaning, too, and qualifies her statements by beginning "Not to deceive you,...." The narrator testifies to her character: "She would deceive you, under any circumstances, as little as might be; but she had a trick of answering in this provisional form" (I, 12).

Another class of characters show their quality of mind by syntax: the nonstop free-associators Mrs. Nickleby and Arthur Clennam's old flame Flora Finching in *Little Dorrit*, whose flightiness shows in their total inability to order their talk rationally. Mrs. Gamp, the gargly-voiced alcoholic nurse in *Martin Chuzzlewit*, is something like them, but the rambling of her discourse is only apparent—she usually has a point to make, and winds it in with boozy shrewdness, as when Mr. Pecksniff engages her to attend the body of old Anthony Chuzzlewit:

> "If it wasn't for the nerve a little sip of liquor gives me (I never was able to do more than taste it), I never could go through with what I sometimes has to do. 'Mrs. Harris,' I says, at the very last case as ever I acted in, which it was but a young person, 'Mrs. Harris,' I says, 'leave the bottle on the chimley-piece, and don't ask me to take none, but let me put my lips to it when I am so dispoged, and then I will do what I'm engaged to do, according to the best of my ability.' 'Mrs. Gamp,' she says, in answer, 'if ever there was a sober creetur to be got at eighteen pence a day for working people, and three and six for gentlefolks—night watching,'" said Mrs. Gamp, with emphasis, "'being a extra charge—you are that inwallable person.' 'Mrs. Harris,' I says to her, 'don't name the charge, for if I could afford to lay all my feller creeturs out for nothink, I would gladly do it, sich is the love I bears 'em. But what I always says to them as has the management of matters, Mrs. Harris:'" here she kept her eye on Mr. Pecksniff: "'be they gents or be they ladies, is, don't ask me whether I won't take none, or whether I will, but leave the bottle on the chimley-piece, and let me put my lips to it when I am so dispoged.'"   (19)

This only begins to open the varieties of individual speech in Dickens, and a beginning is all I can make room for. One more variety of language that Dickens gives to certain characters, however, needs to be mentioned. David Copperfield speaks it, and little Paul Dombey, and Pip, and all the rest of Dickens's heroes, without regard for their social or regional origins. It is characterized by a grammar and vocabulary correct according to educated standards; and spoken by Oliver Twist, and by Pip even as a child, it is certainly not plausible. Neither is it plausible that the prostitute Nancy in *Oliver Twist* is competent in this dialect on occasion, or that Kit Nubbles in *The Old Curiosity Shop*, or (to some extent) Sloppy in *Our Mutual Friend*, should begin by speaking lower-class dialects and end speaking this one. But the use Dickens makes of this dialect tells something about the mode of his fiction. Plausibility, judged by realistic standards, is not the point. A character's use of this dialect is one mark of his or her moral stature and standing in the story; the dialect might properly be called "heroic" English.

This is also the standard language of Dickens's omniscient narrators. Narratorial omniscience as Dickens uses it, however, is a flexible instrument. Obviously the narrator's language may show a rise or fall in spirits, approval or disapproval, and so on. But Dickens's narrator also can reflect the style of a character. The passage quoted earlier from *Martin Chuzzlewit* shows something of this, suggesting in its own substance the character of the Pecksniff sisters. In *Little Dorrit*, Mr. Merdle the financier gives splendid parties to which all society (economically designated Bar, Bishop, Bench, and so on) flock. The narrator reports one such gathering, and without using direct quotation shifts into something like the discourse of one of the guests:

Bar, with his little insinuating Jury droop, and fingering his persuasive double eye-glass, hoped he might be excused if he mentioned to one of the greatest converters of the root of all evil into the root of all good, who had for a long time reflected a shining lustre on the annals even of our commercial country—if he mentioned, disinterestedly, and as, what we lawyers called in our pedantic way, amicus curiae, a fact that had come by accident within his knowledge. He had been required to look over the title of a very considerable estate in one of the eastern counties—lying, in fact, for Mr. Merdle knew we lawyers loved to be particular, on the borders of two of the eastern counties. Now, the title was perfectly sound, and the estate was to be purchased by one who had the command of—Money (Jury droop and persuasive eye-glass), on remarkably advantageous terms. . . .   (I, 21)

This is what Quirk discusses as "free indirect speech" (pp. 30–33), providing an English label modeled on the French term for it. He quotes an example from *Bleak House*, the interrogation of Jo the crossing-sweeper at the inquest into the death of Nemo the copier of legal documents.

Name, Jo. Nothing else that he knows on. Don't know that everybody has two names. Never heerd of sich a think. Don't know that Jo is short for a longer name. Thinks it long enough for *him*. *He* don't find no fault with it. Spell it? No. *He* can't spell it. No father, no mother, no friends. Never been to school. What's home? Knows a broom's a broom, and knows it's wicked to tell a lie. Don't recollect who told him about the broom, or about the lie, but knows both. Can't exactly say what'll be done to him arter he's dead if he tells a lie to the gentlemen here, but believes it'll be something wery bad to punish him, and serve him right—and so he'll tell the truth.   (11)

The passage evokes the illiterate boy's language and suggests the questions being put to him, but the narrator keeps the narrative in his own hands, avoiding the disjointedness of a simulated transcript of the proceedings, and the detachment which his own dialect would create. One more example, to show how supple Dickens's modulation is into and out of free indirect speech, this one from *Dombey and Son*:

The funeral of the deceased lady having been "performed," to the entire satisfaction of the undertaker, as well as of the neighbourhood at large, which is generally disposed to be captious on such a point, and is prone to take offence at any omissions or short-comings in the ceremonies, the various members of Mr. Dombey's household subsided into their several places in the domestic system. That small world, like the great one out of doors, had the capacity of easily forgetting its dead; and when the cook had said she was a quiet-tempered lady, and the housekeeper had said it was the common lot, and the butler had said who'd have thought it, and the housemaid had said she couldn't hardly believe it, and the footman had said it seemed exactly like a dream, they had quite worn the subject out, and began to think their mourning was wearing rusty too.   (3)

The opening sentence is a good example of Dickens's mature narratorial style, tending in complexity of syntax and diction toward the more elaborate end of his range. A long introductory phrase before the main clause gives a periodic cast to the whole, accumulating meaning that is suspended until the main clause unfolds; the introductory phrase itself develops by addition, an idea being followed immediately by its qualifier. The first clause of the second sentence—short, with plain language and only faintly periodic—tends toward the simple end of Dickens's range and moves the reader easily toward the style of the domestics of Dombey's household, simulated in free indirect speech. That simulation, cast in parallel short adverbial clauses, is followed by a second independent clause in language that belongs to the narrator, like the language of the opening clause, and the reader is back in the main narrative medium of the novel.

The great difficulty of discussing Dickens's style is that its operation through a whole extended passage is both of the essence, and intolerable to illustrate by a passage of adequate size.[8] (Other stylistic features having been more discussable, this Dickensian diffusion has tended to drop out of sight.) But this paragraph shows about as much of Dickens's narratorial range as any short passage can, and I think shows him at his best. I must take room to quote another strong passage here, to show Dickens in full control of an extended run in his more ornate style: the opening paragraph of chapter 52 in *Martin Chuzzlewit*, where he gathers up the narrative state of affairs at a climactic stage of the action.

Old Martin's cherished projects, so long hidden in his own breast, so frequently in danger of abrupt disclosure through the bursting forth of the indignation he had hoarded up during his residence with Mr. Pecksniff, were retarded, but not beyond a few hours, by the occurrences just now related. Stunned as he had been at first by the intelligence conveyed to him through Tom Pinch and John Westlock, of the supposed manner of his brother's death; overwhelmed as he was by the subsequent narratives of Chuffey and Nadgett, and the forging of that chain of circumstances ending in the death of Jonas, of which catastrophe he was immediately informed; scattered as his purposes and hopes were for the moment, by the crowding in of all these incidents between him and his end; still their very intensity and the tumult of their assemblage nerved him to the rapid and unyielding execution of his scheme. In every single circumstance, whether it were cruel, cowardly, or false, he saw the flowering of the same pregnant seed. Self; grasping, eager, narrow-ranging, over-reaching self; with its long train of suspicions, lusts, deceits, and all their growing consequences; was the root of the vile tree. Mr. Pecksniff had so presented his character before the old man's eyes, that he—the good, the tolerant, enduring Pecksniff—had become the incarnation of all selfishness and treachery; and the more odious the shapes in which those vices ranged themselves before him now, the sterner consolation he had in his design of setting Mr. Pecksniff right, and Mr. Pecksniff's victims too.

One does not read this fleetly, but the narrative having come to a pause (the preceding chapter ends with Jonas's suicide) is conductive to a deliberate pace here, and dense though the narration is, it is lucid and controlled. When Dickens goes wrong in one way, though, it is in this manner.

It is no great matter what Mrs. Hominy said, save that she had learnt it from the cant of a class, and a large class, of her fellow-countrymen, who, in their every word, avow themselves to be as senseless to the high principles on which America sprang, a nation, into life, as any Orson in her legislative halls. Who are no more capable of feeling, or of caring if they did feel, that by reducing their own country to the ebb of honest men's contempt, they put in hazard the rights of nations yet unborn, and very progress of the human race, than are the swine who wallow in their streets. Who think that crying out to other nations, old in their iniquity, "We are no worse than you!" (No worse!) is high defense and 'vantage-ground enough for that Republic, but yesterday let loose upon her noble course, and but today so maimed and lame, so full of sores and ulcers, foul to the eye and almost hopeless to the sense, that her best friends turn from the loathsome creature with disgust. Who, having by their ancestors declared and won their Independence, because they would not bend the knee to certain Public vices and corruptions, and would not abrogate the truth, run riot in the Bad, and turn their backs upon the Good; and lying down contented with the wretched boast that other Temples also are of glass, and stones which batter theirs may be flung back; show themselves, in that alone, as immeasurably behind the import of the trust they hold, and as unworthy to possess it as if the sordid hucksterings of all their little governments—each one a kingdom in its small depravity—were brought into a heap for evidence against them.   (*MC* 22)

Here is the same elaborate parallelism. Parallelism is a favorite device in Dickens's rhetoric, and he uses it often to good effect; but the parallel elements here are overstuffed to confusion, just as the formal diction is inflated into fustian. It is a kind of debased eighteenth-century prose, the syntax showing balance and contrast, and the diction Latinate, but with the rational clarity of the model cluttered, like a living room done in the worst Victorian taste. When Dickens's characters fall into this kind of talk, say Nicholas and his uncle Ralph, or Edith Dombey and Mr. Dombey's office manager James Carker, we know where we are: in a Victorian theater listening to melodrama. I have the impression that this is more characteristic of Dickens as a young man than later on, but I find the tendency in his journalistic work, too, throughout his career. Perhaps it is a mark of hurry, rather than of youth.

Dickens tends to fall into this style in wrath; his other major stylistic failings are linked to affection. Inflation is sometimes the trouble here, too: the obsolete poeticizing of his apostrophes to saintly characters like Tom Pinch—"Blessings on thy simple heart, Tom Pinch, how proudly dost thou button up that scanty coat," and so on at great length (*MC* 5)—and Agnes Wickfield, the heroine of *David Copperfield* intended from the beginning and beatified at the last: "O Agnes, O my soul, so may thy face be by me when I close my life indeed; so may I, when realities are melting from me, like the shadows which I now dismiss, still find thee near me, pointing upward!"[9] If the young woman is one Dickens feels impelled to call "little," and is reveling in domesticity, like Tom Pinch's sister Ruth, the narratorial voice is likely to rise to some ecstasy over her cleverness and charm: "Pleasant little Ruth! Cheerful, tidy, bustling, quiet little Ruth!" (*MC* 39). Or the chastened Bella Wilfer at work (*OMF* IV, 5): "Such weighing and mixing and chopping and grating, such dusting and washing and polishing, [etc.], and above all such severe study [of the *Complete British Family Housewife*, addressed by Bella "with all her dimples screwed into an expression of profound research"]!" But if the female is a child, and dying, we have the most notorious case, Little Nell, to modern sensibilities the very image of bathos. However far Little Nell's death was inspired by the death of Dickens's young sister-in-law Mary Hogarth—and there is reason for qualifying the tradition that he spoke his still-fresh grief in Nell[10]—there is no question that Dickens loved this child of his imagination, and put her to death reluctantly and in pain.[11]

The failure, if it is one, is less one of narratorial language than of idea. Dickens knew how hard a thing he was trying to do: a narrative event that he had reason to know his readers dreaded, but that he agreed with Forster belonged to the action. His strategy, in the installment where Nell's death is reported, is to anticipate the disclosure and to soften it by focusing before and after on the demented grief of Nell's grandfather, establishing its intensity by the old man's distress and making it bearable by conveying along with it the pathos of his condition. In his senility he can hide from the truth he knows, first by feverishly insisting that Nell only sleeps, and later by accepting the reassuring answers to his anxious questions that nobody is dead, and nobody is being buried today. The inflationary language in the episode is his, not the narrator's. He is given the reverent archaisms to say—"Why dost thou lie so idle there, when thy little friends come creeping to the door, crying 'Where is Nell—sweet Nell?'—and sob and weep, because they do not see thee" (71)—and the studied simplicity of balladlike questions: "Neighbour! how is it that the folks are nearly all in black today?" (72). The language of narration at the center is simple, the syntax uninvolved: "She was dead. No sleep so beautiful and calm, so free from trace of pain, so fair to look upon. She seemed a creature fresh from the hand of God, and waiting for the breath of life," and so on (71). The account of her death is the same: "She had been dead two days. They were all about her at the time, knowing that the end was drawing on. She died soon after daybreak. . . ." (72).

Dickens was not wrong to feel that he had taken great pains in this installment to bring off a narrative development requiring great tact in the rhetorical situation created by periodical publication. The disclosure that Nell is dead, and the account of her death, occupy the exact center of the installment; the narrative ascends to this center and descends from it. Why does the episode not work better on me?—for I must concede that what

I feel about it is more respect for what my study has revealed than sorrow for Nell. I think because between Dickens and me there is Oscar Wilde, who said, "One must have a heart of stone to read the death of Little Nell without laughing."[12] There is more to it than this, but surely Edgar Johnson's observation is fundamental, that our emotional climate is quite different from the Victorians': "[To] large bodies of modern readers, especially those called 'sophisticated,' . . . a heartfelt expression of senti-ment seems . . . exaggerated, hypocritical, or embarrassing" (J323).

Johnson's assertions about the modern emotional climate carry less authority now than in 1952, Hemingwayesque toughness hav-ing lost favor and a cult of feeling moister than any attributed to the Victorians having come into vogue. But he is mainly right; and we are impatient besides, not willing to submit to literary effects that take time to build. However, as George Ford has said, there are limits to explanatory criticism, and the fault may not be our emotional climate if we laugh at Nell's deathbed, or at least remain dry-eyed, or wish Dickens's sympathy for poor saint-ly Florence Dombey, unloved by her icy father, less insistent and tender. Dickens can do better than this, even for us. The death of Mrs. Dombey (1) is effective, and little Paul's death (16)—until the narrator's pious tag—and especially, I think, the death of Pip's sister, as reported to him by Biddy (GE 35). The language in all of these is unaffected and the syntax simple, as is appropriate to narrative carried by the characters themselves (in the latter two instances). But I also find the death of Jo effective, though it is climaxed in quite another style, when after Jo dies stumbling under Dr. Woodcourt's guidance through the Lord's Prayer, the narrator takes over:

> The light is come upon the dark benighted way. Dead!
> Dead, your Majesty. Dead, my lords and gentlemen. Dead, Right Reverends and Wrong Reverends of every order. Dead, men and women, born with Heavenly compassion in your hearts. And dying thus around us every day.   (BH 47)

I will not quarrel with anyone who finds this pretty florid (es-pecially out of context), but there is in it a quality which links it to these other effective deaths, and distinguishes it from

Nell's death. There is restraint. Dickens aims at that in the case of Nell, where the center of the installment is given the calm of a shrine. What goes wrong, I think, is the excess of narrative contrivance, more than of language. Johnson is right to mention the "lugubrious excess in the sobbing iambic rhythms of the close" (p. 323), but more important are the determinedly pathetic details surrounding the account of Nell's death, and the unconvincing consolatory assertions of the narrator—"Sorrow was dead indeed in her, but peace and perfect happiness were born" (71)—and too much more of the like. By comparison, the narrator does no more when Mrs. Dombey dies, clasping her daughter Florence to her breast, than express all he knows about death in an image: "Thus, clinging fast to that slight spar within her arms, the mother drifted out upon the dark and unknown sea that rolls round all the world." That has restraint, the other has not. That is also what the narrator's comment on Jo's death has. It is an oratorical restraint, in the shape of tight syntactical parallelism that holds back the narrator's erupting anger, where the restraint in the examples from *Dombey and Son* and *Great Expectations* consists in simplicity of diction and syntax. But the effect of language *controlling* emotion, rather than of language *simulating* emotion—of emotion revealed by the struggle to contain it, rather than to body it forth—is similar. Dickens, where he is most successful in conveying emotion, demonstrates the worth of his advice to Wilkie Collins, in another connection, "only to suggest." The structural effect his unrestrained narratorial voice imposes on the stuff of feeling is sentimentality; under restraint, the meaning that voice gives to feeling is the truth of emotion.[13]

Before I move on to other qualities of that voice, I will mention one all-pervading feature of Dickens's fictive rhetoric: the cumulative force that arises from those qualities as they occur in the spaciousness of his narrative. It is obviously impossible to illustrate this cumulative effect, given the diffusion of Dickens's style, and indeed illustrations of individual effects lose force for that reason. For example, the death of Pip's sister is moving not only because of the simplicity of Biddy's account (and because Biddy does the telling), but because that account has a past: the sister's short-tempered tyranny of speech and act over Joe and young Pip is in our minds as we read. That simple close to the first Mrs. Dombey's life suffers, too, in my quotation, separated merely from the preceding scene. In context it gains force from Mr. Dombey's pride in the institution Dombey and Son; his sense that having contributed the next Son (six years after turning out a mere daughter) Mrs. Dombey has on the whole justified her existence; his sister's faith in the efficacy of Mrs. Dombey's "rousing herself," and her collapse into alarm; and the professional oil of the attending physicians, and their helplessness becoming patent at last. Conversely, the final sentence gives strength to weakness elsewhere, covering the stickiness of the sentences about the daughter at the dying mother's side.

Such effects belong to the rhetoric of indirection, commanding readers' assent by other appeals than conceptual statements addressed to the intellect: they work in accumulation, in contrast, in rhythms of subject matter arrangement as well as of sentences, and so on. (For discussion of one such device, a kind of counterpoint that Dickens uses mainly for comedy, see the section on humor below.) Criticism can only affirm the existence of such effects, and refer the reader to the text for confirmation. What I have left to say in this section on Dickens's language and rhetoric is about other effects of this kind, the texture of his narration (meaning by "texture" something different from Sucksmith's linguistic surface); and his symbolism and imagery, which lead me to allegory, and thence to the sections on pattern and character.

Alfred Harbage, speaking of what I am here calling the texture of Dickens's narration, calls it simply "mixed narration and description";[14] but it is all narration, really. Dickens mingles assertions—about a character, an event, a state of being, a place—with illustrative detail, as in the paragraphs from *Dombey and Son* quoted above, and below in the section on imagery (it would be easy to illustrate this from anywhere in Dickens; I use these passages to save space). Stating and restating, he emphasizes a point by taking a different angle or setting out a new example, building his characteristic effect of copiousness. His illustrative details are often concrete without being particular, tending to generalize the narrative, implying the thing happens this way as a rule or in many places. Nothing seems to be left out, and in this apparent exhaustiveness consists in large part the rhetorical authority of the narrative; we are convinced because it seems to take account of everything.

This is such an important feature of Dickens's narrative style, and accounts for so much of the rhetoric of his fiction, that what I have said does not seem enough to say about it. But analysis of examples would amount to little more than naming their parts, and I do not really know what to add, except to recommend references to passages from Dickens I have quoted elsewhere in other connections. This is one of the great fundamental things about Dickens's style, the kind that gets overlooked for that very reason: there really is not a great deal to be said, once the thing is seen. So, having pointed to it, and indicated how important it is, I will leave it and move on to Dickens's symbolism.

III *Symbolism*

The fog in *Bleak House*, the prison in *Little Dorrit*, the river and the mountains of garbage in *Our Mutual Friend*—these and other symbols in Dickens, fictive elements that embody connotations appropriate to the theme and action and appear often enough to set the action in a certain light, have been searched out and explicated exhaustively in the last twenty-five years. In fact the study of symbolism in Dickens is as much a phenomenon in the history of literary criticism (particularly in the United States) as it is discovery of a new dimension of Dickens's work. The onset of symbolism studies in Dickens coincides roughly with the success of the New Criticism. The tools and methods come from the New Criticism, with its emphasis on the meaning intrinsic to the text arising from lexical content and grammatical, syntactical, and rhetorical relations. The New Criticism developed in the study of poetry and produced valuable results, and to the extent that poetry inheres in fiction, the results have been valuable here, too. Critics committed to the approach have seen much that passed with relatively little notice before (though not perhaps so little notice as many think). But critical searchlights developed to deal with poems (and most particularly the seventeenth-century poems of John Donne and the other so-called Metaphysical poets) only pick up certain things in novels; the rest of what should concern the critic lies in the shadows. The trouble is not so much what has been discovered, then, as what preoccupation with the newly seen has caused to be overlooked, and the consequent exaggeration of the new as the real explanation of Dickens's power, and the distortion of our understanding of what he did. It has become conventional critical wisdom that the fog permeating the first chapter of *Bleak House* drifts through the whole novel, that the debtor's prison is the master image in *Little Dorrit*, and that the foul Thames and the Harmon dust mounds make a kind of axis for the world of *Our Mutual Friend*. But once Chancery has been introduced, and Esther Summerson brought into connection with Bleak House, fog plays very little part in the novel; it is more accurate to call it a keynote than a symbol pervading the work. The mud "which is made of nobody knows what, and collects about us nobody knows whence or how" (10), and the rain that falls steadily at the Dedlock estate in Lincolnshire, have as good a claim, and the miasma of sickness that rises from the London slums to spread over the city a much better one. The relations among Mr. Casby, Mr. Pancks, and the inhabitants of Bleeding Heart Yard in *Little Dorrit* go as far to embody thematic concerns there as the debtors' prison (I say more of this further on). I can see more merit in attaching symbolic value to the river in *Our Mutual Friend*. The kind of thing people usually call symbolism in Dickens is fairly explicit and precise in its meaning, and would better be thought of as metaphor, or image; but the river in *Our Mutual Friend* does carry a complex of meanings—hard to reduce to conceptual statement, and coming to life in the course of the action—that is properly called symbolic. However, the dust mounds—garbage, even dung, some say—are quite neatly metaphoric; dirt is a traditional emblem for money. The mounds are also the literal source of Harmon's wealth: which brings me to an important point.

Dickens responded powerfully himself to the river; his periodical articles show his fascination with it, and suggest that it had symbolic significance for him.[15] But he gave his imaginings the shape of character and plot first of all; so far as I have ever discovered, the letters he wrote to Forster and others about work in progress are about character and plot, not about controlling symbols.[16] Symbols exist (more often, metaphors and images), but as supporting and harmonizing detail to character and plot.

Our Mutual Friend, like all of Dickens's full-scale novels from
Dombey and Son on, ranges over nearly the whole of Victorian
society. The settings and action are those appropriate to the
characters at their various levels and in their concerns, and to
the themes Dickens had in mind—once again, as nearly everywhere in his work, guilt, the evil consequences of materialism,
the importance of striving, the power of selfless love. The way
the novel works is through the interplay of characters and action
in plot; to make the river, as a symbol, the engine that moves
the novel is to overturn Dickens and to transfer his emphasis from
one realm of understanding to another, to spiritualize him in-
appropriately.[17]

It will be seen that I do not mean to deny symbolism in Dickens,
only to see it in its right proportions. I will take the example
of *Dombey and Son,* which I have been rereading while writing
this section. The dominant theme is pride, embodied in Mr.
Dombey and in Edith Granger, the second Mrs. Dombey;
thematically the action of the novel consists in the fall occasioned
by pride, and the redemption made possible by selfless love.
This theme is carried out in a plot involving Mr. Dombey's immense sense of his own importance as the head of the firm
Dombey and Son, the insults to his pride and the checks to
his plans that he sees in his daughter Florence and her relations
with others, his collision with Edith (equally imperious but
from quite other reasons), the machinations of his office manager James Carker, and his fall, which really becomes his salvation by the ministrations of Florence's love. (See the appendix
for a more detailed plot summary.) Mingled with this is a network of detail which I think is properly called symbolic, associated, with one exception, with the characters who find no
favor in Mr. Dombey's eyes, but who are the bearers of good in
the story. This detail has to do with the sea and the sun. Walter
Gay, who will marry Florence, lives as a boy with his uncle
Solomon Gills, who sells (when any customers show up) instruments for seagoing navigation, and who, in spite of his own
un-seagoing appearance, is quite as taken by the romance of
the sea as Walter (4). Mr. Gills's good friend Captain Cuttle,
simple, devout, and great of heart, is retired from the sea. And
little Paul, in whose death Mr. Dombey's great hopes for the firm
are dashed, hears the waves at the seashore (where he is sent

to recover his health) and wonders what they are always saying. Mr. Dombey, however, has no such wonder: the seas were made to float the ships of Dombey and Son; and when he goes on a holiday to restore his spirits after his son's death, it is not to the Brighton shore, or even to Bath, but to Leamington in Warwickshire, as far from the sea as one can get in England. Only at the end, in autumn, does the chastened Dombey walk by the sea, and the waves speak to him now, of Florence. Paul finds out what the waves were always saying; the river he has felt rushing him away bears him to the sea as he dies, the same sea, no doubt, that his mother drifted out upon at the end of chapter 1. Walter finds out about the literal sea, since when his employer Dombey sends him to the West Indies (to get rid of him), he is shipwrecked, and makes his way home much later, having learned to live on the sea, and not only to dream of its romance. His uncle too finds the sea out by experience, in his travels in search of Walter. He can live in the water—his name is Gills, as his retired seagoing friend's name is Cuttle(fish?)—and so he is Solomon.

But he is also "Sol," and is called by that nickname more often than the other, making me think of the sun, which lights up the world, but scarcely ever strikes Dombey's house. (I quote the passage in the next section.) It does strike into Paul's sickroom; in the evening it does so "through the rustling blinds, and quiver[s] on the opposite wall like golden water" (16). When he dies in Florence's arms, "the golden light came streaming in, and fell upon them, locked together." After she has fled to Captain Cuttle when her father repudiates her, Florence wakes from sleep near sunset, when the sun, *"looked towards, from quiet churchyards,* upon hill-tops in the country, . . . was steeping distant prospects in a flush and glow that seemed to mingle earth and sky together in one glorious suffusion" (49; my italics). What this sun represents is made nearly explicit as Carker the manager lives his last moments at daybreak at the window of a railroad hotel:

After a glance at the place where he had walked last night, and at the signal-lights burning feebly in the morning, and bereft of their significance, he turned to where the sun was rising, and beheld it, in its glory, as it broke upon the scene.

So awful, so transcendent in its beauty, so divinely solemn. As he cast his jaded eyes upon it, where it rose, tranquil and serene, unmoved by all the wrong and wickedness on which its beams had shone since the beginning of the world, who shall say that some weak sense of virtue upon Earth, and its reward in Heaven, did not manifest itself, even to him? (55)

The railroad signal lights, which associate with death both in this context and elsewhere in the novel, are "bereft of their significance" by the glory of sunrise. Surely we are in the presence of word play on the Son, the light of the world (John 9:5), familiar from generations of English poetry.

So we have suggestions of the sea as eternity, and also as a truth of life unattended by the busy world (the nautical instruments no one comes to buy, Dombey's strictly economic concern with rivers and seas), which it is necessary to make one's own by experience; and the sun as spiritual light, which suffuses this world and unites it to the eternal. These details show how symbolism works in Dickens. They fit the thematic movement of the story, as John Holloway says, "not by *augmenting the meaning,* but by *transmuting the nature,* of the book's picture of life. . . . The symbolism is rather a dimension than an ingredient. What it does is modify literality until the work as a whole stands in a new perspective."[18] The story's center of gravity, however, is in the action, in which the symbolism inheres. It is not detachable from the pattern of the story, but is a sign of the pattern in things, visible to those who have eyes to see: the fictive correlative to Dickens's belief about the order behind our world. This is by no means, then, to deny symbolism a place in any account of Dickens's craft and meaning, but rather to define its importance.

Another kind of symbolism appears in the names Dickens chose for his characters.[19] His early practice was fairly obvious. He used names that are really common nouns—*Grub, Dr. Payne,* and so on—a traditional device. *Mowcher* in *David Copperfield* is a late example of this; so are *Dedlock* and *Vholes* in *Bleak House.*[20] There is little need, either, to say much about humorous names like *Wugsby, Fizkin, Smiggers,* or *Buzfuz* (or *Pickwick,* for that matter), or the monosyllabic ones like *Lobbs, Mudge,* and *Slurk* (all these from *Pickwick Papers*), beyond noting that Dickens seemed to find short *u*'s and *i*'s especially funny, and terminal *g*'s and *k*'s. He continued to use humorous monosyllabic names, and names ending in the diminutive-sounding *-in* or *-ins*: *Wegg, Sprodgkin,* and *Tapkins* are all from *Our Mutual Friend.* But he began using names tinged with the fantastic and grotesque, like *Peggotty, Pumblechook, Skimpole, Twemlow.* A name like this, according to Bodelsen, "does not usually have an actual meaning of its own, it does not normally exist as a recognised part of the English vocabulary, but it tells something about the bearer, either by evoking associations with real words or by the symbolism which attaches to certain sounds, or even to the shape of certain letters" (p. 42). Thus *Twemlow* suggests "tremble," as the name's owner, the dependent aged nobleman, might before his irritable rich relative, and "low," as he must feel then. *Murdstone* is pretty transparent; the version Dickens rejected for David's stepfather, *Murdle* (spelled *Merdle* to suggest something else to anyone with a rudimentary knowledge of French), served later in *Little Dorrit. Jaggers* combines "jagged" and "daggers" suitably for that formidable lawyer in *Great Expectations. Wemmick* is suggestive in another way. Saying it stretches one's mouth in such a way as to give nearly a tactile sense of identification with the man: he had "thin wide mottled lips" like a letter-drop. "His mouth was such a post-office of a mouth that he had a mechanical appearance of smiling" (21). *Dombey,* Bodelsen says, sounds

a note of haughtiness and dreary pompousness and self-importance. . . . Besides, it suggests a cold in the head, and thus contributes to the atmosphere of chilly discomfort [in the Dombey household, symbolizing] the great man's lack of human warmth. . . . *Clennam* [clangs harshly, like] the iron sound of bells on that dreary Sunday in Chapter III of *Little Dorrit* (ironically entitled "Home") which epitomizes that character's (and Dickens's own) mood of disillusionment. . . . *Magwitch* clearly belongs in some submerged world below that of Victorian respectability. The name is freakish, and in some indefinable way debased.   (pp. 44–45)

Dickens's movement over the years from names with an obvious meaning to names with the sort of suggestiveness Bodelsen describes is neatly telescoped in his deliberations what to call the child-wife Dora's father and his partner, the team of proctors in

Doctors' Commons. Dora's father meets the public, professes to be very accommodating, but cannot follow his heart in his dealings, he says, because of his stony partner. (Dora's father is of course the stone one himself.) They start out in the number plan as *Aiguille and Tanguille*, then become *Tranguille and Jorker*, before getting their identities as *Spenlow and Jorkins*. Presumably the order is the same in all three pairs: Aiguille is Tranguille is Spenlow. Dora's father is at first a needle, then something like a peaceful person, and finally someone whose name vaguely suggests spending, perhaps. The falseness of *Jorkins* allegedly never compromising on terms is somehow clearer than if his name were *Jorker*; the diminutive suffix *-ins* does the trick.

IV *Imagery*

Imagery is another important structural element provided by Dickens's narratorial voice. An astonishing amount of it is biblical: astonishing, at any rate, to modern readers, to most of whom the Bible is less familiar than Homer, and who have consequently no idea how drenched in biblical phrase, story, and idea English literature is. In fact, public utterances of all kinds in Dickens's time were pervaded by biblical references, as the opening pages of Humphry House's chapter "Religion" show.[21] No wonder then that Dickens's fiction is colored by biblical elements; indeed, almost the last thing he wrote, near the point where *The Mystery of Edwin Drood* was canceled by his fatal stroke, was the paragraph in which "scents from gardens, woods, and fields—or, rather, from the one great garden of the whole cultivated island in its yielding time—penetrate into the Cathedral, subdue its earthy odour, and preach the Resurrection and the Life." But he makes jocular use of his source, too, as in Captain Cuttle's amazing references both to the Bible and the Book of Common Prayer.[22]

There is a lot of touch-and-go metaphor which gives an effect of vivacity and originality of vision—the meal of cold meats and icy wine celebrating little Paul Dombey's christening, "looking more like a dead dinner lying in state than a social refreshment" (5); the valiant member of the Barnacle clan in *Little Dorrit*, "pensioned off as a Commissioner of nothing particular some-

where or other, [who] died at his post with his drawn salary in
his hand, nobly defending it to the last extremity" (I, 17). But
Dickens also uses imagery to provide structure over a larger
expanse of narrative. In this next passage (which follows directly
on the paragraph quoted under "Language and Rhetoric" above)
the description of Mr. Dombey's house and neighborhood is rendered as incident. There is a buried image, a typical day on that
street; and the light and shade, warmth and cold, associated with
that image become qualities of the street, the house, and of course
Dombey himself.

On Richards [the name assigned Mrs. Toodles by Dombey when
he hired her to nurse the infant Paul], who was established upstairs in a state of honourable captivity, the dawn of her new life
seemed to break cold and grey. Mr. Dombey's house was a large one,
on the shady side of a tall, dark, dreadfully genteel street in the region
between Portland-Place and Bryanstone-Square. It was a corner house,
with great wide areas containing cellars frowned upon by barred
windows, and leered at by crooked-eyed doors leading to dustbins.
It was a house of dismal state, with a circular back to it, containing a
whole suit of drawing-rooms looking upon a gravelled yard, where
two gaunt trees, with blackened trunks and branches, rattled rather
than rustled, their leaves were so smoke-dried. The summer sun was
never on the street, but in the morning about breakfast time, when
it came with the water-carts and the old clothes men, and the people
with geraniums, and the umbrella mender, and the man who trilled
the little bell of the Dutch clock as he went along. It was soon gone
again to return no more that day; and the bands of music and the
straggling Punch's shows going after it, left it a prey to the most
dismal of organs, and white mice; with now and then a porcupine, to
vary the entertainments; until the butlers whose families were dining
out, began to stand at the house doors in the twilight, and the lamplighter made his nightly failure in attempting to brighten up the
street with gas.   (3)

In fact, cold even becomes a mode of character analysis. Pompous
self-regard like Dombey's (commonplace enough in itself as a
symptom of pride), the image of cold says, involves denying
proper place to one's feelings: having spoken to Mr. Carker
with unusual intensity of feeling, "Mr. Dombey, recovering his
composure by degrees, or cooling his emotion in his sense of

having taken a high position, sat gradually stiffening again"
(42).[23]

This economy in the midst of Dickens's narrative abundance,
recalling and reinforcing something in the story, sometimes takes
the form of synechdoche, as when Mrs. Merdle in *Little Dorrit*
becomes "the bosom" (I, 21). The choice of anatomical parts is
neither prurient nor random; Mrs. Merdle's value to Mr. Merdle
the speculator is to display his wealth and ornament his societal
display, and Mrs. Merdle's "extensive bosom, [while] not a bosom
to repose upon, . . . was a capital bosom to hang jewels upon."
Calling her by breast thus reminds the reader what she and
Merdle are all about, as well as setting her vividly before the
mind's eye. A similar bit of shorthand is the moral staircase that
Dickens says Mrs. Sparsit in *Hard Times* sees Louisa descending
step by step (II, 10 and after); in that condensed novel where
Dickens complained of so little room to turn in, he could not
show by accumulating incident the progress of Louisa's reluctant
dalliance with James Harthouse.[24] In *A Tale of Two Cities,* another novel requiring shortcuts, the narrator makes use of acous-
tics. The home of the Manettes near Soho Square is a "peculiar
Ear of a place"; quiet and secluded, it nonetheless collects echoes
of passing footsteps with great clarity, and those echoes are
made to foreshadow things to come (II, 6).

But probably economy, real as that may be, is not the main
effect of Dickens's imagery. Imagery gives an edge to his narratorial voice; by it that voice charges the account with its own
intensity and energy and will. This is especially noticeable
where a forceful figure is infused into a whole stretch of narrative.
In *Our Mutual Friend* Mr. Twemlow, being first cousin to Lord
Snigsworth, is of some interest to people like Mr. and Mrs. Veneering, "bran-new people in a bran-new house in a bran-new quarter
of London" (I, 2), who scramble to establish themselves in
society. They use Twemlow as

an innocent piece of dinner-furniture. . . . [H]e was in frequent requi-
sition, and at many houses might be said to represent the dining-table in
its normal state. Mr. and Mrs. Veneering, for example, arranging a
dinner, habitually started with Twemlow, and then put leaves in
him, or added guests to him. Sometimes the table consisted of
Twemlow and half a dozen leaves; sometimes, of Twemlow and a

dozen leaves; sometimes, Twemlow was pulled out to his utmost extent of twenty leaves. Mr. and Mrs. Veneering on occasions of ceremony faced each other in the centre of the board, and thus the parallel still held; for, it always happened that the more Twemlow was pulled out, the further he found himself from the centre, and the nearer to the sideboard at one end of the room, or the window-curtains at the other.

The figure has a certain daring and wilfullness, and worked out with something like the exhaustiveness of a Metaphysical conceit, Twemlow as a dining table expresses with precision the method people like the Veneerings use to climb the social ladder.[25]

The opening chapter of *Bleak House* provides one of the more extended passages of imagery used in this way, in the Court of Chancery, described by the fog and mud of London. But I return to *Little Dorrit* for my final examples of this quality in Dickens. Mrs. General, whom William Dorrit engages to induct his family into the social proprieties after his fortunate deliverance from debtors' prison, has such control over those proprieties as a coach driver has over his horses, and handles them the same way. Her first husband,

enamored of the gravity with which she drove the proprieties four-in-hand through the cathedral town society ... had solicited to be taken beside her on the box of the cool coach of ceremony to which that team was harnessed. His proposal of marriage being accepted by the lady, the commissary took his seat behind the proprieties with great decorum, and Mrs. General drove until the commissary died. In the course of their united journey, they ran over several people who came in the way of the proprieties; but always in a high style and with composure.   (II, 2)

Mr. Pancks, however, the manager of Mr. Casby's rental property, is compared to a more up-to-date mode of transportation. Mr. Pancks is a steam engine, with "a complexion that was very dingy by nature, or very dirty by art"; his hands look "as if he had been in the coals"; at dinner "he took in his victuals much as if he were coaling; with a good deal of noise, a good deal of dropping about, and a puff and a snort occasionally, as if he were nearly ready to steam away." The contrast of his energy with Mr. Casby's torpor, the narrator says, makes Arthur Clennam see the two of them as ships:

[M]uch as an unwieldy ship in the Thames river may sometimes be seen heavily driving with the tide, broadside on, stern first, in its own way and in the way of everything else, though making a great show of navigation, when all of a sudden, a little coaly steam-tug will bear down upon it, take it in tow, and bustle off with it; similarly the cumbrous Patriarch had been taken in tow by the snorting Pancks, and was now following in the wake of that dingy little craft.   (I, 13)

V *Pattern*

My consideration of language has moved by stages to a point where a new heading is required, as not language, but relations of fictive elements, are now my subject. Thus defined, "pattern" is almost as wide a category as I defined "structure" to be at the beginning of this chapter, but I am limiting my discussion of patterns to the topics in the next four sections. The passage just quoted really opens the first of these; it also illustrates how a local pattern makes meaning. It is an epic simile, and by making Clennam perceive the relation between Pancks and Casby in that ancient form Dickens suggests how out of date Clennam's understanding of the English scene is from twenty years' absence. Clennam is wrong about Pancks (as he will discover). But rightly understood, the image of Pancks as a steam tug, taken together with Casby's character and attributes, and Bleeding Heart Yard and its tenants, expresses a significant idea of Dickens's; and the pattern which relates these fictive elements to show that is allegory.

VI *Allegory*

The London tenement called Bleeding Heart Yard is a place in great decline from its ancient greatness, even literally below the general level: "As if the aspiring city had become puffed up in the very ground on which it stood, the ground had so risen about Bleeding Heart Yard that you got into it down a flight of steps which formed no part of the original approach, and got

out of it by a low gateway into a maze of shabby streets, which
went about and about, tortuously ascending to the level again"
(I, 12). Poor people live there, the deserving poor, that is, like
Mr. Plornish the plasterer, who is often unemployed but not
from laziness; they live anxiously from day to day, and their
worst day, coming around with great regularity, is collecting
day, when Mr. Pancks "cruises" the Yard, "haranguing the inhabitants on their backslidings in respect of payment, demanding
his bond, breathing notices to quit and executions, running down
defaulters, sending a swell of terror on before him, and leaving
it in his wake." The tenants are unanimous that Pancks is "a
hard man to have to do with," and that it is a great pity "that a
gentleman like Mr. Casby should put his rents in his hands, and
never know him in his true light." They do not know that even
as they grumble, the Patriarch (Mr. Casby, so called from the
air of benevolent age emanating from his placid face and shining
bald head fringed by flowing silky gray hair),

—who had floated serenely through the Yard in the forenoon before
the harrying began, with the express design of getting up this
trustfulness in his shining bumps and silken locks—at which identical
hour and minute, that first-rate humbug of a thousand guns was
heavily floundering in the little Dock of his exhausted Tug at home,
and was saying, as he turned his thumbs:
"A very bad day's work, Pancks, very bad day's work. It seems to
me, sir, and I must insist on making this observation forcibly, in
justice to myself, that you ought to have got much more money,
much more money."   (I, 23)

So it is Casby, the owner of the property, who is the real oppres-
sor, not Pancks, who is only his agent, under the guns of the old
pirate himself.

Allegory deals with abstractions by story rather than by exposition, making ideas and relations concrete by embodying them
in persons, places, and incidents. The key to the vision embodied
here, as I have said, is the image of steam, the mode of power
that made possible the Industrial Revolution which transformed
England in the nineteenth century; and the whole fictive complex expresses Dickens's view of what modern industrial power
has come to. Working people have not shared in the country's

growth; their dwelling is depressed below the level of the "aspiring city," so that it is a pond for a Casby vessel to sail on. Pancks, the steam tug, is Casby's agent only; therefore, the industrial system which he represents is not by nature oppressive of workers. It is so only because owners make it so.[26] (The factory of Daniel Doyce, fortunately for him, is above the gateway to the Yard. Doyce is an intelligent and industrious engineer; his productive genius is frustrated by the Barnacle bureaucracy of the Circumlocution Office, and Casby was "formerly Town-agent to Lord Decimus Tite Barnacle" [I, 13]. So Doyce's difficulties with the Circumlocution Office are not entirely unlinked to those of the Yard.) That all this hangs together is confirmed by what Mr. Plornish is reported in narratorial free indirect speech to say to Arthur Clennam, explaining how things are with the Yard: "There was people of pretty well all sorts of trades you could name, all wanting to work, and yet not able to get it. There was old people, after working all their lives, going and being shut up in the workhouse, much worse fed and lodged and treated altogether, than—*Mr. Plornish said manufacturers, but appeared to mean malefactors*" (I, 12; my italics).

Dickens's images do not often translate so readily into ideas; it is more accurate, if not very explicit, to say that in his work a strong undercurrent flows in that direction. Still he certainly thought of story material that way. A letter to Bulwer-Lytton shows him responding to Bulwer-Lytton's comments on *A Tale of Two Cities* from exactly that perspective. Bulwer-Lytton must have objected to the Marquis d'Evrémonde; Dickens replied, "[S]urely when the new philosophy [of the rights of man, presumably] was the talk of the salons and the slang of the hour, it is not unreasonable or unallowable to suppose *a nobleman wedded to the old cruel ideas, and representing the time going out, as his nephew* [Charles Darnay] *represents the time coming in. . . .*"[27] The names are interesting. G. Robert Stange has remarked how the family name couples English *every* and French *monde*; "the association is with *tout le monde*, suggesting that Darnay is an Anglo-French Everyman."[28] We are not told where the Marquis's chateau is, but the Anglicization of his mother's family name D'Aulnais that the Marquis's nephew goes by in England means "of (from) Arnay," and Arnay-le-Duc is near Dijon, in wine country: thus the family is associated with wine, and wine—in *A Tale of Two Cities*—with blood.[29] The Evrémondes, then, share the representative quality of Casby and Pancks; however, the key image being buried, their relations do not take on the pictorial vividness, and as a consequence of that the allegorical suggestiveness, that Casby's and Pancks's do in those chapters of *Little Dorrit*.

Neither is the action in Dickens overtly allegorical as a rule. This example from *Little Dorrit* contains incident, and the incident does arrange and distribute story material to express a state of affairs; but it builds the allegorical scene, not a chain of events. Allegorical action may of course follow from the relations expressed in allegory, and show the causal relations that E. M. Forster's handy distinction between story and plot attributes to the latter: " 'The king died and then the queen died' is a story. 'The king died, and then the queen died of grief' is a plot."[30] But if that were to happen in *Little Dorrit*, the action would have to be generated by the elements of the scene: the turbulence created in the pond by the Pancks tugboat, say, might become so great as to swamp the Pancks or even the Casby, signifying elimination of proprietary economic power by the forces of the Industrial Revolution. Casby is in fact finally done in: Pancks denounces him before the Yard and shears him of his awesome presence by snipping off his flowing hair (II, 32). But Pancks does not steam or puff at all during this climax, and his steaming at the beginning of the chapter has only the literal significance of high emotional pressure generated by Casby's injustice. The humanness of Pancks and Casby is uppermost in the narrative here, and their allegorical suggestiveness has submerged.

It is possible, however, that Dickens's image is more complex and incisively analytic than at first appears. Steam stands well for industrialism; but so does the railroad in *Dombey and Son*. There the difference the railroad makes in Staggs's Gardens is Dickens's analysis of the societal effects of the Industrial Revolution. In *Little Dorrit* steam, besides suggesting the nature of the system under which the Yard lives, may also imply the pressure that the system puts the individual human being under. If so, Pancks's final revolt comes about because the system has outraged his selfhood, and Dickens's image, with its allegorical tendency, becomes a kind of prophecy that human nature will not bear forever the insult offered it by Casbian exploitation of industrial power.[31]

VII *Plot and Scene*

What I have been talking about here is one kind of the richness and value that Angus Wilson refers to in saying that Dickens's plots in themselves do not amount to much (above, p. 73). This allegorical way of conceiving action, if we allow it to be operating in Dickens, accounts for a number of things: for example, and notably, all those selfless young women from Mary Graham in *Martin Chuzzlewit* to Lizzie Hexam in *Our Mutual Friend.* They incarnate redemptive love. The success of these characters varies, but they make more sense in this view than they do on the assumption that Dickens simply could not draw credible women.[32]

However, while allegory (as I said) is not overt in Dickens, the scenic quality I have discussed in the Pancks-Casby episode is. Percy Lubbock left something essential out of account, Dickens's narratorial voice, but he was not wrong to say the world of a Dickens novel is a "picture," built up by a succession of particular scenes. A great deal of the business the narratorial voice transacts is to provide for that succession, to link the scenes together plausibly.

In fact, plot in Dickens might better be considered the shaping and ordering of story material to furnish a coherent succession of scenes than the arrangement of it to provide E. M. Forster's train of causally related events. It is certainly possible to discuss Dickens's plots in Forsterian terms. Events do lead one to another; there are subplots, more of them in the later big novels than earlier, and on the whole better integrated to the main plots later than earlier; the chains of events work out to some kind of resolution. And so on; but considered in these terms, as frameworks apart from the life of his scenes, Dickens's plots come off disappointingly. They seem melodramatic, often theatrical in a bad sense (how many times, for example, Dickens puts a character in an offstage room to overhear action on stage). They can be clumsy, as Wilson says the plot is in *Little Dorrit*;[33] and in *Dombey and Son*, in what Alice Brown and her mother Good Mrs. Brown have to do with Edith Granger and her mother Mrs. Skewton (58); and in *Martin Chuzzlewit*, in old Martin's account of his behavior towards Pecksniff (52). They may also seem to develop arbitrarily, without regard to the characters who should be moving them along. And of course they are long on coincidence, which is a conspicuous kind of apparent arbitrariness.

Readers of Dickens will not dispute any of this, and no doubt can add to it. But reading a Dickens novel is a much larger experience than these considerations account for. It is to hear a narratorial voice of great authority and rhetorical resource tell a story consisting, as Lubbock says, in "a succession of particular occasions," which it is the business of plot in the narrow sense to provide and connect; and readers come to know a novel not as a more or less complex train of events lengthening through time, but as a world spreading out about them, the way Esther Summerson gradually discovers the view from her window at Bleak House.

It was interesting when I dressed before daylight, to peep out of window, where my candles were reflected in the black panes like two beacons, and, finding all beyond still enshrouded in the indistinctness of last night, to watch how it turned out when the day came on. As the prospect gradually revealed itself, and disclosed the scene over which the wind had wandered in the dark, like my memory over my life, I had a pleasure in discovering the unknown objects that had been around me in my sleep. At first they were faintly discernible in the mist, and above them the later stars still glimmered. That pale interval over, the picture began to enlarge and fill up so fast, that, at every new peep, I could have found enough to look at for an hour. Imperceptibly, my candles became the only incongruous part of the morning, the dark places in my room all melted away, and the day shone bright upon a cheerful landscape, prominent in which the old Abbey Church, with its massive tower, threw a softer train of shadow on the view than seemed compatible with its rugged character. But so from rough outsides (I hope I have learnt), serene and gentle influences often proceed.   (*BH* 8)

The passage is an emblematic piece of action foreshadowing (as the parenthetical phrase in the second sentence suggests) Esther's eventual enlightenment about her own past, and the serene outcome of her life; it will serve just as well as an image of the reader's experience of a whole novel. One's developing sense of this novelistic world is spatial, so to speak, as much as temporal—

Lubbock's "picture"—and increasing knowledge of it brings increasing awareness of relations, complexity, ambiguity, and potentiality.

But there is another way of defining "plot" in Dickens, suggested by what I have just been saying. Given the breadth and density of the story, plot is the shaping and ordering of incidents, settings, and narrative strands to *suggest*—not lay out baldly, but only to suggest—the sort of thing that I have just said we become more aware of the more we learn about the world of the novel—that is, its complexity, potentiality, and so on. We are perhaps even less conscious, as we read, of these effects on us than we are of the strategies of the narratorial voice: again, it is only when something untoward happens that we will notice, except while reading the way one does to write things like this, perhaps. (It appears that structure, whether of the narratorial voice in its several aspects, of plot in its various dimensions, or of character, works on us mostly beneath the level of consciousness.)

I have touched on this matter in considering how the mechanics and chronology of serial publication affected Dickens's structure. There I was concerned with larger chunks of story, chapters and installments, but it can be illustrated conveniently on a smaller scale, too. In chapter 35 of *David Copperfield* David perceives his aunt Betsey Trotwood's misgivings about the "girl and boy attachment" between him and Dora Spenlow, and protests, "But we love one another truly, I am sure. If I thought Dora could ever love anybody else, or cease to love me; or that I could ever love anybody else, or cease to love her; I don't know what I should do—go out of my mind, I think!" To which his aunt replies ("shaking her head, and smiling gravely"), "Ah, Trot [he is "Trotwood Copperfield" to her]! blind, blind, blind!" Later Agnes Wickfield appears in town, and David is glad to see her as usual, and to make her a selfless chorus to his praise for Dora. Leaving her, he finds a beggar in the street: "and as I turned my head towards the window, thinking of [Agnes's] calm seraphic eyes, he made me start by muttering, as if he were an echo of the morning: 'Blind! Blind! Blind!'" David does not understand then (though he does now as narrator, or he would not tell it) why Betsey Trotwood thinks he is blind, but the reader must, or miss the main interest of the episode. The beggar appears when David has been with Agnes, and is still full of her virtues; and he is blind, to "echo the morning": to enforce the reader's awareness of what David does not realize, and to make Betsey Trotwood's "blind, blind, blind!" mean that she does know.[34]

VIII *Juxtaposition*

The method may be called juxtaposition; unlike causality, which makes one thing develop from another, this kind of pattern brings things together in the text, so that their contiguity, or nearness, may suggest a relationship of some other kind.[35] The method is obviously operating at the beginning of a novel, where in successive chapters Dickens starts various narrative strands; one knows that eventually these apparently unrelated matters will come together. At that stage, however, they are disjointed; all the connections remain to be made. Later, the layering and inter-leaving of events takes place in a spreading context of information, so that potentialities and significances begin to appear. Chapters 26–28 of *Little Dorrit* (Book I) associate the pretensions and falsity of the Gowan-Barnacle realm with the envy Tattycoram feels toward her mistress Minnie Meagles, and finally with Min-nie's choice of Henry Gowan as her husband. The Meagleses regret their daughter's preference, but Mr. Meagles himself is fatuously absorbed in the doings of Barnacles (I, 17); his daugh-ter's mistake and Tattycoram's somehow relate to Mr. Meagles's weakness. Chapters 9–11 of *Our Mutual Friend* (Book I) move from the Boffins' decision to share their good fortune with Bella Wilfer, who was to have married John Harmon, to the marriage of the adventurers Alfred Lammle and Sophronia Akershem, to Podsnappery, the worldview which reduces all things to the categories of "getting up at eight, shaving close at a quarter past, breakfasting at nine, going to the City at ten, coming home at half-past five, and dining at seven" (I, 11); there is a potential connection between Bella's regard for money, and the Lammles' buccaneering, and Podsnappery, standing in contrast to the Bof-fins' low valuation on wealth, and their unaffected goodness. In *Dombey and Son* Staggs's Gardens, scruffy neighborhood though it is, is the home of Mrs. Toodles, a woman of good sense and honest warmth who is little Paul's nurse after his mother dies. Staggs's Gardens is entirely transformed to a bustling commercial neighborhood by the railroad. In the narrative sequence, Paul's health fails in chapter 14, we learn in chapter 15 what the railroad has accomplished in Staggs's Gardens, and in chapter 16 Paul dies. The passing of Staggs's Gardens is in some way the same thing as the death of Paul.[36] In chapters 50–53 of *David Copperfield* the lost Emily is found, Uriah Heep is brought down, and David's child-wife Dora dies. Two of these are happy events, and Heep's destruction is accomplished in Micawberish comedy besides, but in a wide sense they are all alike: they all say no in some way, the last one most piercingly, to youthful innocence and confidence. Emily and Ham can never marry (and this is no cheap "poetic" justice, but a recognition of the profound division Emily's flight has made), the Micawbers will never prosper in England (the unstressed message of sending them to Australia), and Dora sees rightly that love as they did, she and David were too young. No recovery is complete; all experience leaves scars; consequences cannot be avoided. Indeed, David says at the beginning of chapter 54 that the future appeared "walled up" before him—the infinite prospects before the eyes of youth closed off by events.

IX   *Time*

Dickens's vagueness about narrative time is consistent with—even partly consequential to—this style of plot. Where the concern is with causality, chronological relations are important, and switching the narrative focus from one strand of the story to another, for example, must involve some attention to time: "Meanwhile, back at the ranch." (*Bleak House* is nearly unique in having narrative links which do just that: see below, p. 162.) But it is very hard in most of Dickens to keep the passage of time straight. To say this is not really to contradict Humphry House, who says Dickens "had a very acute sense of time . . . [and] went out of his way to indicate precise dates and seasons of the year, and sometimes even used known historical facts to enforce the actuality of a moment." Fiction of which the basic texture is scenic, and characterized by the kind of pattern I have just been describing, needs what House calls "a surface of tidiness and punctuality."[37] Probably monthly part publication had something to do with this chronological indeterminacy—sharply defined chronological flow might make problems for the reader something like the problems created by crudely suspenseful part endings, requiring too precise correspondence of his readers' consciousness at the end of a part to their mood at the beginning of the next.

But the main reason must be Dickens's sense of his fictive reality. On one side, its scenic nature makes the present moment the focus of attention—something like the "exclusive present" of Homer.[38] On another, there is the quality I have just been describing which makes the image of a picture—spatial, not temporal—more appropriate than the image of a stream. What Dickens is building as he writes is a world of layers and connections; they exist out of time, or at any time. Narrative time is often not important—the time when a thing appears to the reader, considered in relation to when other things appear, is.

I suspect this is what makes possible the state of affairs House discusses in his chapter "History": Dickens's novels are often set a generation back, but thematically they are about his own day.[39] *Little Dorrit* is set thirty years in the past, but it is Dickens's vision of grim interlocking realities in the 1850s: in the Pancks–Casby–Bleeding Heart Yard relationship, what industrial power had come to mean in English life; in the Circumlocution Office, the paralysis engineered by the Establishment; in Merdle and his bubble, the fraud of speculative finance.

Summing up "pattern" in Dickens then (to which all the last four sections belong): the business of a Dickens novel is to make a fictive world that appears comprehensive, complex, and puzzling, with the hint of correct order to be finally discovered and a solution to be worked out. This appearance is built by a long succession of scenes, often tinged at least by allegory, and by the juxtaposition of the various parts of the story in the order of narrative. Pattern is the arrangement of materials to provide this; precise chronology, and causality as provided by plot, may be—usually are—decidedly subordinate in the narrative effect. It is not clear how Rosa Dartle knows Emily is in London, and knows how to find her; Dickens faces the difficulty down by making Mr. Peggotty speculate that Littimer, Steerforth's snaky former manservant, may have been responsible. But, he says, "I doen't greatly ask myself. My niece is found" (*DC* 51). That is the important thing to him. To Dickens (except insofar as it is necessary to quiet reader uneasiness) the important thing is the confrontation between Rosa and Emily.

X *Character*

Why does he want that confrontation? The scene is not one of Dickens's successes; Victorian melodrama, again and again his model for scenes involving women in emotional stress (as if he did not know this subject well enough, and invention failed him), has done its worst here. It is painful to read, in more ways than Dickens can have intended. Rosa Dartle, who has loved James Steerforth hopelessly all her life, all edge from the grinding of frustrated passion, cuts deep and salts the wounds: Emily cries, "I have deserved this, but it's dreadful! Dear, dear lady, think what I have suffered, and how I am fallen!" (50). The scene goes on (and on, and on), Rosa taunting and Emily agonizing, David watching and listening from a small adjoining room, and waiting tensely for Mr. Peggotty to come. One reason for the scene is moral arithmetic, no doubt: Emily pays, on stage, for her sin. But that cannot be all, for she is clearly more to be pitied than censured. Her judge is not just, but vengeful; jealousy is Rosa's motive, not outraged virtue, and what she feels is savage joy at the pain of one who has had even for a while what she never has had.

Something else is being deployed here. In the clash between Rosa and Emily, with their widely disparate and yet oddly parallel pasts, Dickens is dramatizing the exactions of love gone wrong. Rosa and Emily are both orphans, Rosa living with Steerforth's arrogant mother as her companion, and Emily brought up by her loving and selfless uncle. Rosa hoards life—she risks nothing, never committing herself in speech, adding each year's interest to her small capital (20). Emily spends it, running away with Steerforth even at the cost of the secure home she has known. Rosa's style reflects Mrs. Steerforth's total absorption in her son, as Emily's abandon is a distortion of Mr. Peggotty's selflessness. So the two women are somehow commensurate, and they live out the costs of love paid by the cautious calculating intellect and the reckless undisciplined heart: jealousy and hate, and shame and remorse.

Dickens's characters embody for us in this way the complexity of the human condition. Looking at them separately, leaving aside the context of the story, and the tonality of the narratorial voice, a reader is likely to find them stagy and two-dimensional. We should not look at them that way, of course. It used to be said that

Dickens's characters are static: they can be counted on to repeat themselves whenever they appear (Mrs. Micawber will vow she will never desert Mr. Micawber, and so on). Taken within a set of qualifications (many do change, others turn out to have depths unrealized at first, though consistent with the major impression), that view has some truth. But the implication that Dickens's vision of character is simple is mistaken. Mrs. Micawber will never desert Mr. Micawber; however, Betsey Trotwood did leave her husband when he proved incorrigible. But in a sense she never leaves him, either. She continues to give him money, more than she can afford, and from her memory of what she once believed him to be she is reluctant to have him dealt harshly with even now when he cadges on her relentlessly (47). Dickens sees, and shows, various forms that loyalty growing out of love can take, but he distributes them between two women, and relates them to two widely different sets of marital circumstances. Mrs. Micawber considered in vacuo may appear simple, and Betsey Trotwood only less so; but together, in the story, they express a range of potential human behavior. In *Little Dorrit* Flora Finching and her late husband's batty aunt are an excellent comic pair, Flora ridiculously affecting girlishness in middle age, but with some shrewd self-knowledge too, and a right heart, and Mr. F's aunt unappeasably hostile, firing off obscurely threatening volleys at any approach. Between them they embody the complex feelings of a woman meeting after twenty years the man, Arthur Clennam, who as a youth had loved her until destiny in the form of parents separated them (I, 13, and after).[40]

Doubles occur often in Dickens (a commonplace critical observation) because he develops character this way. Each member of a pair gives perspective on the other: Samuel Pickwick and Sam Weller, the two Martin Chuzzlewits. In *A Tale of Two Cities*, Charles Darnay is what Sidney Carton could become, with purpose in his life; love gives him purpose, and he ends literally in Darnay's place and actually as good a man as he. (Seeing the pair from the opposite perspective is possible, and confirms the nature of the relationship, but the narrative focus keeps us conscious mainly of Carton.) David Copperfield's shining friend Steerforth, and Mrs. Strong's not so shining cousin Jack Maldon, display various unhappy consequences of purposeless life. Some characters are not strictly doubles, but serve to embody character

complexity in the same way. David does not see the full significance of what he says as he looks forward to friendly relations
between his wife-to-be Dora and his "sister" Agnes: "I saw those
two together, in a bright perspective, such well-associated friends,
each adorning the other so much!" (39). Nor is David aware of
his own "consanguinity" with Uriah Heep.[41] Pip and Orlick (Joe's
helper in the forge) are never friends, and Pip suspects (correctly, as it turns out) that Orlick struck down his sister. Pip is
sure the convict's leg iron that felled her is the one his convict
filed off with the file Pip got him. So Pip connects the attack on
his sister to an act of his own, and feels guilty, which suggests a
concealed wish to do her violence—a wish we can understand,
considering how she treats him. When Orlick is revealed as the
attacker, he is, as it were, Pip's agent. Orlick, then, expresses a
potential for violence in Pip's own character.[42]

This mode of presenting character is consistent with the tendency to allegory that I spoke of earlier. I do not mean to say that
Dickens saw his characters as abstractions; he meant them, and
felt them, as lifelike personages. But as he conceived them, they
express certain qualities and states of being in what they do and
say. The narrative order itself sometimes shows this. As David
Copperfield grows in experience he recognizes that Dora, the
choice of his "undisciplined heart," simply cannot be a grownup
wife. He resigns himself to this and resolves to make the best of
things. But Dora dies, and David eventually realizes Agnes has
always been the right one. Allegorically interpreted, this makes
sense. The male consciousness comes first to sex as play, and the
female as playmate; less exciting but less limited roles women live
do not count for much at that time. So, "Dora" must fade away,
so that "Agnes" may come forward. There may also be a sign here
that fear of sex is overcome: at first tolerable only as play, and
screened off from the rest of femaleness (which is "sisterly"; it
would be interesting to consider what Dickens does with brother-
sister sets), sexuality is eventually fused with housewifery and
soul-communion. In *Great Expectations* Pip's plans to rescue his
benefactor Magwitch (undertaken out of a sense of responsibility
and obligation) are interrupted by the summons to a mysterious
meeting out on the marshes. There Orlick reveals himself and his
intent to kill Pip. Following the analysis I made earlier, this is to
say, allegorically speaking, that the discovery of the murderous

truth in one's own heart first checks and then clears the way to
creative free action: after Orlick's plan is frustrated, Pip returns
to the rescue of Magwitch, and discovers finally that somewhere
along the way he has stopped regarding him as a malefactor to
whom he is unwillingly bound: "For now, my repugnance to him
had all melted away, and in the hunted wounded shackled creature who held my hand in his, I only saw a man who had meant
to be my benefactor, and who had felt affectionately, gratefully,
and generously, towards me with great constancy through a
series of years. I only saw in him a much better man than I had
been to Joe" (54).

The tendency of what I have been saying about character is
Aristotelian: characters, in Dickens, exist for the sake of plot,
not the other way round. This appears at odds, perhaps, with my
earlier support for Angus Wilson, that Dickens's plots are not his
strength, and that the riches of Dickens lie elsewhere. But the
contradiction is only apparent. Plot may be primary in a work—
that is, the thing the writer starts with, and regards as most
important—and still be weak. Furthermore, the way Dickens
worked is consistent with what I have said. However Dickens
began a novel, or whatever the germ of the story was, it jelled
for him when he could put a name to some central idea in it.
Martin Chuzzlewit is about the curse of selfishness, *Dombey and
Son* about pride, *David Copperfield* about the undisciplined
heart, *Little Dorrit* about the paralysis of English society, *Our
Mutual Friend* about money-madness, and so on. All of these are
about more than those labels, but those seem to be Dickens's or-
ganizing ideas, and in developing these stories, Dickens saw
actions, and characters, as embodying parts of these themes.
Dickens does not often analyze what he is doing when he writes
about his own works, but in that letter to Bulwer-Lytton about
A Tale of Two Cities that I quoted in the section on allegory,
defending himself to a friend and fellow novelist whose critical
opinion he respected (especially as affecting sales), Dickens is
very clear. The Marquis d'Evrémonde embodies the old system,
and Charles Darnay the new. The theme is the thing. What they
do, and what is done to them, are significant for that. — This is
not quite Aristotle's meaning, of course. When he says that
characters exist to move the story along, and reveal their natures
incidentally to that, he is talking about the physical actions of

the story. My analysis of Dickens's characters makes them important to plot not only as the doers of actions (they have the large assistance of the narrators in that), but as embodying in themselves aspects of the idea that the novel is concerned to develop. (I am using "plot" here in the wider sense of "pattern" that I described earlier.)

XI *Realism*

So the question how "realistic" or "convincing" Dickens's characters are misses the point. But the debate goes on, though the terms and the categories of success or failure change. E. M. Forster's familiar distinction between "flat" and "round" characters goes back more than fifty years, but it is relevant here both because Forster develops it with his eye on Dickens, and because it bears (erroneously) on a matter that I will touch on here and develop more fully at the end of this section. Flat characters, Forster says, "are constructed round a single idea or quality"; whatever more there is to them begins "the curve towards the round. The really flat character can be expressed in one sentence such as 'I will never desert Mr. Micawber.'" Such a character moves through circumstances unchanged, and is always the same. Round characters, like Jane Austen's, are "more highly organized," that is, more completely imagined, and "new sides of their character" will appear with changing circumstances. "The test of a round character," Forster concludes, "is whether it is capable of surprising in a convincing way. . . . It has the incalculability of life about it. . . ." From this it appears that round characters are superior to flat ones, and indeed Forster says openly "that flat people are not in themselves as big achievements as round ones."[43]

An author of intelligent and distinguished novels (the last of them, *A Passage to India,* one of the major novels in English in our century) is not to be set aside lightly, nor is his criticism lightweight because his style is unpretentious and commonsensical. His dimensional image appeals to all our experience of objects and entities, and his analysis accounts for many unsatisfactory characters in fiction. But it does not apply very well to Dickens. All sorts of characters who are "flat" by Forster's analysis work just fine, as Forster himself clearly recognizes:

"Dickens's people are nearly all flat," he says, "and yet there is this wonderful feeling of human depth." He suggests it is some sort of "conjuring trick"; Mr. Pickwick is as flat as a phonograph record, "but we never get the sideway view" (p. 71). Forster's image is lucid, but not an accurate instrument of analysis. It is not a question of three-dimensionality, of fullness and complexity of characterization. The people at Merdle's great gatherings in *Little Dorrit* named Bar, Bishop, Treasury, and Horse Guards are perfectly convincing though absolutely flat. So are the people similarly engaged at the Veneerings in *Our Mutual Friend*. So are Bounderby the mill owner and Mrs. Sparsit his housekeeper in *Hard Times*. So is the gentleman in the white waistcoat who exists to say "That boy will be hung!" when Oliver asks for more. So are the Americans in *Martin Chuzzlewit*, I am afraid. On the other hand, Mr. Dombey, carefully conceived and central to Dickens's design, is not a total success in my view, nor is Edith Granger, to whom he devotes nearly as much attention, nor is Arthur Clennam in *Little Dorrit*, nor John Harmon in *Our Mutual Friend*.

The trouble with Forster's idea is that it assumes fictive life depends on resemblance to actual life. It does not allow flatness to be better than roundness in a novel, because real people are round, not flat. Nor does it allow truth of character to be rendered in any other way than in individual fictive persons. The example of Dickens makes Forster uneasy about his categories, and he should be, because they really belong only to realistic fiction, and not to the mode in which Dickens worked. If they applied legitimately to Dickens, they ought to account for his failures of characterization. They do not, on Forster's own showing: round characters are superior to flat ones; Dickens's characters are nearly all flat; therefore . . . But instead, Forster's own excellent sensibility compels him to say that Dickens's "immense success with types suggests that there may be more in flatness than the severer critics admit" (p. 72).

I can see a couple of better ways to account for Dickens's variable success with characters. From the side of drama (and with apologies once more to Aristotle), the question is whether character and action fuse. I referred earlier to Aristotle's most effective relation between character and plot: character exists to move plot, plot does not exist to reveal character. There is no reason to restrict the idea to tragedy, or even to drama; it works for fiction, too, and best when we know qualities in the characters appropriate to the action they have to do, and when they have just enough attributes for that. There is identity between character and action. Dickens's work is of this kind, not tragic indeed (tragicomic, perhaps), but sharing this quality of character and action. Thus the examples I mentioned of characters Forster would call "flat," but who even communicate a sense of life, work, because they do exactly what they need to, and the action is such that no more is required of them: we do not wonder about Bar's wife or Treasury's temper. But this symmetry often fails in Dickens. He has a great stock of characters, sharply observed and vividly drawn; he has a theme; he devises a plot (in the narrow sense) to work out the theme in action; the characters must move that plot along. When everything works right, there is fusion. But as Wilson says, Dickens is not a strong plotter: he can not always produce an action that objectively correlates with the human states he so strongly perceives and describes. When that happens, we have obscure action, or unconvincing characters, or both.

From another point of view (or perhaps I had better call it another part of the explanation), the question is which prevails, the rhetoric of exposition or the rhetoric of fiction. It is easier to state than to illustrate in detail, but there is a perceptible difference between Dickens's narrator telling about a character and his narrator presenting them, the distinction Henry James made between reporting and rendering in a novel. In fiction what convinces and persuades best is fiction, not exposition. Dickens is best—and the characters I will turn to next, in moving along to the subject of humor, show this most clearly—when he follows his own advice to let his characters "play out the play" themselves. This does not mean that only in the most purely dramatic parts does Dickens really succeed: as I have argued above, it is wrong to distinguish sharply between scenic and narrative action.[44]

To risk illustration, I turn to *Dombey and Son.* Dickens explained to John Forster in advance, more fully than he ever did before or after, what he planned to do in that novel. Mr. Dombey was to be wholly possessed by the idea of "the Son," and balked by the son's preference for the daughter, and he was to

come to "a positive hatred" for her after the son's death, though
her love for him was to grow. That love, "when discovered and
understood," was to be "his bitterest reproach." In the end "the
sense of his injustice, which you may be sure has never quitted
him, will have at last a gentler office than that of only making
him more harshly unjust." This was to be "the stock of the
soup," to which "all kinds of things will be added," in the course
of "all the branches and off-shoots and meanderings that come
up" (F VI, ii, 472-73).

The whole passage is much too long to quote, but this summary fairly shows that in Dickens's description of his plan the
focus is almost entirely on Mr. Dombey. But how different this
is from the reader's experience, and memory, of the novel. Mr.
Dombey is very far from the center of attention. "All the branches
and off-shoots and meanderings," of course, take attention away
from him. But that only partly explains the difference. Dickens
has simply not provided enough action for Mr. Dombey to reveal himself in; he is explained more than he acts. (Another
way of indicating this, reflecting my point about Dickens's tendency toward allegory, is to say that proud Mr. Dombey becomes Pride; the character disappears and the idea comes to
the fore.) Similarly, Edith Granger's state of haughty self-loath-
ing: only she does the explaining herself, to Mr. Carker, in another of those retrospects by which Dickens accounts for the
state of affairs. She is not given action particularly persuasive
of the condition she describes. It might be argued that pride
such as Mr. Dombey's does not act, but requires to be courted
and attended, and so his passivity is right; he aspires to be the
still center of his turning world. The argument is credible applied to human beings in the world of mass and motion. But
this is a novel, and the novelist must work like a translator, who
sometimes must depart from his literal text to recreate its effect
in another language.

Dickens's success with character depends on the extent to
which the narrative focus stays on the character. The more it
shifts away from the character, so that our awareness begins
to include the skillful and self-conscious voice of the narrator
himself, or the idea rather than the character, the less convincing the character. In the same way, characters explaining themselves, rather than being themselves, often fail.

XII *Humor*

Writing about character in Dickens I have been considering not heroes and heroines, but a much larger class: characters who light up Dickens's themes. There is another large class of characters, partly overlapping with the first, but whose relation to the themes is much less regular; the relation occurs more often in the later Dickens than the earlier, and these characters are more often connected to plot in the narrow sense than to pattern or to theme. These are the humor characters, the grotesques, as they are often called, although I do not want to use that label for the same reason that I resist describing Dickens's characters as "flat": it implies a standard of realism not appropriate to Dickens. At any rate, here are Mrs. Gamp, Captain Cuttle, Bumble the beadle, Micawber, Mr. F's aunt, Mr. Bounderby, and all the characters who as Forster somewhere says "are easily recognized wherever they come in," because they do not change. At least, they do not change their way of talking (they do sometimes change character): it is by their speech that we know them, some turn of phrase, or flow of thought.

I do not undertake to list them, or discern types, because considering them under the head of Dickens's humor, it does not greatly matter what they are, or what they do, except as speaking and thinking are acts. Dickens learned to use these characters to help move his plots along (as in everything else, *Bleak House* furnishes good examples), but there was little excuse in plot for their presence in earlier novels. Or rather, that *was* what plot provided: an excuse for their presence, so that they might do what they were born to do, amuse. Their humor comes from their language and thought, just as it does in the case of the narrator himself. Of course, each successive appearance is also qualified and enriched by the developments of the story. Mr. Bumble's heated response late in *Oliver Twist* to the suggestion that he rules his wife would not be so funny if we had not seen him pompous and single at first, and maritally subdued thereafter: " 'If the law supposes that,' said Mr. Bumble, squeezing his hat emphatically in both hands, 'the law is a ass—a idiot. If that's the eye of the law, the law is a bachelor; and the worst I wish the law is, that his eye may be opened by experience—by

experience'" (51). The humor in Mr. Bumble's choice of metaphor, in fact, depends on the narrative history.

A few more examples. Captain Cuttle's conflations of Scrip-
ture are wonderful: "Train up a fig-tree in the way it should
go, and when you are old sit under the shade on it" (*D&S* 19).
They also show that the Bible was in Dickens's bones. In that
example, Captain Cuttle grafts chapter 4 of the Book of Jonah
(where Jonah sits in the shade first of a booth of his own de-
vising and then of a gourd plant the Lord causes to spring up,
while he waits to see whether the Lord will honor his prophecy
of destruction upon Nineveh) to Proverbs 22:6—"Train up a
child in the way he should go: and when he is old, he will not
depart from it." But Jonah sits under a gourd, not a fig tree. The
gourd, however, withers under attack by a worm sent from the
Lord, which is perhaps why Captain Cuttle thinks of a fig tree:
outside Bethany there was a fig tree that withered away under
Jesus's curse when, hungry, he found it fruitless one morning
(Matthew 21:17–19). — Long familiarity is behind this; it is
not the sort of thing one thinks up—it wells up.

Mr. F's aunt in *Little Dorrit* is implacably hostile to Arthur
Clennam just as concisely, but more unsettlingly, in the oracu-
larly obscure: "He has a proud stomach, this chap. Give him a
meal of chaff!" (II, 9). But conciseness is less characteristic of
Dickens's humorous characters than profusion, as is true of
the Dickens narrator himself. Mrs. Gamp:

> "Now, ain't we rich in beauty this here joyful afternoon, I'm sure.
> I knows a lady, which her name, I'll not deceive you, Mrs. Chuzzlewit,
> is Harris, her husband's brother bein' six foot three, and marked with
> a mad bull in Wellington boots upon his left arm, on account of his
> precious mother havin' been worrited by one into a shoemaker's shop,
> when in a sitivation which blessed is the man as has his quiver full
> of sech, as many times I've said to Gamp when words has roge betwixt
> us on account of the expense—and often have I said to Mrs. Harris,
> 'Oh, Mrs. Harris, ma'am! your countenance is quite a angel's!' Which,
> but for Pimples, it would be." (*MC* 46)

That speech illustrates also what George Orwell calls the
"unmistakable mark of Dickens's writing . . . the *unnecessary
detail*."[45] Orwell meant something like "incongruous," not "unnecessary," as his example from *Great Expectations* shows: in

Joe Gargery's report of what the robbers did to Pumblechook when they broke into his house—"and they took his till, and they took his cash-box, and they drinked his wine, and they partook of his wittles, and they slapped his face, and they pulled his nose, and they tied him up to his bedpust, and they giv' him a dozen, and they stuffed his mouth full of flowering annuals to prewent his crying out" (57)—it is the flowering annuals that Orwell calls "the unmistakable Dickens touch." Mrs. Gamp's effusion contains a handful of such touches—the height of Mrs. Harris's brother-in-law, Mrs. Harris's own pimples, and especially those Wellington boots. It also shows that nonstop associative thought process which is another source of Dickens's humor. Mr. Micawber's profusion is of a different sort, ornate and verbiferous, a parody of all speakers who appear "majestically refreshed by the sound of [their own] words" (as David remarks in chapter 52, while Micawber is reading his statement of Heep's infamy). Micawber seems to recoup his spirits in the very act of reporting his desolation: "'Perhaps, ... madam and gentlemen,' said Mr. Micawber [speaking to Betsey Trotwood, Mr. Dick, David, and Traddles], 'you will do me the favour to submit yourselves, for the moment, to the direction of one who, however unworthy to be regarded in any other light but as Waif and Stray upon the shore of human nature, is still your fellowman, though crushed out of his original form by individual errors, and the accumulative force of a combination of circumstances?'" (52).

Much of what I have written above about the narratorial voice, adjusted to the topic of humor, would fit here, and some of my examples there are appropriate to this context. By way of further economy, I note that the humorous features of Dickens's characters just discussed fit Dickens's narrator as well: with the difference that such instances as Captain Cuttle's quotation will be unplanned by the character, but deliberate in Dickens's narrator. A similar qualification needs to be made about the inflated Micawber style when Dickens's narrator uses it. Micawber believes in his rhetoric, so to speak, while the narrator does not. When Micawber breaks off to say, "—in short," and then restates in simple terms, it is not comic self-deflation but gracious condescension, a recognition that his hearers may be straining a little to soar after him. Dickens's narrator, however, is always conscious of the absurdity. Parody is always present to some degree, and he is inviting the reader to share his ironic delight in the language. Of course, in doing so he is also satirizing the mind of the earnest generator of such language.

These are comic effects on the scale of individual expressions, sentences, and speeches. On a larger scale, Dickens alternates passages of swelling rhetoric with brief narratorial commentary, where the effect comes from the counterpoint:

"My dear Mr. Copperfield, Mr. Micawber's is not a common case. Mr. Micawber is going to a distant country expressly in order that he may be fully understood and appreciated for the first time. I wish Mr. Micawber to take his stand upon that vessel's prow, and firmly say, 'This country I am come to conquer! Have you honours? Have you riches? Have you posts of profitable pecuniary emolument? Let them be brought forward. They are mine!' "

Mr. Micawber, glancing at us all, seemed to think there was a good deal in this idea.

"I wish Mr. Micawber, if I make myself understood," said Mrs. Micawber, in her argumentative tone, "to be the Caesar of his own fortunes. That, my dear Mr. Copperfield, appears to me to be his true position. From the first moment of this voyage, I wish Mr. Micawber to stand upon that vessel's prow and say, 'Enough of delay: enough of disappointment: enough of limited means. That was in the old country. This is the new. Produce your reparation. Bring it forward!' "

Mr. Micawber folded his arms in a resolute manner, as if he were then stationed on the figure-head.   (57)

This is only half of the passage, to show how it goes; imagination must supply the effect of the whole. — I think this disappears in the later Dickens, but I find it often in *David Copperfield*, and without taking time for an exhaustive search, as late at least as *Little Dorrit*.[46]

One more general observation will lead me to my final point on Dickens's humor, and that is, how pervasive it is. The last quarter-century of Dickens criticism has not had much to say of humor, in part for the very good reason that it did not seem to need talking about—everybody saw it. (In fact, Dickens's humor surely had something to do with the condescension toward him from late Victorians like Leslie Stephen, and their unwillingness to rate him very high: greatness was high seriousness, inseparable from solemnity.) But the gathering avalanche of Dickens criticism tended to obscure the humor, and whatever part it had in keeping people reading Dickens, it gained little support from academic criticism until lately.[47] The return to critical respectability of Dickens's humor is welcome, for we see Dickens entirely wrong if we leave that out. One way or another, from imagery to syntax to the larger rhythms of narration, and from the wildest absurdity and the most savage sarcasm to the nearly imperceptible irony of Esther Summerson, humor figures in nearly every chapter of Dickens.

This is to say, finally, that humor in Dickens is structural, not incidental. It cannot be considered separately from Dickens's "real" meaning, because it is a condition of that meaning. A humorous image can be a mode of analysis and a comment. Ironic use of circumlocution and abstraction invites the reader to judge of the discourse that uses such a style with sober intent. Beyond that, humor may license what might otherwise be intolerable for one reason or another. Ernest Hemingway's World War I veterans, walking wounded manfully bearing their losses, kept American fiction hard-boiled into the 1950's; Saul Bellow's Hemingwayesque Eugene Henderson, by his comic earnestness and spontaneity, reopened subjects that had been closed to fictive treatment for thirty years. Edgar Johnson argues that this effect of humor partly offsets Dickens's sentiment for modern readers: "They can bear the Marchioness in *The Old Curiosity Shop* [because] Dickens disinfects her pathos by infusing it with humor" (J 323). Walter Allen is mistaken about Silas Wegg in *Our Mutual Friend*, I think, in saying that "his viciousness becomes very much a secondary consideration" under Dickens's humor, but he is making a point about humor that is closely related to mine: "The character has been translated in [*sic*] a realm in which moral considerations are irrelevant. The comic becomes an aspect of Dickens's charity, indeed in these instances it is the expression of his charity."[48] Mrs. Gamp, he says, is the supreme example of such a translation, and indeed nurses before Florence Nightingale are not easy to look at in their own realm; the humor makes Mrs. Gamp not only bearable but a joy.

Satiric humor licenses another sort of study. Instead of disinfecting what would otherwise be painful, it lets us set aside the grave or the admirable to show us what those qualities ordinarily keep us from seeing. The 1963 film *Dr. Strangelove* is not likely to be surpassed as a vision of our flirtation with thermonuclear extinction; its caricature and parody go straight by tragedy, courage, and self-sacrifice to show us the banal heart of our love affair with death. Allen notes how savage Dickens is with characters like Uriah Heep in *David Copperfield*, the bullying schoolmaster Squeers in *Nicholas Nickleby*, Gradgrind and Bitzer and Bounderby in *Hard Times*, and Podsnap in *Our Mutual Friend*. They seem to me (except Squeers, who belongs elsewhere) instances of the effect I am here considering. They all have qualities that Victorian readers would value in real life. But Dickens will not let us see those, or rather, by means of humor, he turns them over to show the grub life that lives beneath them.

Another way of looking at this licensing function of Dickens's humor is to say that by inducing us to receive something we might otherwise reject, it works like rhetoric. It would be too much—or perhaps, the wrong order of statement—to say that humor convinces, or persuades, or renders credible. I do not expect to see (or hear) Mr. Micawber or Mrs. Gamp, or walk into the sort of household where a cold buffet instantly strikes me as a dead dinner lying in state; my life is more humdrum. But the humor in Dickens's conceptions does something like sandpapering my sensibilities, so that I sense something true in his conceptions. Or perhaps the humor gets his ideas past my defenses. (It is impossible to avoid figurative speech here.) In any case, humor does, in the mode that Dickens writes in, what verisimilitude—photographic and phonographic lifelikeness—does in realistic fiction: it authenticates the text that it inhabits.

XIII   *Mode*

What exactly is the mode of Dickens's fiction?—not quite an unnecessary question. A text must finally do its own work with readers, and the work of criticism ideally is to turn them back to that text with renewed interest and expectation, not to provide them with an alternative text answering as many critical questions as space allows. Once granted the willing suspension of disbelief that every imaginative work deserves in the reading,

Dickens stands less in need of support from criticism perhaps than any other major novelist in English. But there is an obstacle to that surrender which criticism may try to remove: not Dickens's alleged sentimentality as such, or his plot devices as such, or his characters as such, but his fictive mode, to which these belong.

It is an obstacle because most of us are deeply committed to matter-of-fact vision, and the world of a Dickens novel is not a matter-of-fact world. It is a world that expressed the consciousness of its maker, modulating from novel to novel as he moved through life, but maintaining always qualities that answer to his imaginative intensity, his energy, and his will. Matter-of-fact vision will see only blatant coincidence in a plot that walks Pecksniff past the seaport inn where young Martin Chuzzlewit and Mark Tapley alight directly on coming home from America, and will not see that Pecksniff appears there so that his fraudulence, and the fraudulence of America, are juxtaposed to each other: in Barnard's phrase, "Eden is merely a geographical Pecksniff."[49] It will see only "flat" characters in Flora Finching and Mr. F's aunt, and not the complexity of human emotion that they express in their meetings with Arthur Clennam. It will not see that the phenomena of Dickens's novels exist to embody his vision of human life, shaped and arranged in ways that answer to his vision.

The right name would distinguish Dickens's mode from realism without implying something less valuable than that. "Surrealism" fails this test. So does "fantasy," for much the same reason, that it implies a greater distance from fact, and a more merely private vision, than is appropriate. The adjectival form "fantastic" might do, if understood in the sense used to describe *Gulliver's Travels* as "fantastic" voyages: explorations of realities that correspond to the readers' "objective" realities, as Swift perceived and imaginatively embodied them. The distance between Dickens's fantastic reality and ours is not so great as in Swift's case, however, and "fantastic" has been hopelessly devalued by overuse as a mere intensive, anyway. My objections to "symbolism" I have already stated.

I have not found a name for Dickens's mode that satisfies me, although I hope explaining why some do not begins to indicate the nature of that mode. The objection to Dickens met by Santa-

yana long ago (quoted above, p. 31), that he exaggerates, is another clue, as is Santayana's response to it. Dickens's mode is
such as to provide an image of reality, to our eyes intensified, or
magnified (which is not the same as "exaggerated"; that implies
a tampering with proportion). Intensified: like a landscape photo-
graphed in color, with filters that cut through the haze which
softens and obscures precise outlines, and perhaps a telephoto lens
that foreshortens distances between objects in the scene. Or magnified: as a pointillist painting is magnified by viewing it from too
close, into an arrangement of points of color; one must back off
for the spots to blend into recognizable shapes. Metaphors break
down, and this one may raise a wrong question: how does one
"back off"? The parallel, for my present purpose, is between looking at the painting from close up, and the actual reading of the
text: the particular parts may appear disjunct as the eye, or the
reading consciousness, passes from one to the next. — As to that
"wrong" question, the metaphor probably helps explain why a
Dickens novel accumulates to something greater than is often
accountable from moment to moment in the reading: spatial distance, in viewing the painting, is equivalent to temporal distance
in reading, and as backing away from the painting organizes it,
moving the text through one's consciousness into the distance
of memory organizes the novel.

To our eyes intensified, or magnified—as Dickens somewhat
plaintively said in his "Charles Dickens Edition" preface to
Martin Chuzzlewit, really there is a legitimate question whether
the alleged defect belongs to the writer or the reader. But in
the absence of a bureau of standards to which all sensibilities may
be referred, majority prevails. We can admire Dickens without
blaming ourselves. What remains to do here is simply to review
how Dickens's image of reality impresses itself on us, when we
submit our belief to his mode. (We cannot tell how that image
appeared to him, though there are some clues which I follow up
at last.)

Perhaps most importantly, there is no such thing as a narrative
essence apart from the narration. Reading a Dickens novel, we
are—Robert Garis would say—in the Dickens theater, where the
voice from the stage creates all the reality we experience. Not
only that, but the will of the creator that shapes the creation is
everywhere present. This is not dramatic fiction after Stephen

Dedalus's model, where the author is "invisible, refined out of existence." The creator's intent appears in explicit narratorial statement, but it is also in the narrator's imagery, in symbol, in the orchestrated rhythms of narration, in pattern and plot and sheer narrative mass. Even when the characters are doing the work of the novel themselves, they do it in a way that expresses that will, they are if nothing else insistently *themselves* to express that will.

This fiction thus expresses in itself an immanent will, a continuous commentary alloyed with the narrative (I am reminded again of Geoffrey Tillotson's book on Thackeray cited in n. 44 above). It is all fiction and all commentary. The pressure on the reader is insistent and intense. When the narrator's voice thins and the creator's emotion breaks loose of that restraining form, the damage is correspondingly great. But if the narrator holds, even weakness can become a strength. The nearly unbearable coyness about "pleasant little Ruth! Cheerful, tidy, bustling, quiet little Ruth!" in chapter 39 of *Martin Chuzzlewit* seems about to be duplicated in chapter 53, when John Westlock finally opens his heart to Tom Pinch's sister. But the narrator takes off the excessive sweetness with humor, jauntily estimating the progress of John's suit by the changing prospects of his surly laundress, Fiery Face, for continued employment. (Besides, of course, the accumulated mass of the narrative provides indefinable but tangible support.)

Pattern (not plot) from juxtaposition of narrative blocks is another feature of Dickens's mode. The order of narration affects readers' perception of relationships, of complexity, and potentiality. I have mentioned as an example how putting Barnacle pretensions, Tattycoram's envy, and Minnie Meagles's marital mistake into narrative neighborhood in *Little Dorrit* suggests that Mr. Meagles himself, with his grave regard for Blood, is more than a little to blame for the unfortunate marriage of his daughter to the lounging Henry Gowan. Mr. Meagles's character is thus not the simple one we would conclude from any single episode, and his moral implication (and that of the class he stands for) in the condition of England is more complex than it would seem from his indignation at that happy hunting ground of Blood, the Circumlocution Office.

Pattern is a more indirect, and more subtle, way Dickens proposes his image of things than commentary. It works more slowly, too; the layers and segments must be introduced sequentially, narrative being what it is, and the impression of complexity and all the rest must coalesce gradually. Also Dickens is usually not precise, or at least not insistent, about the passage of time in his story. He is much more concerned about narrational time: the contiguity of narrative events in the reader's experience, rather than in the story. (There are reasons in serial publication for this, but it is consistent with his vision of things that time is less important than relations and stages of being, as I have suggested above.)

The effect for readers is that much of what we come to know, we know without any clear sense of when we found it out. We just know it. This is unexpectedly lifelike, for it is like the growth of our own experience. It is the way we know our own stories.

This in itself must go a long way to authenticate Dickens for us, even though his mode is distinctly not realism. Having noted this turn back toward the reader's own reality, I may wind up this section on the differences between that reality and Dickens's mode of fiction with the reminder that that mode *was* reality to him. He always said so. He never conceded, answering attacks on the accuracy and truth of his fictions, that he had written mere fancy, or hyperbole, let alone falsehood. Instead he insisted that what he had written was true. That he recognized his mode was not precisely literal is indicated by his reply to some critic of his "too great imaginative wealth":

It does not seem to me to be enough to say of any description that it is the exact truth. The exact truth must be there; but the merit or art in the narrator, is the manner of stating the truth. . . . And in these times, when the tendency is to be frightfully literal and cata-logue-like—to make the thing, in short, a sort of sum in reduction that any miserable creature can do in that way—I have an idea (really founded on the love of what I profess) that the very holding of popular literature through a kind of popular dark age, may depend on such fanciful treatment.   (F IX, i, 727–28)

Sometimes he defended unwisely, where a prudent reference to literary artifice would have deflected criticism. But his very insistence on an implausibility is significant: if the thing was consistent with the intrinsic order of things as Dickens understood that order, it could be true, and therefore must be.[50] So if the

Court of Chancery, as he saw it, was an oppressive judiciary system in mid-nineteenth-century England, the reason to him could be that it embodied some fundamental evil. *Bleak House*, the novel to which I now turn, is persuasive about the evils of Chancery partly because Dickens shows them working through the lives of his characters by his rhetoric of fiction. But the other reason is that in the mode of Dickens's fiction, Chancery, looked through and through by that magnifying imagination, is at the same time an affliction of these people in this place, and a sickness as wide as the world and long as time.[51]

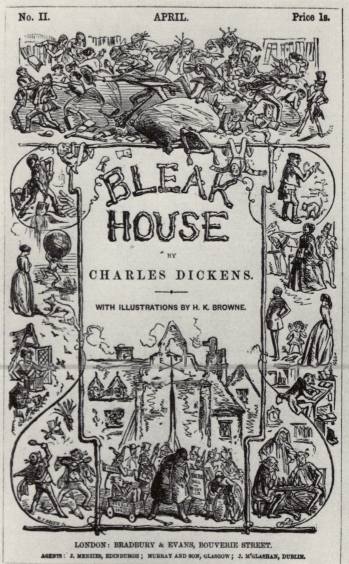

No. II.   APRIL.   Price 1s.

BLEAK HOUSE

BY

CHARLES DICKENS.

WITH ILLUSTRATIONS BY H. K. BROWNE.

LONDON: BRADBURY & EVANS, BOUVERIE STREET.

AGENTS: J. MENZIES, EDINBURGH; MURRAY AND SON, GLASGOW; J. M'GLASHAN, DUBLIN.

NOTICE is hereby given that the Author of "BLEAK HOUSE" reserves to himself the right of publishing a Translation in France.

CHAPTER 5

Bleak House

T HIS chapter is an essay at finding a way into *Bleak House* by some of the approaches to Dickens's work that I have been discussing. It would be pleasant, for the sake of symmetry, if the chapter might unfold in exact parallel to the preceding one. But working through a particular novel is a different matter from describing Dickens's work in general, and my order of development, the scale of the parts, and the parts themselves, do not tally precisely with the preceding discussion. (As will appear from my final chapter, this irregularity is appropriately Dickensian.)[1]

I *Summary*

The main parts of the story are Jarndyce and Jarndyce, the suit in Chancery which involves everyone in the story directly or indirectly; Lady Dedlock's secret, which generates most of the physical action; and Esther Summerson, whose importance as the central character is not of a nature to be evident in a summary such as this. The first three chapters introduce these parts in the order given here: a session of the High Court of Chancery, on a question of costs in Jarndyce and Jarndyce ("a mere bud on the forest tree of the parent suit, [which] really will come to a settlement one of these days"); the agitation of the usually haughty and controlled Lady Dedlock at seeing the copyist's handwriting on a document in the suit being routinely presented for inspection by the Dedlock legal advisor Mr. Tulkinghorn; and Esther's account of her orphan childhood with her aunt Miss Barbary (her only family so far as she knows, and she did not know that while Miss Barbary lived), and her history to the present moment, when she is about to join the household of John Jarndyce as a com-

panion to Ada Clare, who with her cousin Richard Carstone is a
ward in Jarndyce and Jarndyce; both are coming under the
guardianship of John Jarndyce. Jarndyce, it turns out, has been
Esther's secret benefactor for years, and she so well pleases him
now that he gives her the responsibility of managing Bleak House.
(Anything but bleak now, it was but a ruin when he took it over
after Tom Jarndyce's suicide; it was Tom Jarndice who named
the house out of his despair over the suit.) The qualities Jarndyce sees in Esther are continuously evident, in the way she
turns to immediately in any situation where a helping hand
is needed: in Mrs. Jellyby's chaotic household of neglected
children, with the brickmaker's family where she accompanies the
overbearing charity worker Mrs. Pardiggle, and throughout the
story.

Tulkinghorn, made curious by Lady Dedlock's uncharacteristic
perturbation, locates the copyist at lodgings above Krook's rag
and bone shop, but finds him dead of an overdose of opium (an
accident, the inquest concludes). So Tulkinghorn's quest for his
identity seems at an end. Nemo—as he called himself—appears
to have been a man who knew better fortunes once, and had the
gratitude, for occasional kindnesses, of Jo the crossing-sweeper,
who testifies at the inquest. (Jo is some time later engaged by a
woman unknown to him to show her the various places associated with the case, including the reeking churchyard where
Nemo is buried.)

Interest at the Jarndyce household centers for the time being
on the question of a profession for Richard, who has no strong
inclination in any particular direction, and makes no headway
at his first choice, surgery. He develops some interest in the
Chancery suit, to the disquiet of the Jarndyce circle, and consequently turns to law. But that does not do, either, especially
as he becomes more and more preoccupied with the suit; and he
finally determines on the army. In the meantime he and Ada have
become engaged, and his fascination with the suit has led to
estrangement from Jarndyce (Richard cannot endure Jarndyce's
anxious remonstrances). In the meantime, too, the Jarndyce
household has visited for some weeks at the home of Jarndyce's
friend Boythorn, which adjoins the Dedlock estate, and they
have met Lady Dedlock, who impresses and affects Esther greatly
without her quite knowing why.

Tulkinghorn however has not closed his inquiry; at his direction Inspector Bucket locates Jo, who finds the woman Bucket shows him like in dress but not in voice to the woman he escorted to Nemo's burial place; she is Lady Dedlock's former maid Hortense. Tulkinghorn now learns (from his contacts lower down in the legal world) of a former soldier, George Rouncewell, who has some letters from his former officer, a Captain Hawdon, that Tulkinghorn wants; George however declines to give them up. At about this juncture Mr. Guppy, a young law clerk who is interested in Esther, lays his research in progress into her identity (set on by her remarkable resemblance to Lady Dedlock) before Lady Dedlock, who receives the fragmentary information coolly, concealing the agony of the revelation: that the child of her liaison with Captain Hawdon did not die at birth, as her sister (Miss Barbary) told her. Her secret is now known to the reader (in ch. 29, about halfway through the novel). Seven chapters later Esther learns who she is, when a distraught Lady Dedlock reveals the truth to her, saying however that they must not meet again. Her secret appears to be safe, since Guppy concludes that Nemo-Hawdon's papers, which would prove his hypothesis, were consumed along with Krook in his sensational death by spontaneous combustion. But Tulkinghorn, in his pursuit of Lady Dedlock, has forced George to give up his letters from Captain Hawdon, and now he knows; he tells Lady Dedlock to do nothing while he considers the best interests of the Dedlock family in all this. Tulkinghorn is found murdered; George is arrested; Inspector Bucket finds the real murderer, Hortense; Lady Dedlock, unaware of Bucket's coup and with good reason to think her secret out, flees, to spare her husband humiliation. Sir Leicester however loves her deeply and orders Bucket to find her, which he does, but too late: she lies dead at the gate of the churchyard where Nemo—Captain Hawdon—lies.

Richard and Ada have meanwhile been secretly married, following the collapse of Richard's army career; henceforth his attention is entirely given over to Jarndyce and Jarndyce, as he feverishly hangs on the opinions of his lawyer Mr. Vholes. His health is going, as Esther learns from Allan Woodcourt. Esther met this young doctor during Richard's surgery phase, and the obstacles to their interest in each other being at last overcome, they now marry. Shortly thereafter Jarndyce and Jarndyce really does end: the estate has been consumed in costs. It is too much for Richard, and he dies, happily not before being reconciled with John Jarndyce. Ada takes Esther's place as mistress of Bleak House, and Allan and Esther set up in a new Bleak House of their own in Yorkshire, where Allan practices medicine among a grateful populace.

I have omitted from this summary the action involving such characters as Mrs. Jellyby, Mrs. Pardiggle, Harold Skimpole, Rev. Chadband, and the Smallweeds; to include them would have damaged the impression of unity more than omitting them damages the impression of the book's texture. But in aggregate, these parts are very important to the effect of the whole.

II *Voice and Point of View*

Bleak House, as the reader discovers at chapter 3, has two narrators. The reader gets the story not only through the filters of two different intelligences, but from two perspectives. The omniscient narrator is detached, with a breadth of vision that makes it possible to depict a large-scale scene, as well as to direct the narrative spotlight now here, now there. His is a public voice. Esther's is private, and anything but detached, and tells a story from ground level and from within a web of human relationships, reporting only what Esther experiences herself (with, so far as I recall, a single exception, where in chapter 51 she reports conversations of Allan Woodcourt with Vholes and Richard as told to her afterwards by Allan). Dickens seems to have felt that the scope of his story would be broadened by as wide a contrast between his narrators as possible, as if to enclose between them as much as possible of the potential meaning of his story: one narrator anonymous, presumably male, widely experienced in the world, and ironic; the other a personal identity, female, without direct knowledge of the world outside home and school, and unshakably earnest.[2] Logic and experience would suggest extending the contrast to say that Esther is subjective and the anonymous narrator objective, as we have come to expect of two such positions. Actually more like the reverse is true; or rather, Esther is in her way just as objective and trustworthy as the anonymous narrator. More of that later.

Esther speaks in the conventional past tense of narration, while the anonymous narrator uses the historical present tense. It is usual, and I think true, to say that this tense carries a sense of immediacy, so that we feel the action as going on now. What Esther reports is over and done, according to her verb tense, and although she does not usually color the narrative with her afterknowledge, still that she has come through provides a kind of assurance about the outcome to set against the indeterminacy conveyed in the narrator's present tense. (Reversing the tenses would have given a radically different tone: the narrator reporting the wider scene, all complete, and Esther telling a story with un- certain outcome—we would not be so secure, unsure what her place would be in the end.) The use of the two tenses also widens the way we experience time in reading the novel, to something like the way we experience it in living, where our past exists in memory the way it came into being, as the unfolding now.

The anonymous narrator, whom I shall call simply "the nar- rator" hereafter, speaks with assurance and (of Chancery and Dedlock affairs) sardonically, his grim wit expressing his disil- lusion with what he reports. It is he who introduces the famous fog (and mud) in describing London at Michaelmas term of the law year, and indeed, if his implied experience of the world is regularly compounded of such elements, his tone is understand- able. He has also been around the Court of Chancery long enough to see it as a ritual without end and its participants mere mechani- cal pieces of the machine—"Eighteen of Mr. Tangle's learned friends, each armed with a little summary of eighteen hundred sheets, bob up like eighteen hammers in a piano-forte, make eighteen bows, and drop into their eighteen places of obscurity" (1)—and to have learned to hear what is spoken there as mere ritual code: "Mlud, no—variety of points—feel it my duty tsubmit—ludship." He may turn where he likes, as to the town house of Sir Leicester Dedlock in the next chapter (I have quoted the third paragraph above, p. 91). His tone would imply a moral unity between the two scenes, even if his words did not indicate it (which in this instance they do, though later the tone informs of such connections unaided). Still he is able to see merit where it exists; Sir Leicester Dedlock is immovably feudal, "re- gards the Court of Chancery . . . as a something, devised in con- junction with a variety of other somethings, by the perfection of human wisdom, for the eternal settlement (humanly speaking) of everything": but he is also "a gentleman of strict conscience, disdainful of all littleness and meanness, and ready, on the shortest notice, to die any death you may please to mention rather than give occasion for the least impeachment of his integrity."

This narrator may then be trusted in spite of his sustained disillusion. He also presents character without by his omniscience violating the character. Tulkinghorn's nature is to be secret, as is Lady Dedlock's need, and the narrator presents both of them without fully exercising his omniscience: "Has Mr. Tulkinghorn any idea of this himself?"—that is, that Sir Leicester Dedlock finds Mr. Tulkinghorn's air, and dress, agreeable, "in a general way, retainer-like," and "receives it as a kind of tribute." After a paragraph describing the ways tradesmen manipulate the great they serve, the narrator concludes, "Therefore, while Mr. Tulkinghorn may not know what is passing in the Dedlock mind at present, it is very possible that he may."[3] Neither does he take the liberty (reporting how it comes about that the Dedlocks are in London) of explaining why Lady Dedlock said she was "bored to death" at the place in Lincolnshire, though the order of narration shows he knows: she, "(who is childless)," had just been "put quite out of temper" watching the reunion at day's end of an estate keeper with his wife and child (quoted p. 92 above). So early Dickens's narrator hints at Lady Dedlock's case, but without disturbing the secrecy that is her prime motive. This is his regular method with Mr. Tulkinghorn and Lady Dedlock. He looks into the minds of both characters only when more of the story has come out, and only when those characters are by themselves. Thus the mystery in the novel comes appropriately from the narrator, who knows the duplicities of the world. His rhetorical authority comes from that worldly wisdom, and from the ethical commitment evident both in his judgment of the world, and his fairness to an individual like Sir Leicester Dedlock.

Esther's rhetorical authority is based elsewhere. She is not weary of the world, or at all disposed to blame it for her troubles, which from the dawn of her consciousness are not inconsiderable. Told on a childhood birthday by Miss Barbary, "Your mother, Esther, is your disgrace, and you were hers," she cries herself to sleep. But her resolve is "to repair the fault I had been born with (of which I confusedly felt guilty and yet innocent), and would strive as I grew up to be industrious, contented, and kind-hearted, and to do some good to some one, and win some love to myself if I could" (3). She does behave that way, and all who know her love her and praise her and look to her for guidance, and she is grateful, though she thinks it is all a conspiracy of kindness toward her, believing as she does that she is "not clever," and that "to have done so little and have won so much" is almost occasion for shame (3). She weeps with gratitude—"I hope it is not self-indulgent to shed these tears as I think of it" (3)—and wonders again and again at the generosity of everyone toward her: when Mr. Boythorn compliments her for her consideration for others, "(They all encouraged me; they were determined to do it)" (9); when John Jarndyce (whom she calls "Guardian") asks her opinion, "He who was so good and wise, to ask *me* whether he was right!" (13); when she comes back to Bleak House after a trip to London, "They were so glad to see me when I got home, as they always were, that I could have sat down and cried for joy, if that had not been a method of making myself disagreeable" (23). Once, in fact, she sounds like Mark Tapley in *Martin Chuzzlewit* complaining he can win no credit for being "jolly" in adverse circumstances because everybody is so good to him: "in short it was the old story, and nobody would leave me any possibility of doing anything meritorious" (38). Other characters' regard for Esther, implied by her own protestations, is universally high; Ada and Richard invent affectionate nicknames for her and depend on her for advice, John Jarndyce turns the management of Bleak House over to her as soon as she gets there, Caddy Jellyby owns her debt to Esther for helping her to a new life, little Charley is devoted to her, and so is George Rouncewell, and so on. She is herself endlessly affectionate—Richard is "dear Richard," Ada is "my darling," John Jarndyce is her "dear Guardian"—and her kindliness and charity are always on tap.

No wonder that Esther has stuck in many a modern throat. It is not just her sweetness and awesome steadfastness in doing good; that may bother us more than it did Victorians, though one reviewer did find her "a prodigious bore, whom we wish the author had consigned to the store-room the moment she was fairly in possession of her housekeeping keys," and others protested less vehemently.[4] The main trouble is the same one that reviewer complained of: the paradox of a selfless heroine "who notes in her journal every thing that a self-forgetting mind would not note." Dickens himself was surely conscious of the difficulty; he has Esther begin chapter 9 with this paragraph:

I don't know how it is, I seem to be always writing about myself. I mean all the time to write about other people, and I try to think about myself as little as possible, and I am sure, when I find myself coming into the story again, I am really vexed and say, "Dear, dear, you tiresome little creature, I wish you wouldn't!" but it is all of no use. I hope any one who may read what I write, will understand that if these pages contain a great deal about me, I can only suppose it must be because I have really something to do with them, and can't be kept out.

But as even this brief example shows, Dickens tarnishes his effect by overdoing it: Esther is just too cute, calling herself names. Furthermore, Dickens gives her intelligence and sensitivity, which makes her self-forgetful self-consciousness even harder to accept. John Forster himself (in a generally glowing unsigned review) conceded that Esther was not a complete success: "[W]e suspect that Mr. Dickens undertook more than man could accomplish when he resolved to make her the *naive* revealer of her own good qualities."[5]

The question is, then, why? Partly, no doubt, the dare in it: Dickens mounts the high wire, scorning a net. We should not underestimate that motive in accounting for things in Dickens, the pleasure he took in his own skill. But there is in Dickens's conception of his novel a structural reason for the character, and for the point of view. Dickens conceived this novel in polar terms. Chancery is not the whole of reality; there is another, in which needs are seen and met in love. Participants in this reality do not make much of themselves—"Charity vaunteth not itself, is not puffed up" (I Corinthians 13:4)—and when the professional benevolence people urge their line, as Mrs. Pardiggle does in commanding Esther to help her in her visiting of the poor, Esther explains why she would rather not: she has good intentions but she is inexperienced, and she does not have "that delicate knowledge of the heart which must be essential to such a work." But the core of her reluctance is what she tells Mrs. Pardiggle at last: "For these reasons, I thought it best to be as useful as I could, and to render what kind services I could, to those immediately about me; and to try to let that circle of duty gradually and naturally expand itself" (8). In the case of the neglected Jellyby children, whose plight so disturbs John Jarndyce when Ada and Richard and Esther tell him about them, Jarndyce's solution is sweets: "Couldn't you—didn't you—now, if it had rained sugar-plums, or three-cornered raspberry tarts, or anything of that sort!" But Ada says, "It did better than that. It rained Esther"; and goes on to specify: "Esther nursed them, coaxed them to sleep, washed and dressed them, told them stories, kept them quiet, bought them keepsakes . . ." (6).

Esther is right to conclude "I have really something to do with [the story], and can't be kept out." She embodies and enacts this other reality, the reality that opposes (and is threatened by) Chancery. How shall it (she) be presented with the least distortion? The logic of evidence rates firsthand accounts higher than secondhand ones; by some such logic, I suppose, Dickens decided that Esther should tell her own story. He might have done Esther's part of the novel in the dramatic mode, with no narrator at all, or an entirely neutral one—but to voice that thought is to dismiss it, so foreign is it to Dickens's style. Certainly he was right not to use that other narrative voice; the tonalities would have altered her essence. Some other voice would have had its distorting tones, too, especially for us, trained as we are to distinguish the tale from the teller. There remains the option he chose. The difficulty with Esther as a narrator that Dickens's reviewers saw is inherent, given Dickens's basic conception of his material. But the regard in which she is held by other characters provides the ethical proof we require to accept both her protestations about herself, and what she tells us as a narrator. Dickens's solution is defective, partly from the nature of the case and partly from his own mistakes. But in the whole stretch of the novel, it works well enough, and from time to time, much better than that.

III *Language*

As Esther's nature is different from the narrator's, so is her language. His shows all the variety usual to Dickens, in syntax from plain to ornate and in vocabulary from Latinate complexity to street vulgarity. His tone runs from the heavy but cultivated

irony of the opening chapters through the lighter but still satiric
style of the Smallweed episodes; there is friendly humor mingled
with solid respect for Inspector Bucket and the Bagnets and
George Rouncewell, and solemn simplicity for the emotional
climax of such a passage as Jo's death. His language is laced with
imagery; it would be the work of a monograph to trace it all out,
and dull to boot, coming at it that way instead of in context.
This imagery is profuse and not necessarily systematic; the office
of Vholes the lawyer ("field mouse" by name) sounds like a
mouse nest, but Vholes is also a cat watching a mouse, and there
is a prominent image of a snake, too, when he and Richard return from court with "several blue bags hastily stuffed, out of
all regularity of form, as the larger sort of serpents are in their
first gorged state . . . " (39). It may be much to see a reference
to the serpent in Eden here, but there is a great deal of biblical
reference in the imagery: to stay with Vholes, earlier in the chapter he is reported to be always at work, "making hay of the grass
which is flesh." If all flesh is grass, as Isaiah 40:6–7 has it, "and
all the goodliness thereof is as the flower of the field: the grass
withereth, the flower fadeth"—the allusion is highly appropriate to
a lawyer who makes his living disputing over wills in the Court
of Chancery, and the fusion with a slangily commercial phrase
like "making hay" neatly conveys the haymaker's motive and outlook. This is another image like Captain Cuttle's biblical montage that I traced out in the preceding chapter, evidence of how
integral the Bible was to Dickens's thought.

Esther uses some of this imagery, too; the allusion to Revelation 6:8 ("And I looked, and behold a pale horse: and his name
that sat on him was Death") is clear in the scene that she describes earlier, lit in her memory by afterknowledge of Richard's
fate, of Richard and Vholes in a gig about to leave for London:
"I have before me the whole picture of the warm dark night, the
summer lightning, the dusty track of road closed in by hedge-
rows and high trees, the gaunt pale horse with his ears pricked
up, and the driving away at speed to Jarndyce and Jarndyce"
(37). The whole scene has allegorical suggestiveness: a road
(of life), night, storm in the offing, death. And perhaps it is not
too much after all to see the snake in Eden two chapters later,
when Vholes here, tall and thin and dressed all in black, is
seated by Richard in the gig "quite still, black-gloved, and but-

toned up, looking at him [no doubt in that "slow fixed way he had of looking at Richard," as Esther says earlier] as if he were looking at his prey and charming it": as a snake is said to do, rendering it powerless to move and escape devouring. (One may also see a suggestion here, in the image of a snake's prey, of Miss Flite's caged birds, emblems of all the Chancery-prisoned joys of life; and a link to the whole network of bird imagery in the novel.)[6]

I have been carried from my starting point, but this will serve as an instance of how Dickens's imagery intersects and weaves through the narrative, qualifying its tone. By and large, however, Esther's language is less vivid with imagery than the narrator's. It is consistent with her domesticity and modesty that this is so, as it is consistent with the platform personality of the narrator to be more decorative. Esther describes what she sees, and what passes, simply. Her imagery is not a rhetorical instrument, but a sign of her own character: the allusion to Revelation 6:8, unobtrusive and uncontrived, shows what her consciousness is stocked with.

This is not to say that Esther's narrative is neutral, but that it is charged with a different energy than the narrator's. Hers is the energy of love, his the energy of judgment. There is judgment in Esther, too, very occasionally made mildly and soberly explicit, and more often purely dramatic in form, where Esther lets what she reports make its own impact. The rhetorical force of the method can be great, as the example of Harold Skimpole shows. Time and again Esther presents him in his own words, spining his gauzy evasions of responsibility, with no more explicit commentary that she sets down the first time: "If I felt at all confused at that early time, in endeavouring to reconcile anything he said with anything I had thought about the duties and accountabilities of life (which I am far from sure of), I was confused by not exactly understanding why he was free of them. That he *was* free of them, I scarcely doubted; he was so very clear about it himself" (6). The second sentence is a mistake on Dickens's part; without it, Esther's puzzlement is unmistakable, and reinforces the effect made by Skimpole's own words. But the second sentence smacks of irony, which if present makes the first one insincere. Dickens does not always keep himself clear of Esther. The description of dinner at Mrs. Jellyby's is all right (4); it is ludicrous, but Esther remains herself, she is simply reporting what happened, even when she says so many letters about Borrioboola-Gha kept arriving "that Richard, who sat by [Mrs. Jellyby], saw four envelopes in the gravy at once"—even if that is a comic invention, it is Richard's, not Esther's. But the description she gives of old Mr. Turveydrop ending "he was not like youth, he was not like age, he was not like anything in the world but a model of Deportment" (14) is not all right—it is Dickens, making a mask of her. He does the same in chapter 35, where Esther is made very knowing about the conferring of titles in England, away outside her experience; the deadly matter-of-fact concision of her comment on Miss Flite's innocent misconceptions of the matter sounds very nearly Swiftian: "I am afraid she believed what she said; for there were moments when she was very mad indeed."

Still these slips are exceptional.[7] For the most part Esther is herself, and she lets other characters judge themselves before the reader, in the acts she reports them doing. As herself she expresses love, and the narrator expresses judgment: Dickens gives the reader these two perspectives on his story, and from the collisions and minglings incident to them will emerge his theme.

IV   *Plot and Pattern*

It is a little surprising to find contemporary reviewers of *Bleak House*, praisers and dispraisers alike, complaining that the novel has no plot. The *Illustrated London News* reviewer did not finally mind, so much else is there to be entertained by—"*Bleak House* . . . has beauty enough, and power enough, and is full of passages which those who read them find reason to be glad they have read"—but George Brimley in the *Spectator* was more severe: "Mr. Dickens discards plot, while he persists in adopting a form for his thoughts to which plot is essential, and where the absence of a coherent story is fatal to continuous interest."[8] Brimley understood something about novel-writing, to have put it that way. How did he miss seeing the plot?—for surely modern critics are not wrong to find Forster's judgment sensible that *Bleak House* is Dickens's best-plotted novel: "Nothing is introduced at random, everything tends to the catastrophe, the various lines of the plot coverage and fit to its centre, and to the larger interest all the rest is irresistibly drawn" (VII, i, 560).

Brimley seems to have disapproved of Dickens's work in general, and so found much in *Bleak House* to dislike. Serial publication could be much to blame, too, more especially for a Brimley, interested in the consistency of thought and aesthetic form, than for the uncritical reader. The reviews which I have referred to were all published at the end of the nineteen-month serialization, but even if the reviewers had the entire text before them, they wrote remembering it as they had read it, month by month. The mass of detail in each part, the large number of characters and the complexity of the action, the deliberate pace of the action (until the climax), the sidelong and infrequent references to the passage of time in the story: all this, together with the fact of month-long intervals between parts, certainly could operate to keep the plot well covered. Plot, at any rate, as Brimley conceived it: a "close and necessary connexion" of incidents "which form the outward life of the actors and talkers," and which are interesting because they "powerfully aid in modifying and developing the original elements of human character" (p. 283).

Such a conception of plot is certainly not eccentric, and in fact working from that conception Brimley does not see things in *Bleak House* far wrong. The Chancery suit of Jarndyce and Jarndyce, he says, exists apart from such plot as there is ("the series of incidents . . . connected with the relationship of the heroine . . . to her mother"), and it "has positively not the smallest influence on the character of any one person concerned. . . ." As for that "meagre and melodramatic" plot, "it is so unskillfully managed that the daughter is in no way influenced either in character or destiny by her mother's history; and the mother, her husband, the prying solicitor, the French maid, and the whole Dedlock set, might be eliminated from the book without damage to the great Chancery suit, or perceptible effect upon the remaining characters" (p. 284). Allowing for a little overstatement, it is a view that might be defended easier than Forster's. The plot *is* melodramatic, with secret sin, hidden identity, and murder. Brimley's assertion that even Richard's deterioration is uncaused by the Chancery suit is arguable: Richard is not "made reckless and unsteady" by it, he says, but "simply expends his recklessness and unsteadiness on it, as he would on something else if it were non-existent": but which comes first, the chicken or the egg. But Esther *is* entirely different from her mother, and certainly not from her bringing up, since her aunt is at least as proud in her severely religious way as her mother is in the fashionable world. (Esther's intended, Allan Woodcourt, is not much like his mother, either.) And the case of Richard aside, shoals of characters, both admirable and otherwise, do seem to have little or no connection to the suit in Chancery, and pursue their lives unaffected by it: the Bagnets, the Rouncewells, the Dedlock clan.

There is a difficulty, however. Brimley's sort of plot is generally supposed to produce realistic action and believable outcomes, and so it finds favor, then and now. Actually such a plot is simplistic and mechanistic, expressing a wish for order, perhaps, and the author's enormous faith in his own knowledge of character; but it is not like life, because it leaves too much out—a feather's fall may be timed in a vacuum, but in the lives of birds, feathers fall through unpredictable currents of air. So the objections Brimley raises are less weighty than they appear. We really cannot decide the point he makes so confidently about Richard. And Esthers do come inexplicably from mothers like Lady Dedlock. As Raymond Williams says, "The inexplicable quality of the indestructible innocence, or the miraculously intervening goodness, on which Dickens so much depends, and which has been casually written off as sentimentality, is genuine because it is inexplicable."[9] Realistic fiction limits what may be said to what may be rationally traced out, and will not admit intuitive perception, which is what we get along on most of the time in dealing with the much larger class of phenomena that surround us, the things we understand dimly or not at all.

So Forster has the better grasp of the novel. He conducts his analysis in the same categories as Brimley, but when he says, "the various lines of the plot converge and fit to its centre," the tangle of his image shows that he sees something not wholly describable in those categories. A plot "line" suggests a train of events, beginning at a certain time and ending at a later time; but lines that "converge and fit to its centre" make a design in space, to which the idea of time is irrelevant: a system of relationships. And Forster's mixed image is finally right. There is a train of events, which the plot summary at the beginning of this chapter summarizes. But it moves through, and reveals, a vast system of relationships in which the characters live and move and have their being; this system is more or less independent of time, a condition, not a sequence; and the suit of Jarndyce and Jarndyce in the Court of Chancery is its name.[10]

Once again, and as usual, I find E. M. Forster's suggestive term "pattern" more satisfactory to describe Dickens's story than "plot." Plot establishes personal relations of greater or less intimacy among many of the characters, but the larger system of relationships, the pattern of *Bleak House*, consists in the relations between people imposed by Chancery. Imposed by Chancery, and insisted on by Dickens: "He makes the connections," Williams says, "forces the involvements, and directs the conclusions."[11] Lady Dedlock has some unspecified interest in the case, and in that connection is startled out of her usual ennui, which in turn surprises Tulkinghorn and sets the plot moving; the events which the action of the plot are to uncover are not part of the suit, but the suit draws them in. Esther has no connection with the suit, but it makes part of chapter 3 anyway, as Conversation Kenge introduces it by way of introducing the subject of her unknown benefactor, who does have a part in it. (It is not unrealistic, but characteristic and appropriate, that the lawyer Kenge should derive the personal identity of John Jarndyce from his involvement in the suit.) Mrs. Jellyby has no part in the suit, but her home is near the court, in Thavies Inn, one of the nine Inns of Chancery, and out for a walk after staying there overnight and before going to Bleak House, Esther and Richard and Ada and Caddy find themselves without having planned it once more near the Court, and once more in conversation with Miss Flite, the eccentric old perpetual attender at the Court. Others, of course, are closely concerned, like her: Gridley, the man from Shropshire; Ada and Richard, participants in the suit; John Jarndyce himself. Still others make their livings by it: not only the lawyers Kenge and Carboy, and Vholes, but Mr. Guppy in the office of Kenge and Carboy, and Mr. Snagsby the law-stationer, and Nemo the copier of legal documents, and even, in a sense, Jo, who sweeps a crossing in the neighborhood for his bare living. Some few characters, like those I mentioned earlier, and Harold Skimpole and the Turveydrops and Mrs. Pardiggle, seem not to be linked to the suit, but as we shall see shortly, they too have their place, Jarndyce and Jarndyce, and the Court of Chancery, being what they are in Dickens's vision.

Connecting people up this way, Dickens establishes a human world dense with parallels and contrasts. Jo, Snagsby's servant Guster, and Esther are all parentless, at different levels. John Jarndyce's benevolence and selflessness are matched in the younger Allan Woodcourt and contrasted in the self-proclaimed child Skimpole. Charley is as cheerfully industrious at her level as her mistress Esther; both of them do the work at hand, unlike Mrs. Jellyby and Mrs. Pardiggle. The retired soldier Bagnet family is a model of cooperative endeavor and self-help, in contrast to the Dedlock relations who descend on Chesney Wold at intervals. Krook the junk collector proclaims his resemblance at his lower level to the Lord Chancellor: Richard, trusting to the suit in Chancery to set all things right, is like Guppy's friend Jobling, jobless but trusting in "things coming round" (20). The list of such resemblances can be extended to great length, attesting to Dickens's intensity in working out his idea.[12] Everyone is part of the pattern and contributes to the whole, one way or another.

V *Juxtaposition and Time*

This is accomplished gradually, and within the context created by Chancery, mainly by juxtaposition. Esther meets Ada, later Mrs. Jellyby and Mrs. Pardiggle, later still Charley and Jo; as we come to know them by their works, we see them in correspondence or in contrast with her. But juxtaposition operates more broadly than along the line of a single character's encounters; the plot, involving as it develops a wide range of characters and events in various locations, requires recurrent shifts of actors and scenes from chapter to chapter. Chapter 18 is Esther's narrative —she and Ada, and Skimpole and Mr. Jarndyce, go to visit Mr. Boythorn in Lincolnshire—and the next four chapters are the narrator's, reporting events in London. The narrative's vagueness about time helps suggest connection. It is just past Midsummer (June 21) when Esther and her party set out in chapter 18; in chapter 19, "It is the long vacation [i.e., summer] in the regions of Chancery Lane"; in chapter 20, "The long vacation saunters on toward term-time"; and chapter 21 is established by internal events to be continuous with chapter 20. Chapter 22 opens on a hot evening during "the sultry long vacation weather" in Tulkinghorn's chambers, and Esther returns from Lincolnshire in chapter 23, which begins, "We came home from Mr. Boythorn's after six pleasant weeks." The potential connectedness of the three distinct episodes in 19–22 is suggested by the characters who figure in them, and intensified by the imprecise stretches of time separating them: if we knew exactly how long it was after Guppy learned how Jo got hold of a whole sovereign (chapter 19) that he had dinner with Bartholomew Smallweed (chapter 20), and that Trooper George discussed Captain Hawdon with Bart's moneylending grandfather (chapter 21), we would have somewhat less a sense of floating mystery. These events take meaning for us from juxtaposition in an indefinite time, which creates our expectation that they all hang together somehow. Similarly, Dickens has Esther (back again at Bleak House) report how during the Boythorn visit Lady Dedlock's discharged maid Hortense applied to her for a job. But before that, in chapter 22, Hortense appears in Tulkinghorn's chambers in London to mystify Jo, looking and yet not looking like the woman he guided to Nemo's grave. This must be *after* the interview Esther reports in chapter 23, because that takes place in Lincolnshire during the visit at Boythorn's. But to the reader the close juxtaposition of the two incidents made possible by the indefiniteness of time suggests a connection of the London events to Esther's doings.

Chapters 45–51 show Dickens using this method with striking boldness to keep the pattern imposed by Chancery plain while he moves the plot through it. The sequence of events in these chapters can be worked out, though the exact time covered is not clear. Esther visits Richard at Deal, where his military career has just blown up; she returns to Bleak House and commutes to London daily to attend Caddy, who is sick; after three days Mr. Jarndyce proposes that she and Ada and he go to London for a while; about at this point Allan Woodcourt visits Richard in his London lodgings. For the next eight or nine weeks Esther spends most of her time with Caddy, and about the time Caddy begins to recover, notices a new reticence in Ada. Somewhere near the end of this period Allan runs across Jo in the slum called Tom-All-Alone's; Jo is sick, and Allan takes him to George's shooting gallery. He lingers for some days before he dies. That same day Esther finds out the reason for Ada's reticence: she and Richard have been secretly married. That evening at the Dedlock's London house, Lady Dedlock sends her maid Rosa away in the charge of the ironmaster Rouncewell, to Tulkinghorn's displeasure. That night Tulkinghorn is murdered. Next day at dinner time George is arrested on suspicion.

The order of narration is quite different: Esther's visit to Richard at Deal (45); Tom-All-Alone's, and Allan's discovery of Jo (46); Jo's decline and death (47); the events at the Dedlock house, and Tulkinghorn's murder (48); the arrest of George (49); Esther's nursing of Caddy, and the change in Ada (50); Allan's visit to Richard's lodgings, and Esther's discovery of the marriage (51). Dickens is able to do this because he suppresses time references when he changes the scene, or keeps them vague. The effect, from the force of juxtaposition created by his narrative order, is to imply connections between events that strict chronological order in narration would keep separate.[13] Thus the ruin of Richard's military career, the consequence of his preoccupation with the suit in Chancery, is placed next to Tom-All-Alone's, the property that has fallen to ruin because it is a subject of Chancery litigation (16), and so worth no one's while to keep up until the case is settled; and Richard's continuing decline after he leaves the army is placed next to Esther's discovery of the marriage.

This sacrificial consequence of the suit in Chancery is linked in Esther's account to Jo's death. When she returns to her lodgings after leaving Richard and Ada, Mr. Jarndyce is out to inquire about Jo, who "was lying at the point of death; indeed, was then dead, though I did not know it" (51). The detail comes in unexpectedly, and the precision about time is nearly unique; one looks for a reason and finds it two pages on, in the opening sentence of the next chapter: "But one other day had intervened, when, early in the morning as we were going to breakfast, Mr. Woodcourt came in haste with the astounding news that a terrible murder had been committed, for which Mr. George had been apprehended and was in custody." Together the two details establish a relation in time between the cluster of events around Tulkinghorn's murder and Esther's discovery of Ada's marriage to Richard, and so connect this fateful development for the wards in Chancery with the event that motivates Lady Dedlock's flight (55) and death.[14]

The chronological order of events does make for one juxtaposition which Dickens leaves intact. After the narrator's denunciatory epitaph on the death of Jo ("Dead, your Majesty. . . ."; quoted above, p. 102), the narrative moves directly to the Dedlock house in London, and we are made to feel where the blame partly belongs. But if Jo dies because he has been endlessly "moved on" at Tulkinghorn's will, or from the sickness born in Tom-All-Alone's, the implications of narrative order are wrong here, unless the Dedlocks too somehow embody the evil in Chancery. It is time to consider what Chancery and the suit of Jarndyce and Jarndyce mean.

VI *Symbolism*

Medieval allegory rests on the assumption that reality, created by God and shadowing Him forth, is a vast and intricate and symmetrical system, in which the infinite variety of the parts is harmonized by correspondences which extend throughout the whole: thus, the microcosm, the little world of man, bodies forth the macrocosm. The medieval allegorist could then think of his symbol as real in a sense other than metaphorical, not merely yoked by human imagination to its referent, but perceived by imagination to be somehow identical with it, or corresponding to it. Dickens's symbolism is something like that, or as Trevor Blount puts it in the article I have already referred to, "The load of symbolical significance he wanted to put on the metaphor was only relevant [to him] if it was based in attested fact."[15] There had to be actual correspondence, in other words, between the "fact" and the meaning he wanted the fact to stand for. Williams has hold of the wrong end when in his admirable essay he says Dickens can make "an abstraction into a dramatic force." Dickens can make a dramatic force body forth an abstraction. He can make the Marquis d'Evrémonde represent "the time going out," or a piece of the Victorian world—a bureaucracy, or a court of law—show a moral and spiritual idea.[16]

The Court of Chancery epitomizes something so various in its manifestations that its essence is easiest to see by contrast, in its opposite: as is implied by the very narrative strategy in the book, not an anonymous voice but a personal one, not an institution but a human being—Esther. Esther's nature, the positive force of which Chancery represents the negation, is summed up in the resolution she takes on first hearing from her aunt some hint of her unhappy origins: to try "to repair the fault I had been born with" and strive "to be industrious, contented, and kind-hearted, and to do some good to some one, and win some love to myself if I could" (3). And she believes the way to do this is to brighten the corner where you are: and as she tells Mrs. Pardiggle, "to try to let that circle of duty gradually and naturally expand itself" (8). That is not how Chancery works. Dickens's opening chapter emphasizes how inaccessible the court is, in the very name of its presiding judge, "the Lord High Chancellor in his High Court of Chancery" (1). The Lord High Chancellor sits on his padded dais, "softly fenced in with crimson cloth and curtains," above the solicitors in the cause before the court, who are in "a long matted well (but you might look in vain for Truth at the bottom of it)"; as the case drones on the Lord High Chancellor is "outwardly directing his contemplation to the lantern in the roof, where he can see nothing but fog."[17] There is no getting next to him, as the ruined suitor from Shropshire relearns whenever he appears, for the instant the day's docket is cleared, the Chancellor vanishes before the suitor's call "My Lord!" can arrest him. And doing good is not what members of the Chancery bar are about. They are "mistily engaged in one of the ten thousand stages of an endless cause, tripping one another up on slippery precedents, groping knee-deep in technicalities, running their goat-hair and horse-hair warded heads against walls of words"—in sum, "making a pretence of equity with serious faces, as players might."

This is the worse because doing good is what Chancery is supposed to be all about. According to Blackstone's *Commentaries*, the Chancellor, "being formerly usually an ecclesiastic, . . . became keeper of the king's conscience. . . . He is the general guardian of all infants, idiots, and lunatics; and has the general superintendence of all charitable uses in the kingdom."[18] *Bleak House*, then, is about responsibility, as Robert Donovan says, "a series of studies in society's exercise (more often the evasion or abuse) of responsibility for its dependents."[19] Chancery in *Bleak House* has declined a long way from its original purpose of caring for the helpless: "The one great principle of the English law is," the narrator says, "to make business for itself" (39)—at the people's expense.

How has this happened? Blackstone's language describing the origins, taken with Dickens's description of the present reality, is a clue: the personality of the Chancellor's office and function has become the system of Dickens's Chancery, and in the maze of system responsibility has been lost or transformed. We may say then that Chancery is a symbol of irresponsibility, and get nearer the heart of the matter by going on to define irresponsibility as Dickens does in that sentence from chapter 39, as self-interest. It is significant that Esther (and Ada when she returns to Bleak House) calls Mr. Jarndyce "Guardian"—he whose care for others is continuous and varied and personal.

But Esther herself is still the best commentary on the deficiencies represented by Chancery. She is (as Harold Skimpole tells her) "the very touchstone of responsibility. When I see you, my dear Miss Summerson, intent upon the perfect working of the whole little orderly system of which you are the centre, I feel inclined to say to myself—in fact I do say to myself, very often— *that's* responsibility!" (37). We need not think Skimpole perfectly sincere to see the truth of his words. She *is* responsibility. But Skimpole has it just a little wrong, in exactly the way he may be expected to get it wrong. Esther is *not* intent on the perfect functioning of the little society "of which [she] is the centre"; that is a by-product of what she *is* intent on, the well-being of those immediately around her. In other words, she is not possessed by self-interest. What she is possessed by is its opposite, love that fulfills itself in others, love in the biblical sense: charity, that "vaunteth not itself, is not puffed up," that "seeketh not her own, is not easily provoked, thinketh no evil" (I Corinthians 13:4–5).[20] Take away St. Paul's negatives, and there is Chancery. George Bernard Shaw sees Dickens "declaring that it is not our disorder but our order that is horrible."[21] The horror that Dickens sees in *Bleak House*—irresponsibility, which self-interest is if you believe in Christian love—is the lovelessness of his society; and Chancery is its symbol.

So the suit of Jarndyce and Jarndyce, and any suit in such a court, is doomed. The advocates may have the tongues of men and of angels, but they have not charity; Conversation Kenge and all his tribe are mere sounding brass and tinkling cymbals. Useless to appeal to judgment where there is no love, indeed worse than useless. John Jarndyce knows that, and it is why he charges Rick ("with a sudden terror in his manner," on detecting that Rick is counting on the suit to replenish his resources), "For the love of God, don't found a hope or expectation on the family curse!" (24). The little madwoman Miss Flite knows it, too, even though (like Gridley, the man from Shropshire, and like Richard later) she cannot help attending the court, for she says, "I expect a judgment. Shortly. On the Day of Judgment" (3)—that is, at the end of the world, and not before.

VII *Characters*

Having argued earlier that characters in Dickens exist to move plot (or more appropriately to Dickens, "to fill out the pattern which embodies the theme"), and having explicated the central symbol of *Bleak House,* I need not spend much time on the characters of the novel now. They span the whole Dickens human world, they exist to the breadth necessary to fill their part of the design, and they are, in their mode of being, as true to life (Harold Skimpole, for example) as any in Dickens. But their significance in my analysis is that in the succession of scenes (narrated or dramatized) provided by the action, they illustrate varieties of responsibility and irresponsibility, the degrees of love and lovelessness, and their consequences. Allan Woodcourt is a fitting mate for Esther; he is not trying to get on in the world, but takes to the profession of medicine—an image of selfless concern for others—"from a strong interest in all that it can do" (17). Skimpole trained for medicine, too (6), but has no such interest, except where his training may benefit himself, as in helping reduce risk of catching Jo's smallpox (31); Jo himself he simply wants out of the way. Every time Skimpole appears he illustrates the most complete self-interest and the most complete denial of responsibility, until in the end his airy manner is positively sinister. Mrs. Pardiggle may have faith to move mountains— or perhaps only small chairs, which her skirts knock over when she enters a room (8)—but she has not charity, and so is a tyrant to her children (forced to contribute their allowances to her causes) and to the poor she relentlessly visits. (The small chairs get knocked over even though "quite a great way off," so it is probably her capacity to disturb, not her powerful faith, that the force of her skirts' passage signifies.) Mrs. Jellyby, the tireless correspondent on the African project to colonize the left bank of the Niger with "from a hundred and fifty to two hundred healthy families cultivating coffee and educating the natives of Borrioboola-Gha," has "a curious habit of seeming to look a long way off" (4): she sees Africa well enough, but not the needs of her own family.[22] What moves Mrs. Pardiggle is the love of power and charitable "business"—"I love hard work," she says, "I enjoy hard work. The excitement does me good" (8); Mrs. Jellyby needs the romance of the faraway and exotic to water her efforts— there is "nothing interesting" about Jo, "the ordinary home-made article," the product of "native ignorance, the growth of English soil and climate" (47), unhelped by the Mrs. Jellybys, who do not apply themselves like Esther to the work that lies at hand. Or by institutions: Jo breakfasts meagerly on the steps of the Society for the Propagation of the Gospel in Foreign Parts, "and wonders what it's all about. He has no idea, poor wretch, of the spiritual destitution of a coral reef in the Pacific, or what it costs to look up the precious souls among the cocoa-nuts and bread-fruit" (16); on another occasion, having endured the gaseous preaching of Mrs. Snagsby's spiritual leader the Reverend Chadband, he sits eating the leftovers from the Chadband table, "looking up at the great cross on the summit of St. Paul's Cathedral, . . . so golden, so high up, so far out of his reach" (19).[23]

The gulf between the careless and the uncared-for shown here also exists between Jo and those classes holding political power. The implicit connection Dickens makes between Jo and the Dedlocks from chapter 47 to chapter 48 (I noted it just before beginning "Symbolism") is not, after all, a mistake. Chapter 16 begins with Lady Dedlock's restlessness (the fashionable world don't know "where to have her"; they are of course unaware of the secret visit she is about to make under Jo's guidance to Nemo's grave) and moves to Jo through a paragraph where the narrator makes the same link more openly:

What connexion can there be, between the place in Lincolnshire, the house in town, . . . and the whereabout of Jo the outlaw with the broom . . . ? What connexion can there have been between many people in the innumerable histories of this world, who, from opposite sides of great gulfs, have, nevertheless, been very curiously brought together!

The immediate reference, of course, is to Lady Dedlock, who has denied, in the interest of a place in the world of privilege, her connection to Captain Hawdon. But the Dedlocks are not less guilty. Self-interest is also the Dedlock master motive, taking in Sir Leicester's case the form of pride in a family "old as the hills"—which hills the world could get on without, in his view, much better than without Dedlocks (2). The same outlook characterizes those dependent Dedlocks who "lounge in purposeless and listless paths," though they are "likely to have done well enough in life if they could have overcome their cousinship . . ." (28). It also dominates the assonated -oodles and -uffys, who regard government as their affair—the "People" existing "to be occasionally addressed, and relied upon for shouts and choruses, as on the theatrical stage" (12), but certainly not to be served. The outlook of these self-servers is Dandyism (12), a term Dickens probably owes to Carlyle, and by which he means the sort of consummate self-absorption and indifference to the realities of life that he sees in the figure of the social dandy from Regency days.[24] He provides a literal example in Mr. Turveydrop, whose sole occupation is to model Deportment to the world and shame this "levelling age" (14).

That trio of investigators, Guppy, Tulkinghorn, and Inspector Bucket, represent further variations on the theme of love and responsibility. Guppy's search for Esther's identity is not disinterested; he hopes success might earn him favor in her eyes (29). Tulkinghorn's pursuit of Lady Dedlock's secret is in the service of preserving the Dedlock honor; this is a doubtful enough merit, but there are many signs that his real motive is his own love of power. Inspector Bucket, however, like Allan Woodcourt, is entirely devoted to his profession from interest in what it can do; and if discovery of truth is not always pleasant, still such a man as Bucket does it with real consideration for the people involved. But there are other worthy characters besides Inspector Bucket, who do the best they can in this world of Chancery— Mr. Snagsby, the henpecked merchant of the legal supplies, whose remedy of dispensing half-crowns does Jo more good than all the Jellybys there are; the former trooper George Rounce-well, who rescues Phil Squod from the street, and shelters both Gridley and Jo in their last days; his friends the Bagnets, models of the deserving poor who combine proper benevolence and sturdy independence. Indeed, such people suggest that self-interest is tolerable, even admirable, when it takes the form of self-help, and if it does not extinguish love, the necessary concern for other people.

There is an end to the characters in *Bleak House*, but it is still a long way off, and I have worked through enough of the list to illustrate how they ring changes on the theme of responsibility, defining it, in their persons and works, as the care for other people meant by the word the King James Bible gives as "charity"; and how the greater the distance across which duty must operate (in time, or space, or societal contrivance), the more charity appears to be translated to self-interest. The action of the novel provides for a profuse succession of appearances by these characters, who develop the plot across the mosaic of love and self-interest, and restate themselves as individual variations on the theme.[25]

VIII *Humor*

There is no way for one person to experience one thing for the first time twice; if there were, we could tell more exactly whether the pattern and the humor strike one the same way in reading Dickens by the monthly part and in reading him in the larger chunks and closer intervals made possible by having the entire work in hand. The latter is the mode now, and may have more to do than we think with the revaluation of Dickens that makes more of his structural patterns and less of his humor. If, as I suspect, Dickens's humor was more evident to his monthly audience than to us, the complaints about "dreariness" that Collins says began to be alleged against Dickens beginning with *Bleak House* make sense.[26] Readers would have found humor enough through the first part of the book (though *Bentley's* reviewer claimed to find almost none anywhere, "the grotesque and the contemptible" having replaced it);[27] there is an array of "Dickensians" from Conversation Kenge to the old gentleman in the coach who turns out to have been John Jarndyce to Guppy to the

Bayham Badgers and their joint reverence for the husbands whom
Mr. Badger has had the honor to succeed. But this humor begins
to thin out a third or so of the way through, and from the four-
teenth number on there is scarcely any, as the tragedy of Lady
Dedlock gathers momentum, and the pathos of Richard's decline
comes to an issue.

It is not correct, however, to imply that humor is unimportant
in *Bleak House*; it is structural, essential there as elsewhere in
Dickens to his meaning, though the tone and distribution differ
from earlier works. There are still humorous characters who help
move the action along—I think of the suspicious Mrs. Snagsby and
her harried husband, who implores the unmarried Woodcourt,
"Would you make the attempt, though single, to speak as low as
you can? For my little woman is a listening somewheres . . ." (47).
And Inspector Bucket, who runs things through most of Nos.
XVI–XVIII, is another, with his confidential forefinger and his
manner of bustling people along. (His name is another sign:
Truth being proverbially at the bottom of a well—as the narrator
remarks in the opening chapter—who else would be better formed
to bring it up?)[28] There are instances of humor making tolerable
what would otherwise be painful, as the treatment of the ancient
Smallweeds crippled by age. (As the names of their grand-
children show, the Smallweeds are instances of conventional Victorian anti-Semitism in Dickens.)[29] Vholes, so far as he is funny—
which I admit is not very far—illustrates the use of humor to shut
out from our perception what might keep us from seeing, or
taking seriously, what Dickens wants us to see. Vholes is a hard
worker, and he is responsible toward his family, those three
daughters and his aged parent in the Vale of Taunton (37). All
that is respectworthy, so to keep it from standing between us and
Vholes's function to provide Chancery fodder, Dickens makes
the family ridiculous.

But the main use of humor in *Bleak House* is in the form of
ironic narration. From that we get the humorous images working
as analysis and criticism: Guppy "oscillating" on seeing Esther's
scarred face (38), the great house in Lincoln's Inn Fields, cut
up into offices where "lawyers lie like maggots in nuts" (10), the
groom who precedes Sir Leicester to Chesney Wold, "the pilot-
fish before the nobler shark" (40), the "singular kind of parallel"
between Volumnia Dedlock (her name itself is ironic) "and the

little glass chandeliers of another age . . . with their meagre stems" (66). Some of this ironic narration belongs to Esther, but most of it comes from the narrator, and a distinctive feature of it, conveying the narrator's attitude both toward the subject of narration and toward the forces that have formed his own language, is the ironic use of conventional cliches. Thus Mr. Smallweed the grandfather, that "good old man," keeps by his side a cushion to throw at Mrs. Smallweed, "the sharer of his life's evening," whenever in her senility she begins gabbling, especially about money (21). This resource of the narrator appears often when he talks about the law and lawyers, and the "bee-like industry" over which in their own version of Isaac Watts's industriousness, "these benefactors of their species linger yet, though office-hours be past; that they may give, for every day, some good account at last" (32). It is also characteristic of narration about the Dedlock circle (more properly, "the brilliant and distinguished circle," as in chapter 12): who are "the great world," whose morning is "afternoon according to the little sun," and where on one particular such morning, "Sir Leicester, in the library, has fallen asleep for the good of the country, over the report of a Parliamentary committee" (48)—a compact irony expressing both Sir Leicester's view of his attempt to read the report, and the narrator's view of his falling asleep. F. R. Leavis speaks of "the inexhaustibly wonderful poetic life of [Dickens's] prose";[30] in *Bleak House* the ironic narration seems to me the main source, and the tension between that and the affirmation of love incarnate in Esther is the force holding the book together.

IX *Theme*

This tension does not mean an opposition between the narrator's irony and Esther seen as love acting. The irony is the voice of sorrow, disillusion, scorn, and anger (the proportion depending on the object) at absence of love: whether evident as mere detachment, or as the self-interest that geographical or social detachment, by a deadly and inevitable logic, generates: unconnected to any other being, the spirit more and more contemplates itself. So the ethical stance of the narrator, and of Esther, are the same; it is what they see that is different. The narrator sees the dreadful condition of Tom-All-Alone's, the property in Chancery, and knows that it will repay the neglect "through every order of society, up to the proudest of the proud, and to the highest of the high. Verily, what with tainting, plundering, and spoiling, Tom has his revenge" (46).

Geoffrey Thurley, commenting on the whole passage, says it goes beyond social protest. The narrator, "certain to the point of neurosis of punitive retribution, . . . simply goes too far—unless we read him as we read the great prophetic poets of the Old Testament."[31] The narrator is not neurotic; there *is* retribution in the blow that strikes Sir Leicester Dedlock down, payment for the injury to a handsome and haughty Dedlock wife in a former generation, who swore to walk the terrace at Chesney Wold until the pride of the family was humbled (7). She was not unlike the present Lady Dedlock, whose own pride, in the mysterious ways of Providence, brings the justice by which the sins of the Dedlock past are punished in the Dedlock present. So the analogy to Old Testament prophecy, the truth-telling to the age, is not inappropriate. There are also some tentative signs of prophecy in the popular sense of the word: ironmaster ideas of the shape of the future, and on the other hand a hope. The son of Sir Leicester's housekeeper Mrs. Rouncewell is a man of intelligence and purpose, confident from the knowledge of his own powers, and courteous toward Sir Leicester without being in the least obsequious (28). His son's name Watt, as Louis Crompton has also noted, calls to mind both the inventor of the steam engine, and the leader of the fourteenth-century peasant rebellion Wat Tyler.[32] In his usual way, Dickens is putting an idea into fictive form: the new age has in it the potential for overturning the old.

Once again we see Dickens's ambiguous attitude toward the Industrial Revolution. He did not look forward to an ironmaster future with pleasure. From his radical criticism of his society he hoped for transformation rather than revolution, and there is a suggestion in that direction, too. The home of Chancery is London, where Chancery has made Tom-All-Alone's, filthy, ruinous, death-bringing. The traditional refuge for English writers who see in the city the corruption of human history is the country. But the country, Chesney Wold, is held by Dedlocks, and the narrator's accounts of that place are dominated by flood, cold, shadow, autumn—intimations of the end. Bleak House is a refuge, but only in the tenure of John Jarndyce; and it is in Hertfordshire, closed in between London and Chesney Wold in Lincolnshire. Esther and Allan, however, settle in a new Bleak House, as desirable a place as the old one, but out beyond the sphere of either London or Chesney Wold, in Yorkshire, in "a thriving place, pleasantly situated; streams and streets, town and country, mill and moor," as John Jarndyce describes it to Esther when he first apprises her of this opening for Woodcourt (60). This is Dickens's hope: not a return to the old agricultural society, nor yet some Wat Tylerish overturning of it, but a harmony between human society and its home in the natural world, with the necessities of the mill somehow integrated to the moor: the whole a home for the practice of loving concern for other people.[33]

How to get there from here, thinking now of the societal order implied by this outcome, he does not say. As George Orwell saw, Dickens had no design in mind for a new order. But how individual human beings might renew their personal orders—that is another story. There are two sides to the Old Testament prophets, the denunciation of sin, and the call to renewal in the Lord. Dickens's *Bleak House* is a generally somber book, but it does not merely depict the hopelessly tangled net of self-interest that ought to be a web of mutual concern where out of love each is responsible for each. The book points a way out for individual human beings. Stay out of Chancery, the narrator warns at the very outset: "Suffer any wrong that can be done you, rather than come here!" Do not look to be set right by self-interest. If you do, you will be consumed, like Gridley, like Rick, like the estate in Jarndyce and Jarndyce. There is no end to the appetite of that court. Like John Jarndyce, dismiss the appeal to Chancery from your mind, and share your substance with the needy, or better yet, like Esther, devote your thoughts and efforts to helping others. The theme of *Bleak House* is prophetic, in the biblical sense: a revelation of a sick society, and of medicine that anyone may have.

X   *The Bible in* Bleak House

There is plenty to see in *Bleak House* even for the biblically illiterate, fortunately, but it requires seeing in the biblical light Dickens set it in for his full meaning to be clear. Stephen Gill's article that I have already referred to (note 6) shows persuasively how ideas and language from the Bible and the Book of Common Prayer light up *Bleak House*. In the preface to their edition Ford and Monod thank various consultants, including, "most extensively, [historians of] religion (Dickens' abundant references to the Book of Common Prayer is [*sic*] a significant aspect of his style in *Bleak House*)" (p. xii). On the evidence of their annotations (and they have not caught all), they should have added the Bible. Biblical details, in form running from specific allusions to verbal parallels to ideas embodied in the action, are so plentiful and strategically placed, that to see Esther as enacting the idea of Christian love—as I do, choosing my words here with care—is to see her as the center of a controlling pattern in the action. The prodigal son lives and moves in George Rouncewell, who has soldiered many years in a far country and returns to gladden his mother's heart. He is the Good Samaritan, too, when he rescues Phil Squod. This biblical reminiscence comes close to the main theme embodied in Esther, but the first is somewhat more distant, and is like a great deal of biblical reference which it would be dreary to catalogue even if I had room, and which is important as texture. Some of it, however, like the "flesh-grass" complex I have discussed, belongs to the pattern of pastoralism that Crompton mentions, in which lawyers are identified with the "traditional symbol for the corrupt functionary in pastoral: the shepherd who plunders his own flock."[34] Shepherds like that, in fields like Tulkinghorn's Lincoln's Inn Fields, "keep their sheep in the fold by hook and by crook until they have shorn them exceeding close" (48). The district of the Law Courts was once countryside where presumably sheep might safely graze; but now "the sheep are all made into parchment, the goats into wigs, and the pasture into chaff" (42)—metamorphoses that leave the sheep worse off, and the goats much better off, than they are in Matthew 25:32 ff., where Jesus explains how the Son of Man, when he comes, will reward all people according to their deeds, first separating the good from the evil "as a shepherd divideth his sheep from the goats." This of course will be on the Day of Judgment, which is when Miss Flite, mad though she be, is sane enough to expect Chancery will render up its judgment (3). The wish at the end of chapter 1, that all the court-caused misery and injustice "could only be locked up with it, and the whole burnt away in a great funeral pyre," has often been seen as a foreshadow of Krook's death by spontaneous combustion. But it looks to a hotter fire than that. The Chancellor's Great Seal, Miss Flite has determined, is "the sixth seal mentioned in the Revelations," and "has been open a long time" (3)—which accounts for all the miseries loose in the world, and will lead to the grand final act, when the heavens depart "as a scroll when it is rolled together" (Revelation 6:14); or, in another and frequently associated vision, "shall pass away with a great noise, and the elements shall melt with fervent heat, the earth also and the works that are therein shall be burned up" (II Peter 3:10). The pyre that will burn away Chancery and its children is the fire at the end of time: which is to say that the evil of Chancery is rooted in the heart of things.

I must emphasize an important distinction: Dickens is not re-telling a Bible story in modern guise, like *Hamlet* set in a story of a corporation takeover; by the power of his imagination Dickens discerns the idea in the biblical source alive in his own time, and tells the story of his own time in which he sees the living idea, helping bring it out for his reader with the language of biblical allusion. I take this to be the kind of thing Raymond Williams means in saying that Dickens makes abstraction into dramatic force, and the Leavises mean in saying that Dickens's ideas are "completely dissolved into novelistic material of action, dialogue and characterization."[35]

I have already discussed Esther's importance, but I must now set her in the focal point of this biblical light. Esther's aunt Miss Barbary (what a name) instructs her to "pray daily that the sins of others be not visited upon your head, according to what is written" (3). She refers to the passage that appears first in Exodus 20, where God delivers the Commandments to Moses, in verse 5, as part of God's explanation why the children of Israel must hold no other gods than He: "for I the Lord thy God am a jealous God, visiting the iniquity of the fathers upon the children unto the third and fourth generation of them that hate me."[36] This sounds ominous, and has always been a favorite of Barbarous Christians, who are likely not to quote the following verse 6: "And shewing mercy unto thousands of them that love me, and keep my commandments." It is also the verse that generous spirits indignant at mean-spirited accountant deities cite in repudiating a God of vengeance: Stephen Crane, for instance, who uses it as an epigraph to a poem beginning "Well, then, I hate Thee." What is usually missed on both sides is that the passage is addressed to fathers, to remind them that their acts have consequences which roll on, and not to children, to explain to them why they suffer. It is then a passage about responsibility *to other people*, to generations unborn, and converted into secular language (whatever set of terms being current) would pass unchallenged through any respectable gathering of intellectuals as a law of life. It is, of course, like the Son of Man's distinction between sheep and goats, absolutely appropriate to a novel asserting the centrality of Chancery, the pursuit of self-interest, in the lives of its characters.

The Dedlock sin of pride is visited upon Sir Leicester, as I said, but this does not quite bear out the passage, since honorable and admirable as he is in his way, he has his share in that sin. The Dedlock lease has fallen in, that is all. But Esther's case is more appropriate. Dickens takes care that we feel the force of the passage as injustice, since Esther hears it as a child, and we know that whatever *her* fathers did she is innocent of. The injustice, however, owes to her aunt and not the Lord, in the circumstances; it is Esther's birthday, and to her hungry plea for knowledge of her mother Miss Barbary returns this stone.

"Your mother, Esther, is your disgrace, and you were hers. The time will come—and soon enough—when you will understand this better, and will feel it too, as no one save a woman can. I have forgiven her"; but her face did not relent; "the wrong she did to me, and I say no more of it, though it was greater than you will ever know— than any one will ever know, but I, the sufferer. For yourself, unfortunate girl, orphaned and degraded from the first of these evil anniversaries, pray daily that the sins of others be not visited upon your head, according to what is written. Forget your mother, and leave all other people to forget her who will do her unhappy child that greatest kindness. Now, go!"

She checked me, however, as I was about to depart from her—so frozen as I was!—and added this:

"Submission, self-denial, diligent work, are the preparations for a life begun with such a shadow on it. You are different from other children, Esther, because you were not born, like them, in common sinfulness and wrath. You are set apart."

Esther cries herself to sleep with her doll in her arms: "Imperfect as my understanding of my sorrow was, I knew that I had brought no joy, at any time, to anybody's heart, and that I was to no one upon earth what Dolly was to me."

So Esther is in the position of the children, bearing the sins of the fathers. Her importance in the moral structure of *Bleak House* lies in what she says next:

> Dear, dear, to think how much time we passed alone together afterwards, and how often I repeated to the doll the story of my birthday, and confided to her that I would try, as hard as ever I could, to repair the fault I had been born with (of which I confusedly felt guilty and yet innocent), and would strive as I grew up to be industrious, contented, and kind-hearted, and to do some good to some one, and win some love to myself if I could.

It is exactly right that she feel innocent, and yet guilty: she knows she has not done whatever wicked deed was done, and to be accused by one in authority generates guilt by itself. But she does not writhe in resentment, or try to escape the condition, or complain of being misjudged: figuratively speaking, she would not go to Court, to have her true identity accredited and affirmed. She would act it out instead, "and win some love to myself if I could." Esther is not a cardboard figure of inhuman disinterestedness; she wants something for herself. But wanting to be loved is not such a bad object, when the love is to flow to one for being "industrious, contented, and kind-hearted"—indeed, "Charity suffereth long, and is kind; charity envieth not" (I Corinthians 13:4) amounts to just that. And in the event, when Esther does "some good to some one," she does not ration her efforts, and her only principle of selection is need, not merit. She does good on the same principle as the sheep on the right hand of the Son of Man, who must ask when it was that they did him the good he credits them with, and who receive the answer, "Verily I say unto you, Inasmuch as ye have done it unto one of the least of these my brethren, ye have done it unto me" (Matthew 25:40).

Thus it seems to me that Esther enacts the idea of Christian love. That cold speech of Miss Barbary's contains something else, however, which is conclusive. When she says Esther is "set apart" and "different from other children," she means branded by her bastardy. That is surely the judgment of fanaticism—illegitimacy has never been all that uncommon. And more important, she is perverting the usual meaning of "set apart" used in a biblical context. Esther's name is significant here. Her biblical namesake, an orphan brought up by her cousin Mordecai, was made queen by the great king Ahasuerus, who reigned from India to Ethiopia, and she was able from her influence to turn the tables on the wicked Haman, who wanted the king to do away with all the Jews in his dominions. This Esther was at first reluctant to try, whether from fear or modesty, but Mordecai convinced her: "Who knoweth whether thou art come to the kingdom for such a time as this?" (Esther 4:14). So if Dickens's Esther is "set apart," it is not in Miss Barbary's sense, but in Mordecai's: chosen to save the people. Given the symbolic imagery of sheep, the Lamb of God is perhaps not amiss to remember, either, when the instrument of salvation is Esther's kind of love. But God's Lamb had to descend into humanity, partake of the human condition to exercise his love, which earned him death. And of course Esther does something like that, too, for in the exercise of her love, caring for the sick boy from Tom-All-Alone's, and then for Charley her maid, she catches smallpox herself.[37] The contagions of the slum, a consequence of Chancery, are everywhere; the rain falleth on the just and the unjust. No wonder Dickens has Esther say at the beginning of chapter 9 that she really has something to do with the story, "and can't be kept out."

I said that Esther enacts the idea of Christian love, and that I chose those words with care. I meant to convey that in the world of *Bleak House*, made of ideas "dissolved into novelistic material," what Esther does has consequences of the kind that tradition assigns to Christian love—the love shown by Christ, which his followers are to emulate. I do not mean that Esther is a Christ, but that in the maelstrom of human behavior shown in *Bleak House*, her behavior affects those around her as Christ's love did those around him. In that sense, *Bleak House* is a novel embodying a Christian vision of human existence. But I feel uneasy going any farther than that along the way toward defining Dickens's intent. Dickens was not the only Victorian writer whose characters fulfill themselves in other people. "When God vanishes," J. Hillis Miller writes, "man turns to interpersonal relations as the only remaining arena of the search for authentic selfhood."[38] Traditional Christianity was in long retreat in the nineteenth century from the complex developments in science, as well as in biblical studies. The moral earnestness that had been yoked to religion was turned loose in the world, to appear in secular forms perhaps even more strongly because of its frustration in the religious sphere, since for many people these took the place of religion. Art, indeed, was to replace religion in the view of many.

At the same time the centrality of a Christian vision of life in *Bleak House* is consistent with what Angus Wilson correctly calls "that very evasive thing, [Dickens's] religious beliefs."[39] In all his torrents of prose there is relatively little about religion, and that little most often about his suspicion of the Roman Catholic Church and his intense dislike of evangelical Protestantism. But Steven Marcus says forthrightly that of course Dickens was a Christian, "which is to say that, living when he did, his involvement with Christian culture was by nature profound, passionate, contradictory and, as frequently as not, adverse."[40] So it is possible to say with some confidence that Dickens was a believer, so long as we understand what we mean by that. Wilson speaks of him as "a simple New Testament Christian" who, "rational and humanistic" by temperament, lived by "the sort of broad New Testament Christianity" that one associates with Charles Kingsley.[41] The most explicit statement we have from Dickens on this is in his farewell letter to his youngest son, Edward (Plorn), who went to Australia in September 1868:

I put a New Testament among your books, for the very same reasons, and with the very same hopes that made me write an easy account of it for you, when you were a little child; because it is the best book that ever was or will be known in the world, and because it teaches you the best lessons by which any human creature who tries to be truthful and faithful to duty can possibly be guided. As your brothers have gone away, one by one, I have written to each such words as I am now writing to you, and have entreated them all to guide themselves by this book, putting aside the interpretations and inventions of Man.

You will remember that you have never at home been harassed about religious observances or mere formalities. I have always been anxious not to weary my children with such things before they are old enough to form opinions respecting them. You will therefore

understand the better that I now most solemnly impress upon you
the truth and beauty of the Christian religion, as it came from
Christ Himself, and the impossibility of your going far wrong if you
humbly but heartily respect it.

Only one thing more on this head. The more we are in earnest
as to feeling it, the less we are disposed to hold forth about it. Never
abandon the wholesome practice of saying your own private prayers,
night and morning. I have never abandoned it myself, and I know
the comfort of it. (N III, 668)

The emphases there upon the New Testament as a guide to life,
and upon Christ as its source and center, and the suspicion of
the institutional church and the impatience with doctrine ("mere
formalities," "the interpretations and inventions of Man")—these
elements bear out pretty accurately Wilson's characterization of
Dickens's religious views.[42] Such a religious position could imply
superficiality—indeed, Wilson also says Dickens "preferred not
to examine sacred subjects too closely"—but having written the
life of Christ for his children that he refers to in the letter,
Dickens was surely familiar enough with the idea of Christian
love to have set it into *Bleak House* in the way I have argued.
Since in his letter he also puts reticence into direct proportion to
strength of belief, it is also consistent with his distaste for preachi-
ness that he should do so. And—to wind this up—it is entirely
consistent with the need that Forster saw in Dickens to convert
his belief and desire into "the real in its most intense form" (F
VIII, ii, 641), and as I argued earlier, with his general method
of embodying ideas in fiction, that he should transmute the Christian idea of love into fiction.

All this considered, then, and leaving the question of Dickens's
intent where this leaves it, I think Esther's centrality to the theme
of *Bleak House* is safe to affirm. But now that she is more than
a narrator, her adequacy as a character seems not just important
—it seems crucial. If she does not hold, *Bleak House* needs other
strengths. On this matter I could use more help than I get from
Esther's defenders, who I wish were at least as convincing as
her detractors. But their cases, solid-seeming in isolation, tend
to wash away when immersed in the text. Geoffrey Thurley makes
an emotionally satisfying statement against the abuse of Dickens's virtuous young women, but the case he goes on to make is
not much more, it seems to me, than a counterposition, and Rob-

ert Donovan's more temperate vindication relies too heavily on her exemplifying "perfectly" the only two qualities he says the novel's design really requires of her: transparency and integrity.[43] From among the detractors I lift two. While it is not true that Esther has "no will, no desire, no ego," as Robert Garis claims—she has them all, and makes clear in many places that she does, and that she subdues them to what she regards as duty—Joseph Fradin's objection is more to the point: "Esther's will does not have a convincing source in some Principle of Good as does the terrible Will which pervades the novel's dark world in some Principle of Evil."[44]

What is to be said in response to this? First, that part of the trouble with Esther comes from the rhetorical necessities in Dickens's conception (pp. 152–53 above). Next, that Fradin's objection is sound; and that all we can do is recognize why, and that the significance I see in Esther as the enactor of the love of Christ is the reason why. Our world resists transformation into Dickens's mode of fiction at this point. Incarnate goodness of such purity is simply out of our experience—indeed, that is a premise of Christian belief—while we have no trouble whatever envisioning evil, on which we all have plenty of data. I really think we have to settle for a less than convincing Esther, just as we do for Florence Dombey, and Amy Dorrit, and Lizzie Hexam.

But *Bleak House* can survive that. It is (as the Leavises say) "a whole which is meaningful when (and only when) it is read with the necessary sensitiveness to the text and when the detail is related to the whole in ways implied in their context."[45] It is not legitimate to test Esther by abstracting her from the world of the novel; as Williams says (about social criticism in *Little Dorrit*, but his point applies here as well), "The question of realism is one of the whole imaginative insight and scale. . . . To take any element out of this whole view, and treat it as a problem on its own, is at once to devalue it."[46] And writing more generally of the period, Hillis Miller says, "A Victorian novel is, finally, a structure in which the elements (characters, scenes, images) are not detachable pieces, each with a given nature and meaning, each adding its part to the meaning of the whole. Every element draws its meaning from the others, so that the novel must be described as a self-generating and self-sustaining system, like the society it mirrors."[47]

Within that system Esther, enacting the Christian idea of love, is Dickens's emblem of hope in a dark world. Chancery works its woe in "implacable November weather"; Esther does not turn the season back, but she brings into it the summer sun. Chancery, that gorged snake, still swallows its blue bags of documents, but it need not swallow us. Bleak House can belie its name; people can be warm in November if they will. All claimants to justice at law, Tom Jarndyce, Gridley, Rick Carstone, will die in Chancery: all givers of love, John Jarndyce, Ada Clare, Allan Woodcourt, Esther Summerson, can live in Bleak House; "the letter killeth but the spirit giveth life" (II Corinthians 3:6).[48]

XI *Theme in* Bleak House, *and the Rest of Dickens*

Somebody has said that most writers work out a relatively small set of ideas and themes over and over: in a sense, write the same book all their lives. It is true of Dickens. *Bleak House* seems to me his best novel: most inclusive of his ideas, best realized. But it is not a new beginning, or a culmination. As to the thematic matters I have been focusing on, it gathers what shows earlier, and later: the connectedness of human society and human affairs, and their complexity; the rootedness of evil in the self-interest of the individual human heart; the remedy of love, exercised in personal responsibility and issuing in personal if not societal salvation. *Bleak House* has passages (born out in the action) that connect high and low explicitly, but so does *Dombey and Son.*[49] In two of the early novels, an unknown father-son relationship implies the same thing: Ralph Nickleby and Smike, and in *Barnaby Rudge* Sir John Chester and Hugh. *Little Dorrit* and *A Tale of Two Cities* show the same tendency clearly in their action. *Our Mutual Friend* seems a bit different, for the characters in the Veneering circle are disconnected, really, from things; imagery of mirrors, and superficiality of action, emphasize their insubstantiality. The issue in *Our Mutual Friend* is not only whether certain main characters will recognize their involvement in each other's fates, but whether they will recognize their flaws of self-interest and escape melting into that shallow crowd.

But the continuity of *Our Mutual Friend* with the rest of Dickens is clear in that motif of self-interest, for one way or another, by whatever name Dickens gives it—hypocrisy or self or pride or the undisciplined heart; or by whatever image—Chancery or the Circumlocution Office or dust mounds; self-love, self-interest, self-will is what Dickens sees is wrong. In the later novels he sees a society grown old in wrong, and beyond remedy by individuals, and generating more evil still; but that individual self-seeking helps keep it going is clear from the actions of his characters.

What he sees to do about it is also the same from beginning to end—I should say, perhaps, from the beginning of that part of his career when he was consciously reconsidering and expanding his art, beginning in *Martin Chuzzlewit* but most markedly and substantially in *Dombey and Son*. It is, to change: to sink self and seek the welfare of others, as the chastened Mr. Gradgrind, for example, was to be seen in future "making his facts and figures subservient to Faith, Hope, and Charity; and no longer trying to grind that Heavenly trio in his dusty little mills" (*HT* III, 9). The theme usually centers in the person of a young woman or a child who grows into a young woman in the course of the story: in *Dombey and Son* Florence Dombey; in *David Copperfield* Agnes Wickfield; Esther; in *Hard Times* Sissy Jupe; in *Little Dorrit* Amy Dorrit; in *Our Mutual Friend* Lizzie Hexam.[50] The conventional narrative interest—the interest generated by the plot—lies mainly with other characters. The action of the novel goes on around this young woman, she is part of it, but her importance is to the pattern rather than to the plot, the train of events that moves through the pattern. Her part is to live for the welfare of others, and to have a transforming effect on others (or not, for some resist grace): not on their fortunes or ease, but on their hearts, so that they live no more for self alone.

So, for Dickens, change is necessary. But his characters do not change themselves. They are changed; and the agent of the change is this young woman. She embodies, as I have argued at length in the case of Esther, the transforming power of Christian love on blighted and struggling humanity: proving, as Mr. Sleary the lisping circus proprietor sums it up for Mr. Gradgrind, "that there ith a love in the world, not all Thelf-interetht after all, but thomething very different" (III, 8).

This is clearest in *Little Dorrit*. The title of the novel is also the name by which Amy is called, because she *is* little—so small that a woman of the street takes her for a child (I, 14).[51] The name is redundant, the idea of littleness conveyed both by the adjective and by the diminutive suffix *-it*. The central element of the name then is *do(o)r*—a transparent enough pun: she is the little door, the way; and the way is love, because that is her given name: Amy. There is another Bible verse enacted here, I think: "Strait is the gate, and narrow is the way, which leadeth unto life" (Matthew 7:14). Hablot Browne's illustrations for the monthly part cover and for the title page of the first edition both bear this out. They show a small female figure standing just outside the narrow slot of the partly open prison door. But stone walls do not a prison make: the shaft of sunlight falling through the door must come, as Michael Steig says, from *inside* the prison, so that "in a sense Amy goes into a world much darker than the prison."[52] This makes sense, for the Marshalsea is where Amy lives, and where love is must be light. Light often has conventional allegorical significance in Dickens (in *Dombey and Son*, as I argued in the preceding chapter under "Symbolism"; at Jo's death, where "the light has come upon the benighted way"), and it does here, too. *Little Dorrit* opens in Marseilles, under the blaze of an August sun; all over the city "blinds, shutters, curtains, awnings, were all closed to keep out the stare." This sunshine comes to look very like the white light of eternity; but the human world, instead of staining the radiance like a dome of many-colored glass, shuts it out.

Little Dorrit is then the bearer of divine love in this dark human world, embodying as J. Hillis Miller says "the mystery of divine goodness incarnate in a human person."[53] As in *Bleak House* Esther is set against the joyless religion of her Aunt Barbary, Little Dorrit is given to say finally to Barbary's spiritual sister, "O, Mrs. Clennam, Mrs. Clennam, angry feelings and unforgiving deeds are no comfort and no guide to you and me.... Be guided only by the healer of the sick, the raiser of the dead, the friend of all who were afflicted and forlorn, the patient Master who shed tears of compassion for our infirmities. We cannot but be right if we put all the rest away, and do everything in remembrance of Him..." (II, 31). And as Esther and her husband find their good life in Bleak House in York, while Chesney Wold darkens in Lincolnshire and Chancery still consumes in London, Amy and Arthur Clennam "went down [after their marriage] into a modest life of usefulness and happiness ... quietly down into the roaring streets, inseparable and blessed; and as they passed along in sunshine and shade, the noisy and the eager, and the arrogant and the froward and the vain, fretted and chafed, and made their usual uproar." It is a personal solution, Esther's solution, and the solution of John Jarndyce figured in the *Bleak House* monthly cover design: a choice of a life to be lived differently in the midst of those who remain noisy and arrogant and vain. As George Levine remarks in another connection, "Mr. Pumblechook remains an unchastened hypocrite. Mr. Trabb keeps selling his wares with oily enthusiasm."[54] It is a narrow road that leads to life, St. Matthew says, "and few there be that find it." The later novels of Dickens go beyond conventionally satisfying readers' desires to know what happens after "the end," to show the central characters established in their new life, and to point out the world of vanity and pride still there, and uncomprehending as ever: the world of Chancery, and the Circumlocution world, and the world of the Veneerings.[55]

Thus George Orwell was quite right to say, "It seems that in every attack Dickens makes upon society he is always pointing to a change of spirit rather than a change of structure." Furthermore, in saying this he was not dismissing Dickens "contemptuously as a 'change-of-heart' man," as Williams thinks; Williams forgets or has missed Orwell's later observation that all systems for improving society are provisional, that every one is subverted sooner or later ("There is always a new tyrant waiting to take over from the old ..."), and his conclusion: " 'If men would behave decently the world would be decent' is not such a platitude as it sounds."[56] Orwell knew, unlike some socialists and some capitalists, that there is more reason for human friction than badly designed bearings in the socioeconomic system, and that solutions are not adopted merely because they are rational. Faith in system implies a faith in human rationality and goodness. Now Dickens had notoriously little faith in system; but the consequence for the rest of the proposition, that he had not much faith, either, in the unreconstructed human will to do what is reasonable and right, is still struggling into the canon of criticism. The darkness in the novels of Dickens's major phase is now widely perceived, but the light that is also there is sometimes missed, or its nature not understood. So excellent a book as Butt and Tillotson's *Dickens at Work*, more important for understanding Dickens's true stature than nearly every book published since, says that Little Dorrit represents "optimism about humanity" and "the strength and indestructibility of natural, innocent virtue" (p. 230). More often and less sympathetically she is scored off, like Dickens's other young women, as another of his sentimental excesses. In the latter case something must be allowed for the change of cultural climate, as I have said earlier; in both cases, there is misunderstanding how pervasive a kind of allegory in Dickens is, and how, in the mode of his fiction, the allegorical circulates through the stock of the soup. Butt and Tillotson show that misunderstanding in conceding, in their next sentence, that Little Dorrit's goodness "may be thought implausible"; and they are on the right track but going in the wrong direction as they conclude, "but it must be seen as expressing what still survived of Dickens's own indestructible faith—expressing it *almost allegorically*, with the validity of a fairy tale" (my italics).

It is true that the survival of "natural, innocent virtue" appears to be a theme in Dickens's first four novels. But a case can be argued against that view in at least three of those novels, too.[57] And the idea that Dickens continued to assert such virtue does not fit with another pattern discerned by Barbara Hardy: that as in George Eliot and in Henry James, in Dickens "the hero is converted by seeing and understanding his defect and its origins." That is, the hero is discovered to be somehow wrong, and the action of the novel is to set him right. Conversion is "the moral change on which action hinges, or appears to hinge"; as the story unfolds, "the character catches up with the reader" and sees himself as he is.[58] The interest of the story thus lies in the *restoration*, not the *preservation*, of the hero.

The old idea, then—of a "Christmas" Dickens, hearty, assured, confident in basic human goodness, who petered out as years went by —has been superseded by the idea of a tragic Dickens, who emerged from the mere entertainer and wrote of the world as it really was, in all its immovable mass of stupidity, selfishness, ignorance, poverty, and despair. But this Dickens embodies as important misinterpretations as the earlier one: not only the misreading of such figures as Little Dorrit as remnants of his faith in "natural, innocent virtue," but also the mistaken conclusion that the grim fictive worlds of his later novels represent new awareness and conviction.[59] There is darkness enough in the early Dickens, too, if one looks for it, in the debtors' prison in *Pickwick Papers*, the thieves' den in *Oliver Twist*, the iron manufacturing regions Nell and her grandfather travel through, and in *Nicholas Nickleby* the Yorkshire schools. These are exceptions, one may say; but a passage quoted by Williams describing "the general condition, as Dickens quite consistently saw it," is from *Nicholas Nickleby*.[60]

Now, when he thought how regularly things went on from day to day in the same unvarying round—how youth and beauty died, and ugly griping age lived tottering on—how crafty avarice grew rich, and manly honest hearts were poor and sad—how few they were who tenanted the stately houses, and how many those who lay in noisome pens, or rose each day and laid them down at night, and lived and died, father and son, mother and child, race upon race, and generation upon generation, without a home to shelter them or the energies of one single man directed to their aid—how in seeking, not a luxurious and splendid life, but the bare means of a most wretched and inadequate subsistence, there were women and children in that one town, divided into classes, numbered and estimated as regularly as the noble families and folks of great degree, and reared from infancy to drive most criminal and dreadful trades—how ignorance was punished and never taught—how jail-door gaped and gallows loomed for thousands urged towards them by circumstances darkly curtaining their very cradles' heads, and but for which they might have earned their honest bread and lived in peace—how many died in soul, and had no chance of life—how many who could scarcely go astray, be they vicious as they would, turned haughtily from the crushed and stricken wretch who could scarce do otherwise, and who would have been a greater wonder had he or she done well, than even they, had they done ill—how much injustice, and misery, and wrong, there was, and yet how the world rolled on from year to year, alike careless and indifferent, and no man seeking to remedy or redress it:—when [Nicholas] thought of all this, and selected from the mass the one slight case on which his thoughts were bent, he felt indeed that there was little ground for hope, and little cause or reason why it should not form an atom in the huge aggregate of distress and sorrow, and add one small and unimportant unit to swell the great amount.   (53)

This passage shows that the tragic Dickens is more than a newly draped model from the critical tailors. He was there all along. Of course it would be a mistake to claim that this Dickens appeared only with the turn of critical fashions; though new critical methods applied to the later novels showed him off, there really was a change of emphasis in his work. His spirits *were* higher in the early years; like Nicholas he could see the wideness of human misery, "but youth [as he wrote in the next paragraph] is not prone to contemplate the darkest side of a picture it can shift at will."

There is a third Dickens, who showed the darkness in the world, but also a light that could push the darkness back. This Dickens has suffered somewhat from the new interest attaching to Dickens the man, from the revelations about his relationship with a young actress, but much more, surely, from the massive critical biography by Edgar Johnson. The gains have been great; the loss, so far as understanding of Dickens's vision of things is concerned, has been considerable. The mass and density and particularity of the new biographical knowledge simply outweigh for many readers (I think for critics especially) this third Dickens, who is taken for a mere plot mechanic, or a sentimentalist or a wishful thinker. This I believe to be a mistake, for the direction and resolution of the story as it develops is as much a part of Dickens's statement as the picture that it moves into and across. It is the answer of his will to the human condition, stated in the terms of his day and place. A clue to the importance he meant the idea of love that seeks not its own to have is the change in title from *Nobody's Fault* to *Little Dorrit*; Butt and Tillotson are surely right to see in this a decision not to focus on the all-pervading irresponsibility implied by the phrase in which officialdom took refuge, but on the hope in Little Dorrit instead (p. 230). It is also significant, I think, that contrary to George Gissing's belief, Dickens's plans for *Our Mutual Friend* show he never intended Noddy Boffin to be ruined by greed: Boffin plays the miser as "the homeopathic cure, staging [Bella Wilfer's] mercenary values and repelling her into the right course."[61]

The Dickens I have been describing may look much diminished to some, and his vision of salvation puny in the scale of the world's evil. Part of the explanation for this is in what V. S.

Pritchett calls "the evangelical Protestantism" of Dickens.[62] The side of evangelicalism Pritchett has in mind in making what may seem an odd connection to many Dickens critics is its religious individualism; organized religion, in the evangelical view, is always at least potentially a threat to the spiritual well-being of the people it supposedly serves.[63] Dickens's distrust of system extends to the institutional church, as I have said, and pointing to a solution on the individual level is consistent both with his own inclination and the evangelical spirituality of the era. It must also be said to be realistic, in a time when, if the conditions of modern life were to be fronted at all, any other resolution could only be fantasy.

But scale is also a question of perspective. We live in particular places, from moment to moment, and not across a whole society or through an epoch at once. The individual solution, from the individual perspective, is as broad and deep as life: the more so, when it involves turning outward to other people, and not fencing oneself round.

CHAPTER 6

The Meaning of Dickens

OF COURSE there is no way to write a chapter elastic enough, and strong enough, to contain Dickens's meaning: just to list what I have not dealt with under that head would be a pretty good start on filling a chapter's space. The characters that keep occurring in Dickens—doubles, all those drifting young men, the orphans, the parentlike children and the childlike parents; his use of fairy tales and legends, for incidental allusion and more essential structure (patient Griselda, for example, in *Bleak House*, where John Jarndyce carries out his secret arrangements for Esther's happiness with Allan Woodcourt);[1] the meaning for Dickens of such seemingly whimsical preoccupations as legs; his attitudes toward women, to class, to the church, to politics, to the effect of environment on life; his life as his source; the works as biography; his reading; his influences—there is room here for no more than passing reference, if any, to all these and other such matters of interest in Dickens.[2]

What I am doing here, accordingly, is carrying on the thread of analysis developed so far, intending to complete a perspective on Dickens from which his work may be seen to have the coherence that I think it has. I do not mean to say that everything in Dickens fits together. I will concede, with Raymond Williams, "that Dickens is often contradictory, often confused, and indeed often . . . unenlightened and unintelligent," the more readily because what he goes on to say seems to me exactly right: "More deeply, however, from his whole experience, and underlying the intellectual formulations which he picked up from so many and so different and so contradictory sources, the total vision, not so much drawn from his material as imposed on it, was always there."[3] I have dealt in the preceding chapter with the theme of Dickens that I find everywhere in the work of his maturity: the necessity of self-conquest, individual responsibility to other people, indivisible from the welfare of the human community.[4] This is Dickens's conscious, willed vision of ideal order. Here I am concerned with his more intuitive perceptions: what he sees as the given in human experience, on which that will works.

In the first place (to recapitulate a point I made in chapter 1), very little of that concerns the world of nature:[5] not Hardy's, where people cling to a planet whirling through space from unimaginable beginnings to some inscrutable end; and not Wordsworth's, infused with a divine presence rolling through all things. Angus Wilson says Dickens's sense of the country, "throughout his life and works, is that of a Cockney on holiday" (*Dickens*, p. 118). Natural phenomena enter the works to serve the human events in some way: a picturesque landscape in *Pickwick Papers* is there to make "the dismal man" ridiculous (5), productive farmland contrasts with muddy foggy London (*BH* 6), storms accompany ominous or catastrophic events—it rains drearily when Arthur Clennam sees Pet Meagles drawn to Henry Gowan (*LD* I, 17), and tempestuously when Emily flees with Steerforth (*DC* 31) and before Magwitch reveals himself to shatter Pip's illusions (*GE* 39).

But Dickens's subject, the human microcosm, is itself part of the given; and so what happens in the little world of humanity provides reliable intimations about the macrocosm. What do human affairs tell us about the given, then?—the substance of things, and the order, that Dickens sees? For he does see order, or rather, the potential for order. First of all, mystery. J. Hillis Miller shows how "in all of Dickens' novels, there is a mystery at the center of apparently unrelated events which will make them turn out in retrospect to be orderly and intelligible"; Miller's book traces out various ways that Dickens's central characters move from "opaque and meaningless" to "orderly and significant" experience.[6] This mystery in Dickens, and what is often called coincidence in his novels, mere contrivances of mechanical plot, should be seen as the transformation worked in his fictive mode upon literal beliefs of his indicated in a few well-known passages from Forster and from his letters: how we are constantly being surprised by parallels, resemblances, and correspondences in the experience of our daily lives; how "the ways of Providence" imprint on our days hints and shadows suggestive of unstated and unseen goals, how our ends are not random but woven, through time, out of character and circumstance, so that even a seeming accident becomes, "as it were, an act of divine justice."[7] Given fictive body in Dickens's novels, these beliefs of his make the mystery in each of them integral, not the mere shifts of a pot-boiler.

Mystery implies order, a hidden pattern that will account for what puzzles us. The characters in Dickens's novels move through hints and foreshadows toward a final accounting for the mystery. But it is not a progress lit by some magical glow. It is true that Pip is perplexed several times by the sense of something just beyond his mind's reach: "What *was* it that was borne in upon my mind when [Estella] stood still and looked attentively at me?"[8] However, Dickens is not laying on a Gothic thrill. Pip almost connects Estella to her murderess mother Molly because Wemmick has told him enough about Molly to raise his interest (24), and because he has seen Molly at Jaggers's house (26). Ordinarily Dickens's characters see the design only in retrospect. The second sentence in Esther's account of getting up her first morning at Bleak House (quoted in full above under "Plot and Scene," ch. 4) shows that she now sees the incident as emblematic: "As the prospect gradually revealed itself, and disclosed the scene over which the wind had wandered in the dark, like my memory over my life, I had a pleasure in discovering the unknown objects that had been around me in my sleep." The phrase "like my memory over my life" makes the dark of the previous night, and her sleep, metaphorical, so that the whole incident becomes for the reader a foreshadow of her discovery who she is, as it is for her now, too, in the retelling. But in the moment of experience, it was just getting up and looking out the window. Similarly David Copperfield remembers some incidents which now impress him as ominous—for instance, little Em'ly running along a timber protruding over the water, as if "springing forward to her destruction" (3)—but he is writing in retrospect, knowing what was in store for Emily. David also remembers Steerforth's way of sleeping with his head on his arm at school; in the meantime he has seen Steerforth drowned, lying just that way (55), but when he first saw him so, at school, "no veiled future dimly glanced upon him in the moonbeams" (6). And Esther's recollection of Rick and Vholes leaving for London (quoted under "Language," ch. 5) is portentous now, when she knows what happened to Rick, but there is no sign she took it so then.

Miller says of the central mysteries in Dickens's plots that "in retrospect" the puzzling events are no longer puzzling.[9] These scenes in Dickens are really more mysterious than that: they were not puzzling at the time, and it is retrospect that gives them their mystery. The wonder is in looking back, knowing now what it all meant, as David and Esther do, and seeing now for what they really were the moments which hinted so mutely then at a pattern beneath the appearance of muddle. There is even a further mystery: why did *these* scenes imprint themselves on their minds? The young James Joyce would say that they are epiphanies, luminous with meaning to the imagination though obscure to the intellect. I doubt it would have occurred to Dickens to put it that way, but he would agree to the hierarchy of faculties. He wrote in the first number of *Household Words*, "No mere utilitarian spirit, no iron binding of the mind to grim realities, will give a harsh tone to our Household Words."[10] I do not suppose that he had consciously in mind anything other than what he gives Mr. Sleary to say, first and last, in *Hard Times*: "People mutht be amuthed." But he understood the kingdom of the imagination to be concerned with more than that.

Imagining is a way of knowing; intellectual knowledge by itself is of another order, from the realms of lead not the realms of gold. In E. M. Forster's *A Passage to India* Mr. Fielding, the English schoolmaster, is sure that "a mystery is only a high-sounding term for a muddle" (7)—beneath the appearance of chaos there really is only chaos, and not order. The events of the novel suggest he is wrong; precisely because he is by temperament and culture a man of reason, he "had not the apparatus for judging" (29). He senses that the echo in the Marabar Cave, a decisive event in the story, has symbolic resonance, but cannot develop it; it "lay at the verge of Fielding's mind. . . . It belonged to the universe that he had missed or rejected" (31).

Forster sets his rational schoolmaster into an experience he cannot understand, in such a way that the rational reader perceives a pattern not available to the character Fielding's reason. It is a brilliant and paradoxical achievement: an imaginative vision of a possibility beyond reason; but projected in rational terms, thus implying an inescapable commitment to intellectual modes of understanding.

Forster says in effect, "If there is design, it is outside the reach of the intellect."[11] Dickens says, "There *is* design, *and* it is outside the reach of the intellect." We may, if we have the imaginative vision to see, wonder at the pattern as we see it fulfilled, but cannot know why, or how, the pattern comes to be: why those epiphanic scenes imprint themselves on Esther's and David's memories.

So far I have been talking about pattern in events, the order in things according to that total vision of Dickens which he imposed on his material. There is another kind of evidence of the given in human experience, according to Dickens, in the glimpses of schematic order seen by peripheral vision rather than straight on: what comes about, again and again, because ultimate reality is of a nature to reveal itself in glimpses of this sort. This order is created by the characters, often in the supporting cast, and described with clear approval, as embodying a desirable state of affairs. Neatness and orderliness are characteristic. The two friends in *Dombey and Son*, Captain Cuttle and Solomon Gills, from habits of the sea keep everything neat.[12] The Captain's rooms "were very small . . . but snug enough: everything being stowed away, as if there were an earthquake regularly every half-hour" (9). Gills's nautical instrument shop seems "almost to become a snug, sea-going, ship-shape concern," so compact is it: "Everything was jammed into the tightest cases, fitted into the narrowest corners, fenced up behind the most impertinent cushions, and screwed into the acutest angles, to prevent its philosophical composure from being disturbed by the rolling of the sea" (4). Lieutenant Tartar in *Edwin Drood* keeps the same kind of quarters: "the neatest, the cleanest, and the best-ordered chambers ever seen under the sun, moon, and stars" (21). Everything is conveniently arranged, everything is snug. "Shelf, bracket, locker, hook, and drawer were equally within reach, and were equally contrived with a view to avoiding waste of room, and providing some snug inches of stowage for something that would have exactly fitted nowhere else."

Snugness, then: a deployment of matter into an orderly arrangement that is compact and humanly appealing. An idea associated with snugness is plenitude: the space is *filled up*. Sol Gills's shop and Lieutenant Tartar's chambers typify the crowdedness of the Dickens world. The bars, like the Maypole in *Barnaby Rudge* (19) and Abbey Potterson's Six Jolly Fellowship Porters in *Our Mutual Friend* (I, 6), contain kegs, casks, bottles, beer taps, tankards, lemons hanging in nets, cheeses, closets and presses filled with eatables and drinkables. And finally, the objects thus ordered are also various, even unique: Lieutenant Tartar's storage is designed to provide spaces for things "that would have exactly fitted nowhere else." This variety is true of Esther and Ada's apartment in Bleak House, and the drawing room of Mr. Wickfield's house in *David Copperfield*.

All the moveables [in Esther's apartment], from the wardrobes to the chairs and tables, hangings, glasses, even to the pin-cushions and scent-bottles on the dressing-tables, displayed the same quaint variety. They agreed in nothing but their perfect neatness, their display of the whitest linen, and their storing-up, wheresoever the existence of a drawer, small or large, rendered it possible, of quantities of rose-leaves and sweet lavender.   (6)

. . . in every nook and corner [of the Wickfield drawing room] there was some queer little table, or cupboard, or bookcase, or seat, or something or other, that made me think there was not such another good corner in the room; until I looked at the next one, and found it equal to it, if not better.   (15)

This variety is matched by the pleasing irregularity of these places. Gabriel Varden the locksmith's house in *Barnaby Rudge* ("a modest building, not very straight, not large, not tall") "was not built of brick or lofty stone, but of wood and plaster; it was not planned with a dull and wearisome regard to regularity, for no one window matched the other, or seemed to have the slightest reference to anything besides itself" (4). Its rooms are not on the same level; one goes up and down steps to get from one room to another. The London tavern where Martin Chuzzlewit and Mark Tapley get their first meal after coming back to England is also a little below street level, and it too is madly but pleasantly irregular (*MC* 35). The outside of Mr. Wickfield's house is all "angles and corners, and carvings and mouldings, and quaint little panes of glass, and quainter little windows." The description of Bleak House is much too long to quote in full, but Esther makes a great deal of how rambling and "delightfully irregular" the place is: one of those houses "where you go up and down steps out of one room into another, and where you come upon more rooms when you think you have seen all there are, and where there is a bountiful provision of little halls and passages, and where you find still older cottage-rooms in unexpected places, with lattice windows and green growth pressing through them" (6).

It also appears that in a couple of ways these snug "good" places suggest right living to be a matter of private individual being. First, they are, as the word "snug" implies, rather small—at least, smallness is somehow associated with them. Miss Potterson's bar is "not much larger than a hackney-coach." Bleak House must be big, but it has many little halls and passages, little galleries, little staircases, a little sitting-room; and the house is described as a succession of small places rather than one large place subdivided. The drawing room in Mr. Wickfield's house is probably good-sized, since it is lighted by three or four windows on the street side and has "great beams" in the ceiling. But it gives the effect of being "all old nooks and corners," and its interest too lies in the parts and not in the whole. Second, these places are located out of the main rush of human affairs, if not actually in the country (although Bleak House and the Maypole are). Gabriel Varden's house is on a quiet shady street in Clerkenwell—a suburb then, Dickens says, where the open country was still close by. Canterbury, where Mr. Wickfield lives, is a quiet country town, not at all like London; Sol Gills's instrument store is in the City, but hardly anybody stops there any more. Captain Cuttle lives down near the waterfront—further isolated, in fact, by the ferocious landlady, Mrs. MacStinger. Miss Potterson's bar is "divided from the rough world" of her waterfront customers in the taproom by a glass partition and a half-door. Lieutenant Tartar's rooms are next door to Neville Landless's, high in the attic of Staple Inn, which is itself located in an out-of-the-way street (17).

An order in things that disposes them to good advantage, out of the traffic of society, and preserves profusion and the pleasing irregularity in variety: this occurs so often in Dickens that it must represent some ideal vision. No doubt, an ideal for domestic economy, at the least: we know about Dickens's obsessive neatness. I think it is more than that. The satisfaction and pleasure that Dickens takes in this sort of order are intense enough to make me think that like the wonder arising from evidence of design beneath human events, these too are intimations: akin, in his mode of feeling, to the moments of joy that convince Wordsworth our birth is but a sleep and a forgetting, the response to something in human experience that for an instant, or in a small place, resonates in harmony with the infinite. I take this ordered density in Dickens's world as a mark of its continuity, and consistency, with the traditional vision of the world as a great chain encompassing all possible variety of being. That chain thrums with energy in place, finally static rather than dynamic. The idea is older than the eighteenth century's image of the universe as a watch, but that image expresses it pretty well: an ordered system of parts in motion, intricate and interrelated, mass in spinning and unending dance. Dickens's world of course is the microcosm, the human center of that chain, expressing in the fullness and variety of human life the nature of the whole of being, and like the macrocosm, it is finally static rather than dynamic. I shall return to this shortly.

Though there is little of nature in Dickens, as I have said, there is a significant touch in that description of Bleak House: the "still older cottage-rooms in unexpected places, with lattice windows and green growth pressing through them" imply an original and intimate connection with nature, and the irregularity of the house makes it seem a living organism which has developed a form answering to the setting and the needs of the people of the house. Human order, when it is wrong, is quite unlike this. Thomas Gradgrind's house in *Hard Times* is "a very regular feature on the face of the country":

Not the least disguise toned down or shaded off that uncompromising fact in the landscape. A great square house, with a heavy portico darkening the principal windows, as its master's heavy brows over-shadowed his eyes. A calculated, cast up, balanced, and proved house. Six windows on this side of the door, six on that side; a total of twelve in this wing, a total of twelve in the other wing; four-and-twenty carried over to the back wings. A lawn and garden and an infant avenue, all ruled straight like a botanical account-book.   (I, 3)

Part of the point Dickens is making, of course, is how boring the straight lines and the symmetry are. But why are they? Because there are no straight lines in nature, nor is there symmetry. To get straight lines and symmetry you leave some things out and rearrange others. E. M. Forster's image of Western order is the plan of the British sector of Chandrapore, with its regular grid of streets intersecting at right angles. "It charms not, neither does it repel" (A Passage to India, 1). In his story, most kinds of reality (and it is suggested, the most meaningful kind) fall through such a net. Straight lines and regularity mean the same in Dickens. Mr. Gradgrind "meant to do great things," but "in gauging fathomless deeps with his little mean excise-rod, and in staggering over the universe with his rusty stiff-legged compasses," he had, "within the limits of his short tether ... tumbled about, annihilating the flowers of existence ..." (HT III, 1).

Contrasted to the irregularity and variety that Dickens favors, and that seem to imply the natural order of things, straight lines suggest a counter-order, Gradgrindian dryness and meagerness instead of the infinite variety of creation. Interestingly enough, Hablot Browne's illustration of Pecksniff and his daughters in their living room shows the wall at the rear hung with four pictures in a perfectly symmetrical arrangement, each of them portraying a perfectly symmetrical and straight-lined design (three buildings and a memorial to some hero), while in the shadows at the left rear the bust of Pecksniff appears to gaze approvingly. Symmetry and straight lines are here also connected to fraud and hypocrisy. There is something else about Pecksniff that fits here, too: his very moral throat. "You saw a good deal of it. You looked over a very low fence of white cravat (whereof no man had ever beheld the tie, for he fastened it behind), and there it lay, a valley between two jutting heights of collar, serene and whiskerless before you. It seemed to say, on the part of Mr. Pecksniff, 'There is no deception, ladies and gentlemen, all is peace, a holy calm pervades me' " (*MC* 2). That kind of insistence on perfect plainness and openness, concealing devious criminality, also appears in the short story "Hunted Down" (1859), in Mr. Sampson, a man whom the narrator distrusts on the instant of meeting (correctly, as it turns out). He parts his hair "straight up the middle," and he makes his hair-part stand for candor: as if he were to say in so many words, "You must take me, if you please, my friend, just as I show myself. Come straight up here, follow the gravel path, keep off the grass, I allow no trespassing" (2). Harold Skimpole, too, affects openness, along with his inflexible claim of childlike innocence. Esther says, "The more I saw of him, the more unlikely it seemed to me, when he was present, that he could design, conceal, or influence anything; and yet the less likely that appeared when he was not present . . ." (*BH* 43); and of course her skepticism is right, for he does nothing else. In *Our Mutual Friend* Eugene Wrayburn imposes on his friend Mortimer Lightwood in a similar way, protesting that he simply doesn't know whether anything in particular has been on his mind lately that would account for a change Mortimer thinks he has noticed in him. (There has been something on his mind, increasingly—Lizzie Hexam.) "So much of what was fantastically true to his own knowledge of this utterly careless Eugene, mingled with the answer, that Mortimer could not receive it as a mere evasion. Besides, it was given with an engaging air of openness, and of special exemption of the one friend he valued, from his reckless indifference" (II, 6). Here, too, the appearance of openness and simplicity is itself a deception.

All this hangs together. Like Forster, Dickens makes regularity and geometricity images of intellect, and like him too he shows, supremely in *Hard Times*, how much the intellect leaves out. Coketown has no place for the knowledge belonging to the fancy; Sleary's traveling circus (to which Gradgrind finally owes much) must set up on the outskirts of the city, and the pointedly named Pegasus's Arms where the circus people stay is "a mean little public-house, . . . as haggard and as shabby, as if, for want of custom, it had itself taken to drinking, and had gone the way all drunkards go, and was very near the end of it" (I, 5). But where Forster suggests reason is simply inadequate to net the world's truth, Dickens indicates it may also be a positive fraud. Reality is *not* open and plain; it is charged with mystery. Representations of it by the reason are utterly inadequate at their well-meaning best, and fraudulent at their criminal worst. To apprehend it fully is the work of imagination.

That is one reason why Dickens has no grand programs to offer: Orwell was right. To Dickens system is the child of intellect, and the complexity of the world is beyond the manipulative grasp of reason. But reason is inadequate not only because it cannot know enough. Love is required for any solution to the world's problems, and reason does not love. Love belongs to imagination —plausibly enough, when imagination includes the power to identify with, rather than merely to describe and anatomize. The explicit link between love and imagination is in *Hard Times*, in the character Sissy Jupe, who is one of Dickens's love-bearers and who comes from Sleary's circus. It is she who ministers to Louisa when Louisa flees from Harthouse, and who sends Harthouse away, and who has made a better home for Louisa's younger sister than Louisa did, and to whom Louisa turns in her trouble (III, 1–2); and who does so miserably in M'Choakumchild's school, unable to tell whether a nation with fifty millions of money is a prosperous nation unless she knows who has them, and taking into account, in computing the percentage of accidental deaths, the intensity of the survivors' grief (I, 9). M'Choakumchild's star pupil is Bitzer, whose heart "is accessible to Reason . . . and to nothing else" (III, 8), and Sissy's place in the schoolroom as well as her coloring emphasize her contrast with him. She sits at the end of a row diagonally across the room from Bitzer, and further back, so that she is also higher up than he is, and the sunbeam that strikes her ends at him. "But, whereas the girl was so dark-eyed and dark-haired that she seemed to receive a deeper and more lustrous colour from the sun, when it shone upon her, the boy was so light-eyed and light-haired that the self-same rays appeared to draw out of him what little colour he ever possessed" (I, 2). Sissy is far from Bitzer in the schoolroom, and in every other way too: higher up and nearer the natural light (and by the same token farther from the factual lectern) which confirms her fullness of being as it reveals Bitzer's deficiency.

No grand program then, but what Sissy has to offer, is what the world needs; and there needs no system for that. Perhaps this explains why Dickens was a radical but no revolutionary: why overturn an imperfect system to set up another? deflate a blustering manufacturer like Bounderby so that a windy labor leader like Slackbridge may swell into his place? What is required is personal determination to make things right within one's own radius; "if men would behave decently the world would be decent." Dickens recognizes the powerlessness of most people to set things right, but does not therefore absolve those "born expressly to do it"—the -oodles and -uffys, "my lords and gentlemen," "Right Reverends and Wrong Reverends of every order"; those Mr. Plornish, one of the helpless, means—"He only know'd that it wasn't put right by them what undertook that line of business, and that it didn't come right of itself"; or those addressed by the narrator in *Our Mutual Friend*: "My lords and gentlemen and honourable boards, when you in the course of your dust-shovelling and cinder-raking have piled up a mountain of pretentious failure, you must off with your honourable coats for the removal of it, and fall to work with the power of all the queen's horses and all the queen's men, or it will come rushing down and bury us alive."[13]

George Ford has explained the apparent contradiction between this characteristic denunciatory stance of Dickens, and his penchant for blaming evil on social and environmental conditions, by the example of *Bleak House*, where "a line is drawn in the social structure between those who are helpless and those who are capable of self-help"; a kind of determinism governs those below the line, but free will exists above it, "and the reader is expected to employ somewhat different standards when evaluating those who are above this assumed line and those who are below it."[14] Self-help as preached by Samuel Smiles is not finally what Dickens is getting at here, though, and if Jo is blameless the drunken brickmaker is not entirely so (*BH* 22, 46). I do not think the apparent contradiction is completely explained Ford's way, any more than Dickens's ideal young women can be entirely reconciled to our reality. With them we are up against the resistance of our matter-of-fact experience to Dickens's mode of fiction. With characters like those below Ford's line, we are up against two things. The first is Dickens's rhetorical strategy, which belongs to

his mode of fiction. In order to emphasize how imperative personal responsibility is upon those who have power, he intensifies
the difference between them and those who do not: Jo is *completely* helpless, so as not to encourage distracting speculations
about how far he is responsible for himself.[15] Secondly, Dickens
knows, like the meek man at the Veneerings' party, that there is
"something appallingly wrong somewhere"; but he also knows
(even if he gives it to Podsnap to say) that it is "easy to say somewhere; not so easy to say where!" (*OMF* I, 11). He knows there
is such a thing as evil, from its evidence everywhere; he does not
know exactly how far personal responsibility for it extends. But
he does know that it lies in every human heart—why else would it
be necessary for his representative human protagonists (which
his Olivers and Nells are not) to change?[16]

Finally, then, I think, there is one more reason besides the inadequacy of the "wisdom of the Head" (*HT* III, 1) why Dickens
promotes no alternative system, and it has to do with the stasis of
his world that I mentioned earlier. A great deal happens; but the
novels, in a sense, do not go anywhere. And while a good deal of
Dickens goes back to the eighteenth century, his pulsing human
microcosm is older than the eighteenth-century idea of the watchmaker's universe ticking on in its cosmic case where everything
that is, is right. Spiritually the affinities of Dickens's cosmos are
with the vision of traditional Christianity. In his novels order does
not *change*: order is *restored*. A Dickens novel begins in a condition of disharmony, usually originating in events antedating the
opening, and moves toward a harmony not new but "old-fashioned"—fashioned like the old, the *original*. All those places of
ideal order are old, or old-fashioned, and the people associated
with them, those bearers of love, have some of the attributes of
age. Staple Inn is old; Mr. Wickfield's house and the Maypole are
both very old; so is Bleak House. Sol Gills admits to being old-
fashioned and out of step, and Captain Cuttle is retired. Esther,
of course, is not old, nor is Agnes Wickfield, nor is Lieutenant
Tartar. But each of these makers of order has some attribute of
age other than actual years. Lieutenant Tartar is retired; Agnes
takes the adult role of housekeeper; Esther is given several significant nicknames from the beginning—Old Woman, Mother
Hubbard, Dame Durden (8). They are, like the furniture of

Bleak House, "old-fashioned rather than old"—which of course is the point of the whole old-new theme. The old—the original—does not need to be replaced; it needs to be recognized—that is, known again.

Change, then, is not linear in Dickens, but something like cyclic. Thus while Dickens is a radical, finding the root of systemic and collective wrong in the personal and individual, he is also conservative—radically conservative, as A. E. Dyson says.[17] He is reluctant to overturn the system of things; it is the given, though fallen. So in the human world of his novels the good people do not break down class lines. Mark Tapley in *Martin Chuzzlewit*, the Toodles in *Dombey and Son*, the Peggottys in *David Copperfield*, Charley in *Bleak House*, Joe and Biddy in *Great Expectations*: all of them know where they belong in society and see worth in being what they are. In *Bleak House* Mr. Rouncewell the ironmaster's sense of his own merit and the merit of iron and steel manufacture do not require him to devalue his mother's service as Sir Leicester Dedlock's housekeeper. Mr. Dombey's awesome sense of his own importance, on the other hand, is out of proportion to his real position. He aspires to a place higher than he deserves. If such people succeed in hoisting themselves up, order disappears. In contrast to this, it is a service to the stability of things to recognize merit and restore it to its rightful place. The whole of *Oliver Twist* is a search for Oliver's true identity, and in *Nicholas Nickleby* the Cheeryble brothers really restore Nicholas to his proper rank.[18]

As the author, so the man. As editor of *Household Words* Dickens refused to let stand an implication that workmen are always wrong to strike, his sympathies were with the Preston textile workers in their 1853–54 strike, and yet he thought them "engaged in an unreasonable struggle, wherein they began ill and cannot end well."[19] The furor raised by *Hard Times* led him to protest that he believed in the virtue of both "Aristocracy" and "People," that he would not submit to being represented as setting class against class, and that he wished to use, "instead of these words, the terms, the governors and the governed."[20] Things ought to be set right by those "born expressly to do it"—the reverends, the lords and gentlemen, the honorable boards—those who ought to help others because, in their places in the system, they can, but

who unfortunately (no, wickedly) do no more than help themselves. If Dickens were a reformer of the revolutionary kind, he
ought to be less angry at their shortcomings. But to him they are
derelict in their duty, shirking what their station in life demands,
and his response is properly seen as righteous wrath.

I *Sources, Influences, Affinities*

It is, in fact, the sort of wrath that we associate with Swift. Only
occasionally does Dickens's tone so precisely remind me of
Swift's as in that lapse where he makes a mask of Esther (see
"Language" in ch. 5 above). But the Swiftian savage indignation
is often lodged in his breast, and its source is the same: in the
recognition by "right reason" of the wide gap between what Christian society ought to be, and what is. The latter eighteenth-century vogue of sentiment and delicate feeling separate Swift and
Dickens, influencing the rhetoric of Romanticism which gave
Dickens his rubric of the two wisdoms, of the head and of the
heart. But Dickens's "wisdom of the Heart" (*HT* III, 1) is Swift's
"right reason"—that is, something like inner light, the power of
full and accurate perception of human realities, unmediated and
unimpeded by the meddling and distorting intellect. As for that
scarecrow "wisdom of the Head," a letter of Dickens makes clear
how near to Swift's his attitude is: "My satire is against those
who see figures and averages, and nothing else . . . the addled
heads who would take the average of cold in the Crimea during
twelve months as a reason for clothing a soldier in nankeens on a
night when he would be frozen to death in fur, and who would
comfort the labourer in travelling twelve miles a day to and from
his work, by telling him that the average distance of one inhabited
place from another in the whole area of England, is not more
than four miles."[21] These calculators are surely descendants of the
projector in "A Modest Proposal" and the scientists of Laputa the
flying island.

They are also near relatives of those blind, as William Blake
saw it, from "single vision and Newton's sleep"—that is, from the
obliviousness that Blake felt intellect commits us to. Joseph Gold
uses epigraphs from Blake to help define the "literary and intellectual tradition of English art and thought" that Dickens must be

seen as belonging to, specifically to indicate "certain complex similarities in his and Dickens' moral or 'religious' views,"[22] and F. R. Leavis argues for "the closest essential affinity between Dickens and the author of 'London,'" particularly in *Hard Times* and the "immensely more complex" *Little Dorrit*: "I have in mind, of course, the way in which the irrelevance of the Benthamite calculus is exposed; the insistence that life is spontaneous and creative, so that the appeal to self-interest as the essential motive is life-defeating; the vindication, in terms of childhood, of spontaneity, disinterestedness, love and wonder; and the significant place given to Art—a place entailing a conception of Art that is pure Blake." On the question how much Victorians knew about Blake ("who was far from being a current author in his time and didn't come in with the Romantic poets"), Leavis thinks someone may someday assemble the evidence to show he was as important an influence as Wordsworth. However, Leavis declines "to commit [himself] to the belief that Dickens had read Blake."[23] I have wondered if the image in *Hard Times* of Mr. Gradgrind "staggering over the universe with his rusty stiff-legged compasses" (quoted more fully above) comes from Dickens's memory of Blake's plate of the kneeling "Urizen" (a punning name), left arm reaching downward, with compasses extending, from the spread index and second fingers, marking off the void; or possibly of Blake's "Newton," seated in profile in a cramped posture, working with compasses on a sheet of paper on the ground before him, oblivious of all else around. Either one would be an appropriate source. According to George Wingfield Digby, the Newton print "is a satire on the limitations of one-pointed concentration, intellectual knowledge, and exclusive reliance on rational measure," and Urizen promulgates error: "This is the image of the mind creating, or projecting, its own Maya."[24] Dickens's earlier development of Gradgrind as dryly factual and literal-minded keeps him very close to earth; these sudden cosmic compasses look temptingly like a response of Dickens's intensely visual imagination to one of those prints of Blake. However, without knowing whether Dickens had seen them, or knew anything about Blake, I will imitate Leavis's prudence here and say "affinity." That much is surely unarguable.

Dickens surely knew Swift, he had at least a remarkable affinity with Blake. As for the Romantics Victorians surely knew about, Dickens was generally familiar, as Leavis and others say, with Wordsworth and Romantic poetry in general, and he knew personally people like Leigh Hunt and Walter Savage Landor. He knew and admired Thomas Carlyle, both man and work. He knew the work of Scott. For earlier English literature, we know on Forster's authority that chapter 4 of *David Copperfield* includes an account of Dickens's childhood reading of eighteenth-century English fiction, *Don Quixote, Gil Blas, The Arabian Nights,* and *Tales of the Genii.* (A little further on Forster adds to this the essays of Addison and Steele, Samuel Johnson, and Oliver Goldsmith.) He owned forty-eight of Hogarth's engravings.[25] He surely knew Bunyan. He knew Shakespeare and Jonson and English drama generally.[26] He knew something at least of Gibbon, certainly more than Wegg does in *Our Mutual Friend,* who misreads "The Decline and Fall-off the Rooshan Empire" to Mr. Boffin. (Angus Wilson sees the basis of Dickens's ironic style of narration from *Nicholas Nickleby* to *Little Dorrit* in Gibbon, "a mocking yet loving parody of the grand Gibbonian language of the previous century.")[27]

One does not finish such listing; one stops. There is not much point even beginning to list sources and influences in Dickens's own time, since anything in his work can turn out to have its roots in something Dickens saw, read, felt about.[28] He usually took pride in this connection between his work and the world around him, though he could deny it sometimes, for whatever reason, as when he refused to concede that his Inspector Bucket had any connection with his experience reporting the detective police. As to the influence of other writers, Wilkie Collins used to be credited often with having taught Dickens a thing or two about plotting. That does not hold up.[29] The sort of early influence cited by Ford and Marcus is usual in a beginning writer, and its interest is more in how Dickens departed from his models and parallels than in how he imitated them. Later on, but not very much later, any question of Dickens's borrowings is not much worth pursuing. To speak only of the most obvious example, how would we begin disentangling Shakespearean substance from Dickens? From very early in his career he consumed what he borrowed, so transmuting it in his own creations that its interest is what it does there, not where it comes from.

About Dickens's own influence on recent novelists in English it would be hard to improve on George Ford's estimate: that it is not a matter of "precisely identifiable" debts but of "overall influence," so that (particularly in England) "presenting man in society" has remained the novelists' job.[30] In the main, that holds for the intervening years, too; Ford says so specifically of Arnold Bennett's generation. Even in Bloomsbury, where all things Victorian were deplored, Dickens was recognized, though mostly in the spirit of that man G. H. Lewes heard first "express measureless contempt," and a few minutes later "admit that Dickens had 'entered into his life.' "[31] But as I have shown, Bloomsbury's E. M. Forster and Virginia Woolf were not so grudging as that.

Any account of Dickens's reputation must begin by saying it is worldwide; from there on what one says depends on room. Dickens studies are vigorous in many foreign languages as well as in English; professors must be teaching him; students must be reading him. I have not pursued publication figures in other languages, but Ford estimated in 1970 that American publishers sold about a million copies of Dickens in 1968, and that in England the popularity of particular titles was generally parallel to their popularity in the United States ("1960s," pp. 170–71). "A fair segment" of those readers would be students, as Ford says. But there must be many who were not, just as in the latter nineteenth century and the post-Victorian years when sophisticated literary opinion was marking Dickens down: publishers, who do not as a rule publish what they cannot sell, kept right on issuing single titles and collected editions. "Readers uncorrupted by literary prejudices," as Philip Collins writes (quoting Samuel Johnson's phrase), "have continued to regard him as 'a classic,' and to read or at least to buy his books. . . ."[32] But Dickens's reputation in our age goes beyond his readership. As Ford says, the stage, the movies, radio, and TV ensure that the remark "that man looks like a Dickens character" will be understood ("1960s," p. 168).

II   *Conclusion*

It is hard to strike the right note in ending. First, a reservation. It has become conventional to attribute the congealing of his creative flow that Dickens began complaining of in the mid-1840s to the cooling of his ardor for Catherine, and likewise to see the somberness in his later novels as the shadows of his marital disappointments. No doubt the personal troubles colored the fiction, but the extent to which this is true is debatable, and that his novels became a projection of his troubles is demonstrably untrue when one considers elements already present in the earlier works. It is surely significant that Dickens's cries of anguish began almost exactly at the point in his career when he lifted his artistic sights much higher, aiming to do much more.[33]

If Dickens had deep roots in the eighteenth century (as his own account of his reading suggests, and such evidence as I have given), he has roots deeper still in the worldview of Christian tradition, as the embedding of biblical and broadly Christian ideas and language in his work shows.[34] When he demanded more of himself and drew more deeply on his powers, after the rushing production of his early career, it is this element in his vision which emerges as controlling. Thereafter what characterizes Dickens's novels (to borrow Williams's phrase again) is "that total vision, not so much drawn from his material as imposed on it."

But Dickens was also a man of the nineteenth century, engaged at all points with his own time, and what he had from the past was at some of those points overlaid and qualified. What he urged was not always easily distinguishable from the vision of more secular reformers. So John Jarndyce's advice to Rick Carstone—"Trust in nothing but in Providence and your own efforts" (*BH* 13), and the narrator's deprecatory aside about the prevalence of trusting to "flat things" somehow "coming round"—"Not in their being beaten round, or worked round, but in their 'coming' round!" (*BH* 20), sound rather like self-help as preached by Samuel Smiles, the practice of industry and thrift in order to get ahead. So, at first thought, does Dickens's suggestion that to cure the unconcern for the sick among them which he noted in the girls at Urania Cottage, the halfway house for prostitutes, they be required to help with the nursing: "I am inclined to think this indifference springs out of our doing too much."[35] But it is not quite that. Dickens's idea is that the well must awaken to *responsibility for* the sick, not simply that they be required to be more self-reliant. The difference is polar. Thus his exhortations to those "born expressly to do it," it seems to me, came at bottom from his conviction that a healthy society arises from the conscious exercise of personal responsibility out of love, that is, charity in the meaning of St. Paul. With his intense dislike for puritanical morality, Dickens might have been surprised how closely this aligned him with the Puritanism of the seventeenth century, over against the self-interest he railed against in his own time: "In one of the most powerful of Puritan sermons the preacher bids his hearers ask themselves every night, 'What have I done today for the Public?', for the Respublica, that is, or the Common Weal. When they ceased to ask, the Puritans became a *bourgeoisie*, and the trouble with the English middle classes in the nineteenth century was not that they were Puritan, but that they were not half Puritan enough."[36]

Dickens's world is in many ways still ours; Victorian perplexities are still with us after more than a century of utilitarian technological revolution and societal change. That of course does not fully explain how Dickens "with his extraordinary intuition," as Angus Wilson says, "leaps the century and speaks to our fears, our violence, our trust in the absurd. . . ."[37] If it did, Dickens would only swell a chorus of Victorian novelists speaking to our fears. What makes him singular is what we keep trying to take the measure of, that "extraordinary intuition." By that power his work lives; and the world's body made by Dickens's imagination, energy, and will still breathes.

Appendix:

Summaries of Novels Most Often Discussed

Martin Chuzzlewit. There are two Martin Chuzzlewits: young Martin, the hero, and the favorite relative of the other Martin, his grandfather, the Chuzzlewit clan's rich patriarch. Martin's interest in his grandfather's young ward Mary Graham is the occasion of a quarrel which impels Martin into Seth Pecksniff's school for architects at a village in Wiltshire; Martin is determined to get a profession, and financial independence, so that he can marry Mary in spite of his grandfather. Behind his shining moral facade, Pecksniff covets old Martin's favor and cash as much as anyone else in the family (most of the principal characters in the book belong to the Chuzzlewit clan, who according to the parodic scholarly account in the opening chapter are "remarkable for taking uncommon good care of themselves," and who have "many counterparts and prototypes in the Great World about us"). He is therefore prompt to send young Martin on his way at the urging of his grandfather, who hopes that without means Martin will submit to him once more. But Martin's prideful will matches his grandfather's, and when London offers no prospect of fortune, he determines to make one in America. Mark Tapley, whose comic fate it is never to gain credit for moral fortitude in trying situations because from the influence of his sunny unselfish nature those situations cease to try, appoints himself Martin's servant; Mark sees in Martin's selfishness the potential for "jolly" situations offering him excellent opportunities for "coming out strong."

While Martin and Mark are in America, Pecksniff sees an opportunity to ingratiate himself with old Martin and invites him and Mary Graham for an extended visit. Old Martin accepts, depleted and meek-seeming in contrast to his earlier wrath and suspicion of his mercenary relatives. Pecksniff's excuse is that he is now alone, his older daughter Charity living now in London, and his younger daughter Mercy having married Jonas Chuzzlewit, the son of old Martin's brother Anthony, recently dead. (The famous Mrs. Gamp

210

first appears as nightwatcher of Anthony's corpse.) Jonas, a thoroughly commercial-spirited young man, invests in Tigg Montague's Anglo-Bengalee Disinterested Loan and Life Assurance Company, a confidence scheme which he recognizes as such, but is happy to join in the prospect of profit. But he soon becomes a victim himself: Montague discovers evidence that Jonas poisoned his father, and blackmails Jonas into helping him ring Pecksniff into Anglo-Bengalee, not a difficult task, Pecksniff coming in with the same understanding and motives that Jonas did. But Jonas, desperate at being in Montague's power, murders him.

Meanwhile Martin has been losing his illusions about the United States, as he and Mark meet a succession of vainglorious Americans and observe the meagre and shoddy reality of American life and institutions. He reaches bottom at Eden, the malarial frontier settlement where he has been tricked into buying property, and where first he, and then Mark, fall desperately ill. Nursing Mark back to health as Mark had nursed him, Martin realizes Mark's true worth and awakens to his own selfishness. A loan from one worthy American enables Martin and Mark to return to England, in time to have a part in the discovery not only that Jonas murdered Montague, but that he need not have done so, since old Anthony did not die of poison, but of the knowledge that his son meant him to. Finally, Pecksniff is brought down. Financially ruined by the collapse of Anglo-Bengalee, he is exposed for his consummate hypocrisy in a discovery scene staged by old Martin himself, who it turns out has lived with Pecksniff only to learn what he was. The two Martins are reconciled as both confess their former injustices to each other. The appropriate marriages follow: Martin and Mary Graham are united, as are Mark Tapley and the comely landlady of the inn where he began as hostler, and Martin's friend John Westlock and Ruth Pinch, sister of the selfless and innocent Tom Pinch, whose importance in the fable is not at all indicated by this summary.

Dombey and Son. While he lives, little Paul Dombey (with whose birth the novel begins) is the crown jewel in his father's pride; the firm name "Dombey and Son" once more will mean what it says. His mother dies at his birth, a matter of regret to Mr. Dombey, but on the whole the event clears a profit, more than offsetting the loss to Dombey that his first child is a mere daughter, Florence. There develops a strong attachment between Paul and Florence, which Dombey is somewhat jealous of; however, Paul's influence with him is great, enough even to secure for Dombey's employee young Walter

Gay a loan to help his uncle Sol Gills, a seller of nautical instruments no longer in demand, meet his debts. In fact Paul is beloved by all, from his wet nurse Polly Toodles even to the Blimbers who run the somber boarding school to which Paul is sent, and at which his frail health continues to fade; and from which he goes home peacefully to die—asking for Florence to be with him in his last moments.

Florence now takes Paul's place at the center of interest, and the narrative emphasizes her solitude. Dombey resents her for having taken (as he sees it) his place in Paul's heart, and he leaves her behind when he goes to Leamington on holiday to recover his spirits. Walter, who might have been some comfort, admiring Florence as he does from afar, is also removed, to a post in Dombey's office in the Barbadoes. (Walter's assignment is the work really of James Carker, Dombey's office manager, who is able to manipulate Dombey by playing on his pride, and does so continually for his own inscrutable purposes.) Walter's ship is soon reported missing, and Sol Gills slips away to search for news, leaving his shop in the keeping of his friend Captain Cuttle, who is doubly affected by Walter's fate, having always seen Walter and Florence as destined for each other.

At Leamington Dombey meets the second Mrs. Dombey, Edith Granger, and her mother Mrs. Skewton; the marriage is a straight trade—Dombey gets beauty, grace, and accomplishments suitable to his estate, and Edith Granger gets wealth and status. The harmony between them is shortlived: Edith feels what she is, a woman who has sold herself. It does not help that Edith and Florence are drawn to each other—Dombey sees Florence supplanting him once again—and Edith, as proud as he, will not be ruled. Dombey employs Carker to humiliate her, and Carker takes the opportunity to persuade Edith to run off with him. In his anger Dombey abuses Florence, who flees, finding refuge with Captain Cuttle. At this juncture Walter reappears, having survived shipwreck, and shortly he and Florence profess their love, to Captain Cuttle's great delight.

Meanwhile Dombey learns with the help of Alice Brown, a returned convict, that Carker and Edith are headed for Dijon. (Alice Brown, it turns out, was ruined by Carker; and her father having been Edith's uncle, she and her mother parallel lower down in society the roles of Edith and hers.) Dombey pursues them, arriving there just after Edith has spurned Carker and gone—she never intended a liaison, but took the opportunity to humiliate Dombey even at the price of her own reputation. Carker flees back to England, followed by his former employer, and is killed by a railroad train.

Walter and Florence marry; Walter departs on a long business voyage and Florence goes with him. For the next year the firm of

Dombey and Son struggles to survive, but fails. Dombey is bankrupt and broken, belatedly aware what a treasure he has thrown away in Florence's love. He is on the point of suicide when Florence and Walter (and their infant son, another Paul) return, and Dombey learns he has not lost all. Florence sees Edith one more time, and though there can be no reconciliation, there is forgiveness. Dombey lives out his days in retirement, the ruin of Dombey and Son having been his salvation.

David Copperfield. David begins by reporting the circumstances of his birth at Blunderstone Rookery to a timid naive young widow, on the March Friday that his peppery great-aunt Betsey Trotwood chose to visit her and, disgusted that he did not prove to be a girl, marched out without so much as a glance at him; nor would she see him until he turned up at her door in Dover years later. His happy boyhood is blighted by the appearance of Edward Murdstone, who charms his vulnerable mother (though not the servant woman Peggotty); he comes back from visiting Peggotty's family at Yarmouth to find Murdstone installed as his stepfather, and shortly thereafter, his sister Jane as housekeeper. All joy is at an end under the cold inflexible Murdstone domestic order; David is sent to the sadistic Mr. Creakle's school, where he meets James Steerforth, whom he idolizes instantly. The death of David's mother cuts his schooling short; Murdstone sends him off to London to a menial job in a warehouse; he is ten years old. It has been arranged for him to live with the Micawbers, which he does until Micawber is arrested for debt (a common occurrence for him). Shortly David determines to run away to his great-aunt at Dover. When she repels the Murdstones' attempt to regain custody of him, a secure future opens: he is enrolled in Dr. Strong's school at Canterbury, and lives with Aunt Betsey's attorney Mr. Wickfield and his daughter Agnes. The school is an excellent one, under the venerable Dr. Strong and his young wife Annie. The Micawbers turn up once during David's school days (as they will do at intervals through the story); the only discordant notes are Jack Maldon's attentions to his cousin Annie, and 'umble Uriah Heep's presence in the Wickfield law office.

His schooling complete, David goes to London, where he meets Steerforth again (and is introduced to his proud mother and her companion the waspish Rosa Dartle). Steerforth goes along to Yarmouth, where he makes a great hit with everyone, including David's childhood playmate little Em'ly, now engaged to Ham Peggotty. Back in London, David is articled to Spenlow and Jorkins (proctors in Doctors' Commons), sets up in bachelor's quarters, and on one memorable drunken evening makes a fool of himself before Agnes. Agnes's warning against Steerforth is borne out when Emily flees with him; her uncle Daniel sets off on a search for her which will last for years.

David meets Dora Spenlow and falls desperately in love; though his prospects have dimmed with his aunt's financial reverses, he hews energetically at the "forest of difficulty," taking a second job as Dr. Strong's secretary and teaching himself shorthand to qualify for a job as parliamentary reporter. Mr. Spenlow's objections being set aside by death, and David having begun to make his way as a reporter and writer of fiction, he and Dora marry and are deliriously happy, though their housekeeping never gets beyond muddle. Dora is lovable, and unteachable; it occurs to David that he had better give up trying to form her character, that it must already be formed. When Annie Strong at last finds opportunity to clear herself of the unjust suspicions that she and her childhood sweetheart Jack Maldon are having an affair, and to express her gratitude to her husband Dr. Strong, some words of hers stick with David: "no disparity in marriage like unsuitability of mind and purpose"; "the first mistaken impulse of an undisciplined heart." By the time their marriage is two years old, and Dora's health has begun to fail following the death of their child at birth, David has come to realize the application of those words to himself.

Some time before this David has had news from Rosa Dartle that Emily and Steerforth have parted, and he has told Mr. Peggotty (whose quest brings him to London periodically) that Emily may turn up in London. Eventually she does, to endure a passage of Rosa Dartle's jealous scorn before David's message brings Mr. Peggotty to the rescue. Peggotty reveals his plan not to bring Emily back to Yarmouth, but to emigrate to Australia with her.

Meanwhile Micawber has been employed by Uriah Heep since about the time Aunt Betsey lost her property. Heep has been exploiting Mr. Wickfield's weakness for wine to get control of his affairs, until now the office is practically his. He has long had his eye on Agnes, too, to David's indignation; Agnes of course will have none of him, and tolerates him only from the uneasy suspicion that Heep may have involved her father in shady transactions and she is hostage to her father's reputation. Micawber now comes to the rescue by staging a dramatic disclosure of Heep's villainy, using the knowledge he has gained of Heep's operations to bring about his downfall; a happy consequence is the restoration of Aunt Betsey's property, which enables her to finance the Micawbers' emigration to Australia. They depart on the same ship as the Peggotty party; David goes down to Yarmouth, to deliver to Ham Emily's letter thanking him for his forgiveness. It is never delivered; there is a great storm at Yarmouth, and

David finds Ham engaged in the attempt to rescue a sailor clinging to a ship breaking up offshore. Both Ham and the sailor are drowned; the sailor is Steerforth.

David goes abroad, being now a widower; the catastrophe of Dora's death occurred shortly before the Micawber and Peggotty emigration. While events rushed upon him David bore up; now, wandering Europe like Carlyle's Teufelsdröckh, he experiences deepening desolation until, three months short of a year after Dora's death, he feels the healing touch of Nature in Switzerland; coincidentally he receives a letter of comfort and consolation from Agnes. For nearly two years more David lives abroad, beginning to write again, and coming to realize what Agnes—whom he has always thought of as a sister, and who was his and Dora's friend and confidant—might have been to him. He returns to England, firmly resolved not to disturb their relationship or any romantic attachment Agnes may have now. But when he goes to see Agnes, something in her manner tells him that what might have been still may be, and he declares his love, and is accepted: to the tremendous joy of Aunt Betsey, who for years had much to do never to interfere by telling David what she plainly saw in Agnes's heart. Another saw it too: David now learns that Dora, on her deathbed, had told Agnes that she must some day take her place.

Hard Times. The framework of the story is the opening of Thomas Gradgrind's eyes to the deficiencies of his utilitarian philosophy, though the focus of the narrative is on nearly everyone else: his daughter Louisa and son Tom, starved, not educated, in the Gradgrind school of fact; Gradgrind's friend Josiah Bounderby of Coketown, the swelling manufacturer, proclaiming his self-manufacture ad nauseam, whom Louisa unwisely marries for love (of her brother Tom, not Bounderby, to help Tom secure advancement in Bounderby's bank); James Harthouse, the effete nearly unprincipled idler whose attempt to seduce Louisa finally drives her back to her father's house; Stephen Blackpool, the virtuous workman martyred first by the muddle of the Coketown world (by his fellow workers for not joining their union, by his employer Bounderby for speaking home truths), and then by Tom, who uses him to deflect suspicion from his own bank robbery; Bitzer, the perfect product of the hard fact school whose exemplary lookout for number one recoils on Thomas Gradgrind when Bitzer foils his plan to help his recreant son escape abroad; and finally two saviors: Mr. Sleary, whose despised circus is the means of Tom getting clear after all, and Sissy Jupe, of the circus herself, who as a member of Gradgrind's household after her father's disappearance exerts a wholesome and healing effect on Louisa and the younger Gradgrinds, and even on Harthouse, persuading him to abandon his campaign for Louisa and leave town. Thus the shortcomings of the hard fact philosophy generate ill in the Gradgrind lives; but the worst consequences are finally averted, as a result of Gradgrind's "factually" unjustifiable benevolence toward Sissy Jupe.

Little Dorrit. The longest thread in the design of *Little Dorrit* is Arthur Clennam's feeling that his dead father might long ago have wronged someone, and having never set it right, commissioned his widow to do so. Mrs. Clennam's refusal to set him at rest on this point, and his puzzlement at the unlikely presence in her household of Amy Dorrit, a young and diminutive seamstress whose father is an imprisoned debtor, lead to Arthur's encounter with the Circumlocution Office, where he goes to find out whether the Clennam firm had anything to do with William Dorrit's imprisonment (so long ago that Little Dorrit was born in the family's prison quarters). This is a blind alley, but Clennam's fears remain, to be quickened when a disagreeable and sinister foreigner who calls himself Blandois turns up at Clennam & Co., in circumstances that suggest to Arthur that firm's involvement in unspecified misdeeds. In the end Blandois's business turns out to have been blackmail, to keep the secret that Mrs. Clennam had suppressed a codicil to her father-in-law's will which would (by a tangle of circumstances too complex to go into here, involving something Arthur is never to learn, that Mrs. Clennam is not his real mother) have benefited Little Dorrit: and so Arthur's intuition, wrong in detail, was right in the main.

But this is only the longest thread; it is crossed by and interwoven with many others, and the nature and tone of the novel is better suggested by naming the principal ones of these than by sketching the action. There is no single element so all-encompassing as the suit in Chancery in *Bleak House,* but two—the Circumlocution Office, the Establishment arm for keeping things from getting done, and the Merdle financial empire, which turns out to be a swindle—fill the same kind of role. The Circumlocution Office has a wide jurisdiction and is defended, "drawn salary in hand," by a numerous bureaucracy, notably the Barnacle clan; the Merdle bubble inflates by the eager puffing of all, Bar, Bishop, Treasury, William Dorrit (whose lucky inheritance that got him out of the Marshalsea is scattered when the bubble bursts), even the canny Pancks whose investigations uncovered Dorrit's claim, and Arthur, who nearly ruins Doyce, the engineer who took him in partnership when Arthur left the Clennam firm.

A third system, paralleling the Circumlocution Office and the Merdle bubble in exploitativeness, is the property Bleeding Heart Yard, whose proprietor Casby squeezes his tenants while emanating benevolence. And working through the whole world of *Little Dorrit* is a worship of status (linked to wealth) which gives the Circumlocution Office and Merdle their power, and of which the emblem is Mrs. General, whom William Dorrit engages to guide and instruct his family in the social intricacies to which their new wealth commits them as it frees them from debtors' prison.

Among the more important characters who people this design (besides those already named) are Mr. and Mrs. Meagles and Henry Gowan. Mr. Meagles introduced Arthur Clennam to Doyce, and he and Doyce between them retrieve Arthur's affairs. At one time Arthur hoped for the favor of the Meagles's daughter; to his disappointment (as well as to her parents', and to their cost), she preferred Gowan, a well-born but indolent painter whose mother looks down on the Meagles connection while content that Henry should draw on the Meagles resources for his worldly needs.

Another romantic disappointment to Arthur is Flora Finching, whose girlhood romance with him was scotched by her father Mr. Casby, and who has aged without maturing. Through all Arthur's disappointments, however, he becomes increasingly attached to Amy—Little Dorrit—whose unassuming service to all is the center of hope and strength in the story; and whose love for him, allied to gratitude for his concern for her family, never wavers, and eventually triumphs over Arthur's dreary certainty that at forty he has left all possibility of love and marriage behind.

Great Expectations. Pip's good fortune, as he sees it then—to be plucked from the village forge of his brother-in-law Joe Gargery and established in London to be educated as a gentleman—combines with his fantasies to convince him that his anonymous benefactor is the recluse Miss Havisham, taking this eccentric course to fit him out as a proper suitor for her ward Estella, with whom Pip has been smitten since first he saw her. As Miss Havisham has Pip escort Estella on the social rounds involved in her introduction to society, his belief in his destiny is strengthened. But when, some years on, the anonymous benefactor chooses to become known, Pip is utterly cast down to discover he has been made a gentleman by the ex-convict Magwitch, to whom the boy Pip had brought food and a file when he found the convict chained and freezing, a fugitive from the prison ship on the river, in the churchyard where Pip's parents are buried. He is further dismayed when he goes back home to bid farewell to Miss Havisham and discovers Estella is to be married to a well-off but brutal young acquaintance of Pip's.

Though his life has turned to ashes, Pip recognizes his duty to Magwitch, and he and his friend and guide to social graces Herbert Pocket plan to spirit Magwitch out of England (for as a transported convict, he is subject to execution if discovered). Pip is almost killed first by an old enemy, Orlick, who tricks him into a rendezvous far out on the marshes near his home village; Orlick was a journeyman smith under Joe Gargery when Pip was in his apprenticeship, and always jealous of Joe's fancied favoritism for Pip; he turns out to have been the one who struck Pip's sister down in an incident that had gone unsolved. In the event, the attempt to get Magwitch out of England is foiled by an old enemy of his; Magwitch is mortally wounded in the attempt. But Pip's resentment and repugnance have melted away, and he stays with Magwitch to the end. Coming out of a serious illness brought on by all the stress he has been through, Pip finds work in the firm that in his expectant days he had secretly enabled Herbert Pocket to become a partner in—an outcome of the one good thing he undertook in those days of illusion. He returns years later to his home village to visit Joe and his second wife, Biddy, and chances to meet Estella at the ruins of Miss Havisham's house; she is a widow, and she and Pip it appears will get on, both of them the wiser for their travail. — This is the published ending; in the original ending suppressed by Dickens, Pip runs across Estella in London some years after her husband's death, and they exchange some few words—enough to recognize that they are the wiser for their travail—and part.

The plot furnishes plenty of mystery and suspense—the identity of Pip's benefactor, the sense of *déjà vu* Pip experiences in the grown-up Estella's presence, the complications attendant on Magwitch's appearance in London. There is also an extraordinary degree of coincidence, in the history of Magwitch's indirect connection with Miss Havisham's unhappy betrothal, and in the identity of Estella. The role of the lawyer Jaggers keeps this acceptable; furthermore, coincidence has less the appearance here of unlikely chance than of strands in a web of enclosing and determining circumstance, harmonizing with the atmosphere of prison that Pip feels clinging about him. Much of that atmosphere, however, is of his own making, since it is a consequence of his snobbish desire to escape his origins (in order to be worthy, as he fancies, of Estella: a considerable irony, in view of her true parentage). The shades of prison that haunt Pip, in fact, turn out really to be cast by his superficial notions of gentility; when he learns better, he is free.

Our Mutual Friend. The mutual friend is John Harmon, heir to a fortune amassed by a garbage contractor and apparently found drowned as the story opens; he is known as John Rokesmith through most of the story, but his real identity is disclosed to the reader before the halfway point in the novel. He is the "mutual friend" of Noddy Boffin, who so calls him, and the Wilfers. He has applied to be Boffin's secretary, and he lodges with the Wilfers. His interest in the Wilfers is that under the terms of his father's will his inheritance depends on his marrying Bella Wilfer, whom he does not know, and he wants to observe her before deciding whether to come to life again. The Boffins worked for old Harmon, and as heirs to the fortune after John, are in possession of the estate. Goodhearted and unpretentious, the Boffins decide to share their good fortune with Bella, and take her to live with them. She is a spirited girl who resents having been a toy of someone's will, and partly from such resentment and partly from frankly mercenary considerations she rejects the interest of the lowly secretary Rokesmith: her expectations qualify her for a higher level of suitor now than he.

The society which beckons to her is the showy but insubstantial Veneering circle, populated by nouveau-riche seekers of status and power: they try to ingratiate themselves with the aristocracy, among them Podsnappery finds favor and mere adventurers thrive, and every now and then some member of the circle crashes into bankruptcy, revealing the shakiness of the whole structure. Bella is saved from her own folly by the strategem of Boffin, who pretends to be transformed by the influence of wealth into a bullying old miser. Her distress at what she thinks is happening is strong enough to turn her back from the path she has chosen, to accept the love of Rokesmith, who has been in on the scheme all along. The Boffins are delighted to relinquish the inheritance to John Harmon and return to their old ways.

A parallel rescue is effected by Lizzie Hexam, the daughter of the river scavenger who found the body supposed to be Harmon's, upon Eugene Wrayburn, another of Dickens's talented but lounging aimless young men. His attraction to Lizzie has the seeds of real love in it, and she is drawn to him as well, but he would drift into the usual way of the upper middle class young man with a working class girl if it were not for Lizzie's strength of character. He has an enemy (though not a rival, since Lizzie fears and dislikes him), the dogged schoolmaster Bradley Headstone, whose respectable exterior conceals a passionate and desperate will. Wrayburn is at crisis, trying to resolve the conflict between his true feeling for Lizzie and the social cost of marrying her, when Headstone attacks him and leaves him for dead. Lizzie nurses him as he lingers between life and death; in this condition he comes to a better awareness than he had in health, and he signifies his desire to marry Lizzie. He recovers; never a devotee of the Veneerings really, he forsakes the circle without regret.

The Veneering circle is to *Our Mutual Friend* about what the Merdle swindle is to *Little Dorrit*, an emblem of what is wrong, created and sustained by the operations of human nature in the system of mid-nineteenth-century England. Parallel in importance for the action, and in a sense underpinning Veneering society as an emblem of the economic foundation on which it is raised, are the Harmon dust mounds, the garbage which is the Harmon wealth. Among the characteristic array of supporting actors, the penniless Lammles try to attach themselves to well-off members of the Veneering circle; lower down, Silas Wegg, a street seller of popular ballads, imposes (for a while) on Boffin. Two of the deserving poor set off the falseness of such people: crippled Jenny Wren, the dolls' dressmaker whose drunkard father is her "bad child"; and Betty Higden, indomitable at eighty, and determined to die on her own terms rather than submit to workhouse degradation. The epitome of patient merit however is Lizzie Hexam, another of Dickens's young women who embody the power of charity that seeketh not her own; she cannot transform the invincible selfishness of her brother Charley, but she is the salvation of Eugene Wrayburn.

Notes and References

Chapter One

1. *Moments of Being*, ed. Jeanne Schulkind (New York: Harcourt Brace Jovanovich, 1976), p. 73.

2. For the composite work see *Charles Dickens' Uncollected Writings from "Household Words" 1850–1859*, ed. Harry Stone, 2 vols. (Bloomington: Indiana University Press, 1968). Information Stone used from the *HW* Contributors' (or "Office") Book has since been published in *Household Words, A Weekly Journal 1850–1859 . . . . Table of Contents, List of Contributors, and their Contributions*, comp. Anne Lohrli (Toronto: University of Toronto Press, 1973).

3. *The Letters of Charles Dickens*, Pilgrim Edition, ed. Madeline House, Graham Storey, and Kathleen Tillotson (Oxford: Clarendon, 1965–), III, 591 (2 November 1843); *The Letters of Charles Dickens*, Nonesuch Edition, ed. Walter Dexter (Bloomsbury: Nonesuch, 1938), II, 649 (3 April 1855). Cited hereafter as Pilgrim (abbreviated P) and Nonesuch (abbreviated N).

4. Gladys Storey, *Dickens and Daughter* (London: Frederick Muller, 1939), p. 100.

5. John Forster, *The Life of Charles Dickens*, 2 vols. (London: Chapman and Hall, 1876), I, v, 76. Cited hereafter as Forster (abbreviated F). Dickens wrote to Georgina Hogarth in November 1867 about a certain book that it was "very remarkable . . . for *its suggestion of wheels within wheels*, and sad human mysteries" (N III, 567; my italics).

6. His experiments in mesmerism are a manifestation of this; see Fred Kaplan, *Dickens and Mesmerism* (Princeton: Princeton University Press, 1975). See also the series of letters in September 1861 about his having intuited the date of an alleged supernatural incident (N III, 235–39). Dickens's strong interest in magic, attested by such a letter as he wrote Forster in October 1854 (F VII, iv, 599–600) and by his own skill as an amateur magician, is perhaps part of this complex of interests too.

7. 6 October 1859; my italics except "suggest" (N III, 124–25).

It is intriguing that Woolf says (p. 73) her thoughts have turned to Dickens just now because she is reading *Nicholas Nickleby*—certainly not one of Dickens's more complexly patterned novels. That she should be reading Dickens late in her life (1939–40, according to the editor of *Moments of Being*, p. 61) is interesting in itself; as a young girl she would have heard from her father Leslie Stephen that Dickens's "merits are such as suit the half-educated" (to quote his article in the *Dictionary of National Biography*), and very likely that Dickens had satirized her grandfather in *Little Dorrit* (C. P. Snow, "Dickens and the Public Service," in *Dickens 1970*, ed. Michael Slater [London: Chapman and Hall, 1970], p. 133).

8. See Forster I, ii, 35 and I, iii, 49 for Dickens's assessments of the shoeblacking warehouse experience and of his frustrated romance.

9. *The World of Charles Dickens* (New York: Viking, 1970), p. 118. Cited hereafter as *Dickens*.

10. *Little Dorrit* II, 1. Dickens remembered the dead travelers from his own trip to the monastery in September 1846 (P IV, 619).

11. Geoffrey Thurley calls this "animistic expressionism" in *The Dickens Myth* (London: Routledge, 1976), p. 74; it is of course John Ruskin's "pathetic fallacy," which, as Dorothy Van Ghent says, Dickens used constantly. She discusses it with something like Dickensian intensity in her chapter on *Great Expectations* in *The English Novel: Form and Function* (New York: Rinehart, 1953), pp. 129–33; see also her essay (often cited in the 1950s and 1960s) "The Dickens World: A View from Todgers," *Sewanee Review* 58 (1950): 419–38.

12. "Expectations Well Lost: Dickens' Fable for His Time," *College English* 16 (1954–55): 13.

13. *Soliloquies in England and Other Soliloquies* (London: Constable, 1922), pp. 65–66; quoted from Edgar Johnson, *Charles Dickens: His Tragedy and Triumph*, 2 vols. (New York: Simon and Schuster, 1952), p. 1138. I cite this biography hereafter as Johnson (abbreviated J).

14. William Axton, *Circle of Fire* (Lexington: University of Kentucky Press, 1966); Robert Garis, *The Dickens Theatre* (Oxford: Clarendon, 1965). See also Sylvère Monod, *Dickens the Novelist* (Norman: University of Oklahoma Press, 1968), pp. 39–44, 343, and elsewhere. (A translation and revision by the author of his *Dickens Romancier* published in 1953.)

15. "But let us not lose the use of Dickens's wit and insight, because he chooses to speak in a circle of stage fire" (*Unto This Last*, in *Cornhill Magazine* 2 [1860]: 159; reprinted in book form in 1862. Quoted from *Dickens: The Critical Heritage*, ed. Philip Collins [London: Routledge, 1971], p. 314).

16. On the grotesque style, Axton draws on Wolfgang Kayser, *The Grotesque in Art and Literature*, trans. Ulrich Weisstein (Bloomington: Indiana University Press, 1963). Arthur Clayborough's *The Grotesque in English Literature* (Oxford: Clarendon, 1965), published too late for Axton to have seen, has been favorably noticed by Philip Collins in his essay on Dickens in *Victorian Fiction: A Second Guide to Research*, ed. George H. Ford (New York: Modern Language Association, 1978), p. 66.

17. "The Comedy of Dickens," in *Dickens 1970*, p. 10. Dickens himself speaks of "the desperate intensity of my nature" (F I, iii, 49), though he means there a general quality of temperament, not specifically of imagination.

18. So Robert Buchanan, reviewing the first volume of Forster's biography in 1872: "We see the mightiness of the genius and its limitations.... He was a great, grown-up, dreamy, impulsive child [etc.]" (*Critical Heritage*, pp. 578–79); and Virginia Woolf: "Dickens owes his astonishing power to make characters alive to the fact that he saw them as a child sees them . . ." (*Moments*, p. 73); and Norman and Jeanne MacKenzie: "Caught emotionally at the threshold of adolescence, he kept transacting the unfinished business of his youth in his writings as if he might there discover some ending that had escaped him in ordinary life" (*Dickens: A Life* [New York and Oxford: Oxford University Press, 1979], p. 212).

19. *Critical Heritage*, p. 571. Lewes's essay, "Dickens in Relation to Criticism" (another review of Forster), was published in *Fortnightly Review* in February 1872. Collins prints a generous portion (*Critical Heritage*, pp. 569–77).

20. Like Pip while Orlick's prisoner (*GE* 53) and at the taking of Magwitch (*GE* 54); and like Mr. Lorry and Dr. Manette seeing the terrible mob, sharpening their bloody weapons, "in a moment, as the vision of a drowning man, or of any human creature at any very great pass, could see a world if it were there" (*TTC* III, 2). I owe the reminder of the latter passage to G. Robert Stange, "Dickens and the Fiery Past: *A Tale of Two Cities* Reconsidered," *English Journal* 46 (1957): 387. – The Christmas story is "The Perils of Certain English Prisoners." The quotation is from ch. 1, "The Island of Silver-Store." Dickens also wrote the third and final chapter; Wilkie Collins wrote the second (Lohrli, p. 174).

21. *Pickwick Papers* 34 (quoted by Allen, "The Comedy of Dickens," p. 19).

22. See for example Dickens's letter about a play he saw in Paris in 1855 (F VII, v, 604–605) and his letter about a Boulogne magician (referred to in n. 6 above). Macready is described in a letter of 15

February 1869 which I quote below (p. 62), and the negotiations in a letter of 5 March 1839 (P I, 518–20).

23. For example, G. L. Brook, *The Language of Dickens* (London: André Deutsch, 1970), pp. 30–36. Clayborough notes this kind of ability in Swift (*The Grotesque*, p. 139); on Dickens and Swift see below, p. 204.

24. *The Speeches of Charles Dickens,* ed. K. J. Fielding (Oxford: Clarendon, 1960), p. xx.

25. Forster II, i, 86. My account here is based on Johnson III, chs. i, iv, v and IV, ii; and on the calendar of Dickens's serial writings in *Charles Dickens: A Critical Anthology*, ed. Stephen Wall (Harmonds-worth: Penguin, 1970), pp. 528–36. Wall's information is from K. J. Fielding's articles "The Monthly Serialisation of Dickens's Novels" and "The Weekly Serialisation of Dickens's Novels" (*Dickensian* 54 [1958]: 4–11, 134–41).

26. Johnson II, iii and III, i, ii, v. It is not clear that Mary was "a permanent guest in the household" (J 133) from the first; certainly she was not in May 1836 (P I, 65n, 689). But the evidence of Dickens's letters to friends about her death (P I, 256–68) is against F. S. Schwarzbach's opinion that "Mary Hogarth lived with the family for only a few weeks before her death . . ." (*Dickens and the City* [London: Athlone Press, 1979], p. 240n). — 48 Doughty Street is now Dickens House, a Dickens museum and library maintained by the Dickens Fellowship.

27. Johnson, p. 193, quoting Frederick G. Kitton, *The Novels of Charles Dickens* (1897), p. 29.

28. Pilgrim II, 141n.; cited from a letter quoted in J. A. Froude, *Thomas Carlyle, A History of His Life in London, 1834–1881* (1884), I, 177. The whole passage is somewhat condescending; Carlyle's full acceptance of Dickens came later.

29. Johnson, p. 370, quoting unpublished letters.

30. Forster II, i, 92–93. The Pilgrim editors say Forster often tinkered with Dickens's wording, but "had his subject remarkably in perspective," and in his "numerous small distortions of fact" had his eye on "a larger, or ideal, truth" (p. xi). The image of Dickens seems authentic here, and I have quoted Forster instead of searching for the Pilgrim texts (Forster gives no dates).

31. Forster III, v, 249 and II, xi, 186–88.

32. 3 August 1857 (N II, 867–68). Harry Stone quotes this letter in his account of the editorial labors Dickens makes so light of here (*Uncollected Writings*, p. 29).

33. Storey, pp. 77–78; Henry Fielding Dickens, *Memories of My Father* (London: Duffield, 1929), p. 25. Dickens described the boys'

regimen himself in a letter to a friend of Miss Coutts (5 July 1856); see *The Heart of Charles Dickens: As Revealed in His Letters to Angela Burdett-Coutts*, ed. Edgar Johnson (Boston: Little, Brown, 1952), p. 320. Cited hereafter as Burdett-Coutts.

34. Johnson, p. 1151, quoting from Frederick G. Kitton, *Charles Dickens by Pen and Pencil* (1889–90), Supp., pp. 30–31.

35. Storey, p. 106.

36. "Dickens on Children and Childhood," *Dickens 1970*, pp. 226–27.

37. 13 December 1856 (N II, 815); quoted by Stone, *Uncollected Writings*, p. 29.

Chapter Two

1. The phrase is from a letter of mid-April to John Macrone (P I, 147); internal evidence disproves the July date indicated by Johnson (J 149).—I owe notice of this correction to the MacKenzies' *Dickens: A Life*, p. 43.

2. *Dickens at Work* (London: Methuen, 1957), p. 36.

3. Ibid., p. 63. Robert L. Patten's chapter entitled "*Pickwick Papers* and the Development of Serial Fiction" in his *Charles Dickens and His Publishers* (Oxford: Clarendon, 1978) is authoritative and comprehensive, setting this "revolution in publishing" in the perspective of "a long, complex, and accelerating series of developments" (p. 46) in the economics of publishing and the technology of printing. — The circulating libraries defended their business by keeping the expensive three-volume format standard until nearly the end of the century. See Royal A. Gettmann, *A Victorian Publisher: A Study of the Bentley Papers* (Cambridge: Cambridge University Press, 1960), ch. VIII, "The Three-Decker"; the fullest account is of course Guinevere L. Griest, *Mudie's Circulating Library and the Victorian Novel* (Bloomington: Indiana University Press, 1970).

4. Archibald Coolidge in *Charles Dickens as Serial Novelist* (Ames: Iowa State University Press, 1967) argues that the serial format *evoked* Dickens's style: "His installments required packing with incidents" (p. 59) to keep up reader interest across the intervals between parts; Dickens therefore multiplied his plots, worked up a wide variety of stock characters, and developed improvisation as a deliberate technique, controlling the whole mass by masterly ordering of parts. (Coolidge's main argument is in ch. 4, pp. 49–58.) There is surely something to this; having space to fill generates filler, as any teacher knows (leaving aside any question of quality). Coolidge ends, however, by making out something most people feel is of the

essence in Dickens to be a consequence of the form he published in. Arguing that the monthly serial required this fullness, Coolidge points out that Dickens's novels published in weekly installments are much leaner (p. 51). But surely Dickens's complaints to Forster about the narrow space weekly installments gave him to work in make sense only if we think of fullness, copiousness, as his natural mode of creation.

5. See below, p. 75.

6. Pilgrim I, 150, 654; Johnson, pp. 792–93; Forster IX, iii, 733.

7. Nonesuch II, 422; quoted in *Uncollected Writings*, p. 663.

8. Nonesuch II, 710; *Uncollected Writings*, p. 541.

9. 31 July and 9 August to Wills (N III, 661–62).

10. Forster IX, i, 719–20; also *Critical Heritage*, p. 574.

11. *Victorian Novelists and Their Illustrators* (London: Sidgwick and Jackson, 1970), pp. 8, 12. Harvey thinks the novelists publishing in illustrated monthly parts were really in "the Hogarthian tradition of graphic satire" (p. 43), and constitute "a remarkable demonstration of a great imaginative mode moving out of one art and into another" (p. 75). On Dickens and the tradition of graphic satire see also F. R. and Q. D. Leavis, *Dickens the Novelist* (London: Chatto and Windus, 1970), pp. 332–35.

Household Words and *All the Year Round* used no graphics, so the novels Dickens published in those periodicals—*Hard Times, A Tale of Two Cities,* and *Great Expectations*—were not illustrated in their first published form, although *A Tale of Two Cities* was illustrated very shortly after by Hablot Browne in the monthly part format. But all the rest appeared in print furnished with two illustrations per installment (as a rule; *Pickwick Papers* began with four, but the number was reduced to two after Seymour's death; and occasionally installments of *Barnaby Rudge* had only one illustration). — Browne, as noted earlier, did more of this work than anyone else. George Cruikshank was well known on his own account when he illustrated first *Sketches by Boz* and then *Oliver Twist.* John Leech, Clarkson Stanfield, Daniel Maclise, and Richard Doyle did most of the Christmas books. Marcus Stone did *Great Expectations,* when it was published in volume form, and *Our Mutual Friend* and several others as they were reprinted in editions of the 1860s. These were the main illustrators, out of nearly two dozen who worked with Dickens at one time or another (Thomas Hatton, "A Bibliographical List of the Original Illustrations to the Works of Charles Dickens: Being Those Made under His Supervision," *Nonesuch Dickensian: Retrospectus and Prospectus* [Bloomsbury: Nonesuch, 1937]).

12. Nonesuch II, 17–18; quoted and discussed by Alan Horsman

in the Clarendon *Dombey and Son* (Oxford, 1974), pp. 868–69, and by Butt and Tillotson in *Dickens at Work*, pp. 17–19 (their italics, for phrases Dickens drew "with little verbal change" from the chapter he was then writing). For other examples, see letters to George Cattermole about illustrations for *The Old Curiosity Shop* (P II, 170–72).

13. Butt and Tillotson discuss the *Dombey* and *Little Dorrit* covers in *Dickens at Work*, pp. 92–94, 224–26. — Michael Steig proves that Dickens must have given Browne "quite explicit directions" for the cover of *Bleak House*; quite a few characters in the design are identifiable, and there are clear allusions to incidents well on in the story (*Dickens and Phiz* [Bloomington: Indiana University Press, 1978], pp. 132–33). However, Steig is less convincing in his argument that "the only element structurally opposed" in the design to the image there of Chancery as a game of blindman's buff (the figure of John Jarndyce at bottom center, facing away from the blindmen at the top) "is not really a very hopeful one" (p. 134). But this posture represents more than Jarndyce's "habitual denial of the unpleasant"— turning away from what Chancery represents is to face toward meaningful life. Nor is the wind clearly from the east (traditionally a bad omen, and Jarndyce's image for a distressing state of affairs) in the design—according to the weathervane it is, but not according to the smoke from the chimneys.—See "Theme," in ch. 5.

14. *Dickens and Phiz*, pp. 15, 139.

15. The foregoing summary is drawn from Johnson, passim. The fullest narrative of Dickens's part in the founding of the *Daily News* is in Johnson (VI, vii); see also Patten, *Charles Dickens and His Publishers*, pp. 163–69. The MacKenzies' account is less sympathetic to Dickens (*Dickens: A Life*, pp. 170–82).

16. He also contributed some articles to the *Examiner*, mostly in the 1840s during the editorship of his friend Forster, who also (as editor of the *Daily News* following Dickens's resignation) printed some of the "Travelling Sketches" published as *Pictures from Italy*.

17. Johnson, p. 304; Patten, *Charles Dickens and His Publishers*, p. 110; both rely on Kitton, *The Novels of Charles Dickens*, p. 64. About keeping the *Clock* going, see below, p. 75.

18. Dickens was also smarting at being bound to contractual terms appropriate when he made them, but totally inappropriate even a few months later. — A brief account of Dickens's relations with Bentley is in Stone's introduction to *Uncollected Writings*, pp. 6–8; my analysis agrees substantially with his. Johnson devotes a chapter to the subject (III, iv); so does Patten (ch. 4).

19. Johnson, pp. 262, 702, 945; the text of the agreement for *Master Humphrey's Clock* is in Pilgrim II, 464–71. — Wills earned

his share; the MacKenzies judge that Dickens "was often too rushed to edit *Household Words* with care" (*Dickens: A Life*, p. 248).

20. *Critical Heritage*, p. 570.

21. Johnson, pp. 151–54, 191, 223–24, 310.

22. Johnson, p. 866. Robert Louis Brannan's analysis of Dickens's work on the play confirms this (*Under the Management of Mr. Charles Dickens: His Production of "The Frozen Deep"* [Ithaca: Cornell University Press, 1966], pp. 22–49).

23. Johnson, pp. 735–36, 842–43, 865–66, 1072, 1098–99.

24. My account is based on K. J. Fielding's introduction to his edition of the *Speeches*.

25. Fielding, p. xx, citing the Duke of Argyll's recollection of an 1855 speech in his *Autobiography and Memoirs,* ed. the dowager Duchess of Argyll (London: J. Murray, 1906), I, 416–17.

26. 15 February 1869 to Fields (N III, 704). That particular reading appears to have had a peculiar fascination for Dickens, and a particular horror for his hearers. Dickens insisted on doing it despite the strain it put him under, and against the advice of Forster, his manager Dolby, and son Charles (J 1102–1105).

27. *Charles Dickens: The Public Readings* (Oxford: Clarendon, 1975), pp. liii–lxiii (Carlyle is quoted on p. lv). Collins has concluded, however, from newspaper accounts of the particular occasion, that biographers have misread Forster (XI, i, 801) in assuming that the famous "contagion of fainting" with "a dozen to twenty ladies taken out stiff and rigid" shows how powerful Dickens's dramatization of Nancy's murder was; it happened during his readings that evening from *David Copperfield* and *Pickwick Papers* (p. 470). The passage in Forster, without other evidence, certainly does seem to be about the "Murder" (as Dickens always called it). — My account of Dickens's readings follows Collins.

28. *Charles Dickens As I Knew Him* (1885), pp. 331–32, 450–51 (as cited in J 1146 and Collins, p. xxix). Dickens's full profits from the tour were nearly £38,000, but his determination to bring home gold instead of the paper money he distrusted cost him nearly 40 percent (Collins). I am at a loss to turn this into a contemporary equivalent. Weighing the case for an American tour, and allowing for the cost of converting to gold, Dickens counted seven dollars to the pound (N III, 554); but calculating actual expenses to Forster in April 1868 he figured three dollars (F XI, i, 798). Further, one must consider what a dollar bought in 1868.

29. Collins notes that Dickens echoed this phrasing in a letter to Forster three years later, about the success of the 1861 reading tour (p. xxii, n. 1; F VIII, vi, 689).

30. James A. Davies, "Striving for Honesty: An Approach to Forster's Life" (*Dickens Studies Annual* 7 [1978]: 47. — An excellent article in defense of Forster's biography).

31. Dolby, p. 451, quoted by Collins, pp. xxix–xxx.

Chapter Three

1. "The Monthly Serialisation of Dickens's Novels," p. 4. Other critics important in this are of course John Butt and Kathleen Tillotson, whose *Dickens at Work* has stimulated many others to similar study, and Sylvère Monod, in *Dickens the Novelist*. In *Charles Dickens as Serial Novelist*, Archibald Coolidge categorizes stock characters, incidents, and motifs in Dickens, and illustrates various patterns of story material in Dickens's individual installments (appendixes 2 and 3).

2. *Great Expectations*, ed. Louis Crompton (Indianapolis: Bobbs-Merrill, 1964), p. xxix. Angus Calder says much the same about "sensational climaxes" in his introduction to *Great Expectations* (Harmondsworth: Penguin English Library, 1965): "Dickens ends many of his serial parts on a note of suspense, in the best cliff-hanging tradition" (p. 32). So do the MacKenzies (*Dickens: A Life*, p. 57).

3. Quoted by Butt and Tillotson, p. 19, from a letter of 21 May 1855 to Mrs. Richard Watson (not printed in N).

4. This, I think, explains more about his struggles beginning *Dombey* than the reason George Ford gives: "loss of nerve" because of *Chuzzlewit*'s disappointing sales (*Dickens and His Readers* [Princeton: Princeton University Press, 1955], p. 49).

5. Forster VIII, iii, 656. Forster remarks on this trait often: see for example II, iii, 111; viii, 159; and VIII, ii, 636.

6. I lack space to quote the passage, which conveys a vivid image of Dickens's working style even though the Pilgrim editors show Forster's montage is inaccurate as to dates and even subjects (P I, 343–44, 425, 439, 471).

7. Mamie Dickens, *My Father As I Recall Him* (New York, 1898), p. 69; Thomas Wright, *The Life of Charles Dickens* (London: Herbert Jenkins, 1935), p. 311.

8. *My Father*, p. 68. Except as otherwise noted, I draw here on this work, pp. 68–69, and Butt and Tillotson, pp. 20–24.

9. The interval between the first and second installments of *The Old Curiosity Shop* (25 April–16 May 1840), concerning which see the next section, "The Influence of Readers' Response"; and June and October 1837. Mary Hogarth's death distracted Dickens in May, and strained relations with Bentley at least partly account for the October

suspension of *Oliver Twist*. See Kathleen Tillotson's introduction to the Clarendon *Oliver Twist* (Oxford, 1966), pp. xix–xx.

10. *Dickens at Work*, pp. 24–34 and ch. 6, pp. 114–76. The Oxford Clarendon edition of *David Copperfield* by Nina Burgis also prints the number plans. Other number plans that have been published include those for *Dombey and Son, Little Dorrit,* and *The Mystery of Edwin Drood,* in the Clarendon editions by Alan Horsman, Harvey Peter Sucksmith, and Margaret Cardwell respectively; *Bleak House* and *Hard Times,* in the Norton Critical Editions by George Ford and Sylvère Monod; and *Our Mutual Friend,* by Ernest Boll in "The Plotting of *Our Mutual Friend*," *Modern Philology* 42 (1944): 96–122. The plans for *Little Dorrit* also appear in R. D. McMaster's edition of that novel (Toronto: Macmillan, 1969); and those for *Bleak House* in the Crowell Critical Library Edition by Duane DeVries (New York: Crowell, 1971) and earlier in Sucksmith's article "Dickens at Work on *Bleak House*," *Renaissance and Modern Studies* 9 (1965): 47–85. Forster prints facsimiles of the plans for the first numbers of *David Copperfield* and *Little Dorrit* (VIII, i, 624).

11. Introd., *The Mystery of Edwin Drood,* ed. Arthur J. Cox (Harmondsworth: Penguin English Library, 1974), p. 12. — One might argue that Dickens did not improvise his plot resolutions, that he had those previous events in mind all along, but that he was no good at Hemingway's method: not saying what you know about the characters that makes them act as they do.

12. Johnson, pp. 297–98, 453–55, 674–75.

13. Butt and Tillotson imply that Mrs. Hill, a professional chiropodist and manicurist, threatened legal action (p. 141). As to why Mrs. Hill was insulted, see ch. 4, n. 20 below, on the meaning of the name "Mowcher."

14. " 'The Story-Weaver at His Loom': Dickens and the Beginning of *The Old Curiosity Shop*," in *Dickens the Craftsman,* ed. Robert B. Partlow, Jr. (Carbondale: Southern Illinois University Press, 1970), pp. 44–64.

15. Forster II, vii, 151; 24 November 1840 to Chapman and Hall (P II, 153).

16. Crompton in his introduction (see n. 2), for one: "Both endings convey the same painful sense of loss and both imply the same consolation: the 'hero' is free at last from the world of guilty terrors and the world of idle dreams" (p. xx). See also John H. Hagan, Jr., "Structural Patterns in *Great Expectations*," *English Literary History* 21 (1954): 65–66; and for an especially full and thoughtful treatment of the relative appropriateness of both endings, Robert A. Greenberg,

"On Ending *Great Expectations*," *Papers on Language and Literature* 6 (1970): 152–62. On grounds suggested by his title, William H. Marshall thinks the original ending is the only possible one ("The Conclusion of *Great Expectations* as the Fulfillment of Myth," *Personalist* 44 [1963]: 337–47). — This is by no means an exhaustive bibliography of articles on the topic, and it leaves out any reference to remarks in broader studies. Let this note stand for the kind of sidelight that could be turned on any number of critical cruxes in Dickens.

17. *An Autobiography* (1883), ch. 8; quoted in Kathleen Tillotson, *Novels of the Eighteen-Forties*, corrected edition (Oxford: Clarendon, 1956), p. 40.

18. I use one of the examples most widely available, the plans for *David Copperfield* in Butt and Tillotson, pp. 116–73.

19. *Novels of the Eighteen-Forties*, p. 45. Tillotson's remark (published in 1954) still could not go without saying a decade later, however, as the comments I quoted at the beginning of the chapter show.

20. *Dickens as Serial Novelist*, pp. 56–57 and Appendix 3.

21. *Great Expectations* (39, which closes the second stage of Pip's expectations); *Hard Times* (28, as serialized in *Household Words*; II ["Reaping"], 12, as renumbered for the one-volume edition).

22. Letter of 31 January 1847, quoted by Butt and Tillotson (p. 101n) from Lord Cockburn, *Life of Lord Jeffrey* (1852), II, 407. Jeffrey was one of those who wanted more sentiment and less satire from Dickens. The success of this "repeat performance" in recapturing Little Nell's mourners held a risk implied in Jeffrey's question: that they would find what followed anticlimactic. The low sales of Dickens's next, *David Copperfield*, probably shows they did (Ford, *Dickens and His Readers*, pp. 58–59).

23. Forster, VII, i, 565 and ii, 568; VIII, i, 623; IX, ii, 729. The simulated title pages are printed in both Crowell and Norton editions of *Bleak House* (see n. 10 above).

24. Crowell edition, pp. 833–41; Norton edition, pp. 778–79.

25. *My Father*, pp. 49–50.

26. Quoted in Philip Collins, *Dickens and Crime* (London, 1962; rpt. Bloomington: Indiana University Press, 1968), p. 1, from *Things I Have Seen and People I Have Known* (1894), I, 76.

27. See also George J. Worth's persuasive argument for an August 1851 book review in *Household Words* as a source ("The Genesis of Jo the Crossing-Sweeper," *Journal of English and Germanic Philology* 60 [1961]: 44–47).

28. Butt and Tillotson, pp. 195, 197–98.

Chapter Four

1. Harvey Peter Sucksmith, *The Narrative Art of Charles Dickens* (Oxford: Clarendon, 1970), p. 44.

2. See, for example, reviews of *Little Dorrit* ("Remonstrance with Dickens," *Blackwood's Magazine*: "We appeal from the author of *Bleak House* and *Little Dorrit* to the author of *Pickwick*, the *Old Curiosity Shop*, and the better parts of *Chuzzlewit*") and *Our Mutual Friend* (Henry James in *The Nation*: "It is the letter of his old humor without the spirit"). But one reviewer complained as early as *Martin Chuzzlewit* ("Boz *versus* Dickens," *Parker's London Magazine*: "Mr Dickens has very much changed, since, as Boz the unknown, he took captive the admiration of all classes of readers.... The style of Dickens—that which distinguishes him from Boz—is laboured and artificial, as unlike the easy natural style of the latter as a statue is unlike a living, moving man"). — *Great Expectations* (1860–61) was "welcomed with vociferous relief," according to Philip Collins, quoting the *Saturday Review* (not usually enthusiastic about Dickens): "*Great Expectations* restores Mr Dickens and his readers to the old level. It is in his best vein, ... quite worthy to stand beside *Martin Chuzzlewit* and *David Copperfield*" (*Critical Heritage*, p. 427. The reviews I have quoted from are all in this collection, items 102, 131, and 48, respectively).

3. I quote from Williams's introduction to *Dombey and Son*, ed. Peter Fairclough (Harmondsworth: Penguin English Library, 1970), p. 11. For Dickens's advice to contributors, see his letters to Collins (7 January 1860 [N III, 145]) and to Mrs. Brookfield (20 February 1866 [N III, 461–62]), whom he advises against telling her story *"in a sort of impetuous breathless way, in your own person.... My notion always is, that when I have made the people to play out the play, it is, as it were, their business to do it, and not mine."*

4. *The Craft of Fiction* (London, 1921; rpt. New York: Peter Smith, 1947), pp. 215–16.

5. James R. Kincaid, *Dickens and the Rhetoric of Laughter* (Oxford: Clarendon, 1971); Garrett Stewart, *Dickens and the Trials of Imagination* (Cambridge: Harvard University Press, 1974). For Axton and Garis, see ch. 1, n. 14.

6. *The Rhetoric of Fiction* (Chicago: University of Chicago Press, 1961).

7. See Brook, *The Language of Dickens*, and Randolph Quirk, "Charles Dickens, Linguist," in his *The Linguist and the English Language* (London: Edward Arnold, 1974). Quirk's chapter is "a conflation, revision and expansion of two earlier studies" (p. 1n):

Charles Dickens and Appropriate Language (Durham: University of Durham, 1959) and "Some Observations on the Language of Dickens," *Review of English Literature* 2, no. 3 (July 1961): 19–28.

8. Walter Allen makes this point about the difficulty of presenting Dickens's comic characters fairly: "To quote speeches from the Wellers, Pecksniff, Mrs. Gamp, Podsnap and the rest . . . takes no account . . . of their cumulative effect. It ignores, also, the contexts in which they appear, . . . characterized by quite extraordinary density of specification, to use James's phrase. They are at the centre of crowded scenes, of great set pieces of wonderfully sustained comic drama . . ." ("The Comedy of Dickens," in *Dickens 1970*, p. 26). See also below, pp. 103–4.

9. Let these two passages and the passage from *Dombey and Son* (1) quoted earlier in this chapter illustrate another failing of Dickens's high-flown style, often noted by his contemporaries as well as by more recent critics: he would fall into something like blank verse. Dickens knew this about himself; in 1846 he wrote Forster, "If in going over the proofs [of *The Battle of Life*] you find the tendency to blank verse (I *cannot* help it, when I am very much in earnest) too strong, knock out a word's brains here and there" (F V, vi, 439).

10. See the Preface to Pilgrim II, p. xii, where House and Storey argue convincingly against any lingering "emotional obsession" with Mary's death. Dickens's letter to Forster written while he was writing Nell's death is especially revealing (?8 January 1841 [P II, 181–82, 182n]).

11. See Johnson, p. 303, and the letters to Forster and others that he quotes, dated from 3 November 1840 to 17 January 1841 (P II, 144–88).

12. Quoted from Hesketh Pearson, *Oscar Wilde: His Life and Wit* (New York: Harper, 1946), p. 208. But the reason Wilde's joke occurred to me at this point is surely that George Ford used it to open his penetrating chapter "Little Nell: The Limits of Explanatory Criticism," in *Dickens and His Readers*.

13. Dickens's letter of July 1848 describing his visit to his sister Fanny, dying of consumption, is written in great simplicity of style, and conveys a depth of emotion that his superlatives miss (F VI, vi, 521–22).

14. *A Kind of Power: The Shakespeare-Dickens Analogy* (Philadelphia: American Philosophical Society, 1975), p. xi.

15. See especially in *Reprinted Pieces* "Down with the Tide" (*HW* 5 February 1853) and a significant paragraph in "On Duty with Inspector Field" (*HW* 14 June 1851). Death by drowning figures in these, and in three *All the Year Round* pieces collected in *The Un-*

commercial Traveller: incidentally in "Wapping Workhouse" and "Travelling Abroad," and more prominently in "Some Recollections of Mortality." In somewhat the same way, Dickens was obsessively interested in the Arctic tragedy of Sir John Franklin's lost polar expedition; two *Household Words* articles on the subject in December 1854 are identified as his work in the Contributors' Book, and it was the inspiration for the play he and Wilkie Collins collaborated on in 1856–57, *The Frozen Deep*. This was about the time Dickens's marriage was becoming unbearable to him: I suggest that he took the image of death in frozen wastelands metaphorically to heart. See George Woodcock's introduction to *A Tale of Two Cities* (Harmondsworth: Penguin English Library, 1970), pp. 9–11.

16. See also K. J. Fielding, "The Critical Autonomy of 'Great Expectations,'" *Review of English Literature* 2, no. 3 (July 1961): 79–80.

17. Similarly, critical preoccupation with the symbolism of the dust mounds in *Our Mutual Friend* owes more to Humphry House's description of them than to Dickens. See Robert Barnard, *Imagery and Theme in the Novels of Dickens* (Oslo: Universitetsforlaget, 1974), p. 125.

18. "Dickens and the Symbol," in *Dickens 1970*, pp. 63–64.

19. Except for my treatment of names from *David Copperfield*, I owe much of what follows to C. A. Bodelsen's discriminating article "The Physiognomy of the Name," *Review of English Literature* 2, no. 3 (July 1961): 39–48.

20. According to OED, *mowche* is an old spelling of the verb form of *moocher*, or *moucher*, "one who loiters about, a loafer"; the phonetic value now usually given to *-ow* conceals the unsavory implications of the name. Supporting citations in OED from 1862, 1878, and later show that the moocher mooches about on the prowl for whatever looks worth laying hands on. Thus Miss Mowcher begins as a wandering hairdresser and manicurist, and possibly a procuress for Steerforth. (Forster, by the way, spells the name "Moucher.")

21. *The Dickens World*, 2nd ed. (London: Oxford, 1942). The reviewer of *Little Dorrit* quoted in note 2 expected his readers to recall Psalm 137: "[In] the wilderness of *Little Dorrit* . . . we sit down and weep when we remember thee, O *Pickwick*!" Barnard agrees that in our day "it is not always realised how closely interwoven into [Dickens's] thought and range of reference the Bible and its message are" (*Imagery and Theme*, p. 87).

22. See my analysis of one of them below, under "Humor." For my detailed analysis of biblical references in *Bleak House*, see "The Bible in *Bleak House*" in ch. 5.

23. See also Barnard, p. 57.

24. Alan P. Johnson traces the fire imagery in *Hard Times* as an example of the "diverse" and "consistent and coherently woven strands of imagery" in that novel (*"Hard Times*: 'Performance' or 'Poetry'?" *Dickens Studies* 5 [1969]: 62–80).

25. Clayborough has also noticed this resemblance (*The Grotesque*, p. 241).

26. Nine years earlier Dickens had used another application of steam, the railroad, as an emblem of the Industrial Revolution. The complex attitude he expressed there is consistent with this in *Little Dorrit*. In *Dombey and Son* the railroad track through the wretched slums has opened their miseries to view, "not made or caused them" (20). People did that. — Schwarzbach, however, thinks the railroad is "wholly for the good . . . making mere change into progress" (*Dickens and the City*, p. 110). But writing of the same novel, Herbert L. Sussman says that "the machine usually works . . . to symbolize the union of economic power with moral indifference" (*Victorians and the Machine* [Cambridge: Harvard University Press, 1968], p. 56. See also my article "Staggs's Gardens: The Railway through Dickens' World," *Dickens Studies Annual* 3[1974]: 41–53).

27. 5 June 1860 (N III, 162): my italics.

28. "Dickens and the Fiery Past," *English Journal* 46 (1957): 386.

29. Further on names: *Carton* means an empty box ("un homme du carton" is a nonentity), *Sydney* comes from English mangling of *St. Denis* (compare the pronunciation *senjen* for *St. John*), and according to tradition, France's patron saint, Denis, was beheaded. Steven Marcus has shown how Dickens played with his own initials in naming characters (*Dickens: From Pickwick to Dombey* [New York: Basic Books, 1965], p. 346). That game—especially if unconscious, as Dickens claimed when Forster noticed it in the name *David Copperfield* (F VI, vi, 524)—is biographically interesting, but the sort of name play I have noticed here is more common and more significant for Dickens's themes. — I wish to acknowledge here the valuable assistance of Martha Perrigaud of the Luther College French department in following up my hunch about the name *Darnay*.

30. *Aspects of the Novel* (London, 1927; rpt. New York: Harcourt Brace Harvest Books, 1954), p. 86.

31. Jane Vogel's *Allegory in Dickens* (University: University of Alabama, 1977) argues that Dickens's Christian convictions and his extensive familiarity with the Bible are set forth in exhaustively allegorical patterns that permeate his work; the principal text for her free-wheeling analysis is *David Copperfield*. My view of allegory in Dickens is quite different from hers, and turns on the question of

Dickens's intentions. I do not think Dickens was one "to shoulder the burden of religious allegory," as Vogel says (p. 20), not at any rate in the near-medieval deliberateness and complexity that she traces out. Most of what Vogel charts painstakingly I regard as the unbidden workings of Dickens's imagination, stocked with materials accumulated in reading and in living in nineteenth-century English middle-class culture. — Vogel's assertion of Dickens's deep familiarity with the Bible, however, is substantially supported in her book. That familiarity cannot be ignored in any assessment of his beliefs and values, and influences on his mind and art.

32. I develop this point below, pp. 175–78, and p. 183.

33. See John Holloway's thorough (if not quite accurate) account of the prehistory of the action in the Penguin English Library edition (pp. 896–97). Ross Dabney has similarly straightened out *Oliver Twist* in *Love and Property in the Novels of Dickens* (Berkeley: University of California Press, 1967), p. 12.

34. George Worth shows how the mature David establishes perspective on his young self in "The Control of Emotional Response in *David Copperfield*," in *The English Novel in the Nineteenth Century*, ed. George Goodin, Illinois Studies in Language and Literature, No. 63 (Urbana: University of Illinois Press, 1972), pp. 97–108.

35. Lance Schachterle has noted the same structural technique, and given it the same name ("*Bleak House* as a Serial Novel," *Dickens Studies Annual* 1 [1970]: 220).

36. My article cited above (n. 26) discusses this more fully, pp. 46–50. Cf. Sussman: "With its simultaneous sense of philosophical determinism, social change, and emotional desolation, the train becomes a complex symbol of Victorian life" (*Victorians and the Machine*, p. 56).

37. *The Dickens World*, pp. 21–22.

38. Eric Auerbach, "Odysseus' Scar," *Mimesis*, trans. Willard Trask (1953; rpt. Princeton: Princeton University Press, 1968), p. 6.

39. House's discussion of anachronisms in *Bleak House* (pp. 30–33) needs to be read with Butt and Tillotson's chapter "The Topicality of *Bleak House*" in *Dickens at Work*; furthermore, in saying that "at several points the time-table is congested and obscure" (p. 31) House seems to have missed how Dickens uses time. See "Juxtaposition and Time" in ch. 5 below.

40. I am developing an idea here that I also find (expressed somewhat differently) in Marcus, who says Dickens achieved subtlety and complexity by "embodying within a single work manifold and significantly diversified images of the same kind of person or relation-

ship . . ." (*Pickwick to Dombey*, p. 40). See also Clayborough, *The Grotesque*, pp. 206–10.

41. "Uriah's role as David's darker self" is underscored by the biblical story of David and Uriah (Harry Stone, "Dickens and Fantasy: The Case of Uriah Heep," *Dickensian* 75 [1979]: 100). Some doubles enforce plot parallelism. Edith Dombey and Alice Brown are cousins and look alike, and the point they and their scheming mothers make is one about society: "Were this miserable mother, and this miserable daughter, only the reduction to their lowest grade, of certain social vices sometimes prevailing higher up? . . . Allowing for great difference of stuff and texture, was the pattern of this woof repeated among gentle blood at all? Say, Edith Dombey! And Cleopatra, best of mothers, let us have your testimony!" (*D&S* 34).

42. Barnard's judicious chapter on *Great Expectations* (also to be found in *Dickens Studies Annual* 1 [1970]: 238–51) sets the theme of guilt in a context of hope: Pip's guilt is "not only a consequence of man's fallen state; it is also a precondition of his regeneration" (p. 119). For a more extended treatment of Pip and Orlick, see Julian Moynahan, "The Hero's Guilt: The Case of *Great Expectations*," *Essays in Criticism* 10 (1960): 60–79.

43. *Aspects of the Novel*, pp. 67–78.

44. My point is similar to Geoffrey Tillotson's in *Thackeray the Novelist* (Cambridge: Cambridge University Press, 1954), where he argues that there is no sharp break of style between passages of authorial narration, and the scenic passages: "[T]he presenter of the scene is always seen performing the act of presenting it, treating it as if it were also panorama" (p. 83). — I find some anticipation here of Robert Garis's *The Dickens Theatre*.

45. "Charles Dickens," *Inside the Whale* (London: Victor Gollancz, 1940), p. 69.

46. Other instances occur in *David Copperfield* 14 and 45, *Little Dorrit* I, 24, and doubtless elsewhere. A variety of the same device, used for narrative condensation instead of humor, appears in *Hard Times* I, 14.

47. Margaret Ganz claims Dickens's humor is "perhaps his most striking and original contribution to fiction" ("The Vulnerable Ego: Dickens' Humor in Decline," *Dickens Studies Annual* 1 [1970]: 23). I have to disagree, however, that humor in his later work falls off; Ganz defines humor in Dickens too narrowly.

48. "The Comedy of Dickens," *Dickens 1970*, p. 25.

49. *Imagery and Theme*, p. 45. John Holloway also makes this

point (at more length) about the coherence of the American chapters
with the rest of *Martin Chuzzlewit* ("Dickens and the Symbol,"
Dickens 1970, pp. 69–70).

50. For examples of Dickens's defense, see his prefaces to *Oliver
Twist* and *Martin Chuzzlewit* (quoted in ch. 1 under "Imagination")
and his "Postcript in Lieu of a Preface" to *Our Mutual Friend*.
Dickens's most notorious absurdity, which he stubbornly refused to
concede he had committed, is the death by spontaneous combustion of
Krook the alcoholic junk dealer in *Bleak House*. It involved him in
a controversy with George Henry Lewes which inspired a paragraph
in the next month's number (XI, in ch. 33) and one in his 1853
preface that he repeated (and added to) in his preface for the Charles
Dickens Edition. (There is a small train of essays on the topic; see
especially Gordon S. Haight, "Dickens and Lewes on Spontaneous
Combustion," *Nineteenth–Century Fiction* 10 [1955]: 53–63; George
Perkins, "Death by Spontaneous Combustion in Marryat, Melville,
Dickens, Zola, and Others," *Dickensian* 60 [1964]: 57–63; and Trevor
Blount, "Dickens and Mr. Krook's Spontaneous Combustion," *Dickens
Studies Annual* 1 [1970]: 183–211).

Interest in the phenomenon in the journalism of curiosities is still
not dead. A syndicated article by Brad Steiger, "The Horror of
Spontaneous Human Combustion," appeared in the Decorah (Iowa)
Public Opinion in 1971, describing instances alleged to have occurred
from 1938 to 1970 in California, Florida, Missouri, and England.

51. My choice of *Bleak House* for analysis in the following chapter
owes importantly to my discussions with Lawrence Frank at the University of Minnesota. (For a different approach to the heroine than
mine see Frank's article " 'Through a Glass Darkly': Esther Summerson
and *Bleak House*," *Dickens Studies Annual* 4 [1975]: 91–112.)

Chapter Five

1. "Dickens, it should never be forgotten, is splendidly resistant
to the critical unifying formula" (Collins, "Charles Dickens," in *Victorian Fiction: A Second Guide to Research*, p. 112).

2. Robert Newsom's tentative proposal (which he does not seem
to take very seriously himself) is unconvincing: that "the only way
to explain the double narrative according to even the loosest standards
of 'realism' is to say that Esther has chosen to write in the first person,
but has written an 'other,' third-person narrative to cover those
events of her story in which she has not directly participated" (*Dickens
on the Romantic Side of Familiar Things: "Bleak House" and the Novel
Tradition* [New York: Columbia University Press, 1977], p. 87). Ad-

mitting this proposal admits its opposite too, with equal plausibility. Fortunately "standards of realism" do not govern here.

3. Dickens's narrator treats another close character, Mr. Dombey's manager Carker, the same way (see for example *D&S* 27 and 33).

4. *Critical Heritage*, item 86, p. 295 (James Augustine Stothert in *The Rambler*, January 1854). Reviewers for *Athenaeum* and *Bentley's Miscellany* were less acid about Esther, and respectful of *Bleak House* as a whole (items 81, 84). And Collins says in his headnote, "The feminine ideal represented in Esther was widely admired . . ." (p. 273).

5. *Critical Heritage*, item 85, p. 291 (*Examiner*, 8 October 1853).

6. Stephen C. Gill includes the detail of the pale horse in his concise and suggestive study of how allusions, particularly to the Bible and the Book of Common Prayer, contribute to Dickens's tone and meaning ("Allusion in *Bleak House*: A Narrative Device," *Nineteenth-Century Fiction* 22 [1967]:145–54. On birds, see Cynthia Dettelbach, "Bird Imagery in *Bleak House*," *Dickensian* 59 [1963]: 177–81).

7. Newsom, who has also noticed Esther's Dickensian picture of Turveydrop, is mistaken to say she speaks in the other narrator's voice often (p. 87). The illustration he offers in a note to his remark, Esther's description of a Chancery session in ch. 24, tells against him, as one can readily see by comparing Esther's account there to the anonymous narrator's handling of the subject in ch. 1.

8. *Critical Heritage*, pp. 281, 283 (items 82 and 83).

9. "Social Criticism in Dickens: Some Problems of Method and Approach," *Critical Quarterly* 6 (1964):223; quoted from DeVries's useful collection of criticism and textual and background material in his Crowell edition of *Bleak House*, p. 962. Since DeVries is out of print, I provide the pagination in the original source as well.

10. See n. 25 below.

11. "Social Criticism in Dickens," p. 219; in DeVries, p. 957.

12. "[H]e was very much a man of one idea [at a time], each having its turn of absolute predominance; and this was one of the secrets of the thoroughness with which everything he took in hand was done" (F VIII, ii, 637).

13. Moving Esther's nursing of Caddy, the change in Ada, and Woodcourt's visit to Richard back to chs. 50 and 51 also enables Dickens to end the fifteenth number at a less sensational point than his disclosure of Tulkinghorn's death.

14. There is some fitness, too, in making Tulkinghorn, who was responsible for Jo's harassment, die so soon after Jo dies. The only other place where Dickens explicitly correlates events in different locales is at the beginning of ch. 55; the opening sentence makes chapter time approximately the same as in ch. 54, where In-

spector Bucket discloses Lady Dedlock's secret, and Mlle Hortense's, to Sir Leicester, who suffers a stroke. Lady Dedlock's agony and flight gain tragic irony from this, since we know from ch. 54 that whatever necessity her own pride enforces, the circumstances she fears do not.

15. "Dickens and Mr. Krook's Spontaneous Combustion," p. 186.

16. Williams, "Social Criticism in Dickens," p. 224; in DeVries, p. 963. The younger Dickens, still more journalist than artist, might interrupt the action to make his point in a passage of unlikely dialogue rather than embody it in his characters' minds and flesh: for example, Fagin's explanation to Noah Claypole of the criminals' code (*OT* 43) is a "burlesque [of] the Utilitarian doctrine of enlightened self-interest" (Axton, *Circle of Fire*, p. 94).

17. The lantern, according to Ford and Monod, was "a lantern-shaped structure surmounting the roof, designed to provide ventilation" (Norton Critical Edition, p. 6n).

18. *Commentaries on the Laws of England* (London, 1800), III, 48; quoted by Robert A. Donovan, "Structure and Idea in *Bleak House*," *English Literary History* 29 (1962):180; in DeVries, p. 1019.

19. Ibid., p. 176; in DeVries, p. 1015. It is about many things else too, of course; Collins is surely right to say Dickens has been "subjected to far too much reductive tidying-up" ("Charles Dickens," p. 112). But responsibility is a more useful thing to say it is about than "the interpretation of documents," as J. Hillis Miller writes in his introduction to the Penguin English Library edition (Harmondsworth, 1971), p. 11.

20. My view of Esther runs parallel to W. J. Harvey's in *Character and the Novel* (Ithaca: Cornell University Press, 1965), but the biblical perspective I see her in makes her more than a "moral touchstone [whose] judgments are rarely emphatic but we accept them." She incarnates the force of love in Dickens's design, and because of her *Bleak House* is not finally a novel of despair (see "Theme" below). — I quote from Harvey's chapter as reprinted in Wall's *Charles Dickens: A Critical Anthology*, p. 507.

21. Introduction to *Hard Times* (London: Waverley, 1911); reprinted in Ford and Monod's Norton Critical Edition and quoted from there, p. 334. Shaw takes the view that this insight begins in *Hard Times*, which I think a mistake—it is in Dickens from early on. See the quotations from *Nicholas Nickleby* in n. 23, and near the end of this chapter.

22. Mrs. Jellyby must be wearing the new eyeglasses described in Dickens's 1837 "Report of the Mudfog Association" that let the wearer see "faraway things, such as West-Indian slavery," but not "near things, such as the plight of Manchester cottonmill operatives"

(Axton, *Circle of Fire*, p. 100). — The Borrioboola-Gha project gathers up Dickens's view of a disastrous missionary expedition to the Niger in 1841 and his acquaintance with Mrs. Carolyn Chisholm, founder of the Family Colonization Loan Society; see his 1848 *Examiner* review of a book on the expedition (to be found in the National Edition of 1906–1908 and editions deriving from it), and his letter to Angela Burdett-Coutts: "I dream of Mrs Chisholm, and her housekeeping. The dirty faces of her children are my continual companions" (4 March 1850; Burdett-Coutts, p. 166). Compare Esther's idea of her duty (ch. 8) to Dickens's advice to mission societies: "[T]he widening circle of enlightenment must stretch and stretch . . . until there is a girdle round the earth; but no . . . far-off aim, can make the last great outer circle first. . . . The work at home must be completed thoroughly, or there is no hope abroad." See also House, *The Dickens World*, pp. 86–90.

23. The narrator in *Nicholas Nickleby* talks about what Mrs. Jellyby and Jo illustrate: "There are not a few among the disciples of charity who require in their vocation scarcely less excitement than the votaries of pleasure in theirs; and hence it is that diseased sympathy and compassion are every day expended on out-of-the-way objects, when only too many demands upon the legitimate exercise of the same virtues in a healthy state, are constantly within the sight and hearing of the most unobservant person alive" (18).

24. Ch. 10 of Carlyle's *Sartor Resartus*, "The Dandaiacal Body," ranges Regency fops against the hungry Irish. — I owe this reminder to Louis Crompton ("Satire and Symbolism in *Bleak House*," *Nineteenth-Century Fiction* 12 [1958]:292).

25. Donovan, I take it, sees *Bleak House* about as I do, convinced that it is impossible to trace out causal relations between events that would account for their being there; it is necessary "to define the organization of the book in terms of discovery. . . ." The chief business of the novel, he says, is to show a certain pattern of human relations; "the progressive discovery of that pattern is, then, the 'plot' of the novel . . ." ("Structure and Idea in *Bleak House*," pp. 188–89; in DeVries, p. 1027). Donovan is talking here about events in their narrative relations, however, not in the thematic dimension I have been considering.

26. *Critical Heritage*, p. 272.

27. Ibid., p. 288.

28. Alexander Welsh has noticed how often Dickens refers to this proverb, and speculates whether he meant to allude to it in the well that Nell is shown by the sexton in ch. 55 of *The Old Curiosity Shop* (*The City of Dickens* [Oxford: Clarendon, 1971], p. 206).

29. Dickens protested charges of anti-Semitism vigorously (J 1010–12), no doubt sincerely. But he was capable of the kind of private slur revealed in his direction to Browne to alter the Native in the illustration for *Dombey* VII: "[H]is fashion must be of Moses, Mosesy. I don't mean old Testament Moses, but him of the Minories" (N II, 19). The "excitable Jew" suing for Mr. Jaggers's services (*GE* 20) is given a lisp that marks him as a theatrical stereotype. Perhaps Dickens was making amends for this when he gave the saintly Riah in *Our Mutual Friend* "heroic" English to speak.

30. *Dickens the Novelist*, p. 27. The Dedlock doze, turning commentary into character, is an improvement over Dickens's use of the joke in the first "Mudfog Paper," where the municipality of Mudfog's "little body of legislators, like a larger and better-known body of the same genus . . . are patriotically dozing away in company, far into the night, for their country's good" (*Bentley's Miscellany* [January 1837]; quoted from Axton, *Circle of Fire*, p. 88).

31. *The Dickens Myth*, p. 180.

32. "Satire and Symbolism in *Bleak House*," p. 287n. Sir Leicester's general objection to Wat Tyler is stated in ch. 2. In ch. 28 Dickens mentions "all Sir Leicester's old misgivings relative to Wat Tyler" in connection with the ironmaster, and in ch. 7 he cancelled in proof a sentence which makes the link explicit: "Sir Leicester once remarked, in a moment of inspiration, that he considered the coincidence between the Christian name of his rock ahead the archrebel Tyler, and the surname of the inventor of the steam engine, to have meaning in it" (restored in DeVries, pp. 85–86; in Ford and Monod's textual notes, p. 824).

33. DeVries's edition has a note to this passage in ch. 60 about the variety of agricultural and industrial activity in different parts of Yorkshire today (p. 767).

34. "Satire and Symbolism in *Bleak House*," p. 295.

35. "Social Criticism in Dickens," p. 224 (in DeVries, p. 963); *Dickens the Novelist*, p. 281 (Q. D. L.). — I hope it is clear that I am not claiming the concurrence of either Williams or the Leavises in my entire analysis here of *Bleak House*.

36. Also in Exodus 34:7, Numbers 14:18, and Deuteronomy 5:9.

37. Ch. 31. Dickens does not specify smallpox, but Esther's scarred face suggests it strongly, and she goes blind temporarily, which happened to an acquaintance of Dickens during a severe case of smallpox (P I, 420 and n. 1; letter to Madame Sala [?23 July 1838]. One sometimes wonders if Dickens did not manage to fit most of his experience into his fictive systems—Robert Newsom has even found the name Guppy in a Chancery Commission report of 1826 [*Dickens on the Romantic Side of Familiar Things*, p. 97]).

38. *The Form of Victorian Fiction* (South Bend: University of Notre Dame Press, 1968), p. 33; see also p. 5.

39. Introd., *The Mystery of Edwin Drood*, p. 26. Harry Stone thinks that Dickens's vision of life is secular, not religious: "His imagination is engaged by the strong hidden connections among things, connections that defy rational analysis, but that also defy the rigidities of dogma," and he depicts "a fairytale or anagogic universe, not a theocentric one." The fairy tale, Stone says, "permits Dickens to affirm his sense of the wonder and mystery of life without committing himself to doctrine or dogma" (*Dickens and the Invisible World* [Bloomington: Indiana University Press, 1979], pp. 275, 197; both passages are from the chapter "*Copperfield*: The Fairy-Tale Method Perfected"). — Stone's book brings together much of the work that he has done over the years on Dickens's use of fairy tales; I list two of his individual essays in my bibliography.

40. *Pickwick to Dombey*, p. 68. The whole paragraph is an excellent brief statement. — Norris Pope's *Dickens and Charity* (London: Macmillan, 1978) deals extensively with evangelicalism, since so much of Victorian charity owed to evangelicals, and demonstrates that Dickens substantially agreed with evangelicals on many matters of social welfare—however much he detested the likes of the Reverend Mr. Stiggins (*PP*), the preacher at Little Bethel (*OCS*), the Reverend Melchisedech Howler (*D&S*), the Reverend Mr. Chadband (*BH*), and Mr. Luke Honeythunder (*MED*).

41. Introd., *Drood*, p. 26; also *Dickens*, pp. 296, 144.

42. I am aware that doubts might be raised about Dickens's sincerity, given his audience; but just as strong arguments can be raised on the other side.

43. *The Dickens Myth*, pp. 175–77; "Structure and Idea in *Bleak House*," p. 199 (in DeVries, p. 1031).

44. *The Dickens Theatre*, p. 142; "Will and Society in *Bleak House*," *PMLA* 81 (1961):97 (in DeVries, p. 1056).

45. *Dickens the Novelist*, pp. 118–19 (Q. D. L.).

46. "Social Criticism in Dickens," pp. 216–17; in DeVries, p. 954.

47. *The Form of Victorian Fiction*, p. 30.

48. *Little Dorrit* and *Our Mutual Friend* recapitulate this idea; Daniel Doyce the inventor learns not to expect fair treatment from the Circumlocution Office (*LD* I, 10), and Eugene Wrayburn from Society (*OMF* IV, 16).

49. Quoted above, ch. 4, n. 41.

50. *A Tale of Two Cities* and *Great Expectations* are somewhat out of the mold, but Lucy Manette is a more passive agent of the same type, and in the latter novel Biddy is clearly a relative of these others though not as central to the action. Helena Landless in the

unfinished *Mystery of Edwin Drood* shows signs of belonging to the same order, too. — In *Martin Chuzzlewit* Tom Pinch really fills this role better than Mary Graham, another sign of what Ross Dabney's analysis shows (*Love and Property*, ch. 2): that in this novel Dickens had not yet fully realized his characteristic design.

51. It is perhaps not amiss to recall that a little child shall lead them (Isaiah 11:6).

52. *Dickens and Phiz*, p. 159. The narrowness of the slot through which the light falls, together with the fact that Little Dorrit is a seamstress, reminds me of the needle's eye in Luke 18:25; and Dickens does refer specifically to Jesus's remark there about the trouble a rich man has entering the kingdom of God, in I, 33 (about Mr. Merdle). Furthermore, the theme is the same as in Matthew 7:14.

53. *Charles Dickens: The World of His Novels* (Cambridge: Harvard University Press, 1958), p. 243; cited hereafter as *Charles Dickens*. Cf. Joseph Gold: "Amy is the embodiment of love and devotion and compassion and represents Dickens' ultimate statement on Christianity in the humanist form which he endorsed" (*Charles Dickens: Radical Moralist* [Minneapolis: University of Minnesota Press, 1972], p. 226). Gold also notes the significance of Amy's name (p. 211).

54. "Communication in *Great Expectations*," *Nineteenth-Century Fiction* 18 (1963):180.

55. Marcus thinks that by *Dombey and Son*, Dickens had changed his mind about "the personal as a necessary mode of existence" (*Pickwick to Dombey*, p. 310). I obviously think he is wrong about this; I have argued the case of *Dombey and Son* in my article previously cited, "Staggs's Gardens."

56. "Charles Dickens," *Inside the Whale*, pp. 30–32; "Social Criticism in Dickens," p. 221 (in DeVries, p. 959).

57. Not to argue the cases, but to suggest them: Pickwick has been educated by the end of his story, Oliver is a character conceived only to the depth needed for the story, and so is Smike (Nicholas is hardly the requisite figure of innocence). Nell, I have to agree, is indestructibly innocent.

58. "The Change of Heart in Dickens' Novels," *Victorian Studies* 5 (1961):49, 51, 56. I do not mean to claim Hardy's support for my belief that Little Dorrit and others embody the divine love that enables the heroes to change, since her article does not deal with the question of where the energy to transform the will comes from.

59. Philip Collins wrote in the early 1960s that the image of "a 'dark' tortured Dickens, fundamentally at odds with society . . . has been a useful, indeed an invaluable, corrective; but the corrective has too often become the whole of the picture" (*Dickens and Education*

[London: Macmillan, 1963], p. 210). He says much the same in "Charles Dickens," p. 110 and elsewhere.

60. "Social Criticism in Dickens," p. 222; in DeVries, p. 960.

61. Hardy, p. 63. Gissing's view is in *Charles Dickens: A Critical Study* (London, 1898; rpt. Port Washington, N.Y.: Kennikat Press, 1966, from the Dodd, Mead edition of 1924), p. 89. (Dickens's plan for Boffin is clarified by Fr. Francis X. Shea in "No Change of Intention in *Our Mutual Friend*," *Dickensian* 63 [1967]: 37–40.)

62. *New Yorker*, 21 August 1978, p. 93; in a review of *Tolstoy's Letters*, ed. R. F. Christian (New York, 1978).

63. I draw here on my doctoral dissertation "Evangelicalism in the Novels of Charles Dickens" (Minnesota, 1959), p. 250; cited hereafter as "Evangelicalism in Dickens."

Chapter Six

1. There are touches for the reader at least as early as ch. 44, but Esther's patience is of course most sorely tried just before Jarndyce springs his surprise in ch. 64. Dickens must have had this effect in mind by the sixth number, for Michael Steig, describing Browne's illustration of the little church where Esther first sees Lady Dedlock (18), says that among the details is a memorial inscription "Patient Grissle" on a pillar above Esther where she sits in Boythorn's pew (*Dickens and Phiz*, p. 147).

2. Ada Nisbet's essay surveying the enormous body of writing on Dickens through 1962 runs to more than a hundred pages; Collins's for 1963–74 is very nearly as long. Both are superb. See my bibliography.

3. "Social Criticism in Dickens," p. 220; in DeVries, p. 958. I have referred to this article often, admiring its humane spirit and its rightness of perception very much, especially the premise that critics of Dickens will get him right only as they realize how pieces of Dickens receive their fullness of meaning from the imaginative wholes they belong to. Angus Wilson makes the same point, explaining why he thinks *Our Mutual Friend* does not succeed as well as recent criticism has made out. Modern criticism has worked by abstracting, by examining parts closely. *Our Mutual Friend* is well equipped with good moving parts of the kind modern criticism has attended to, but the whole novel does not come off in a connected reading so well as *Bleak House*, *Little Dorrit*, or *Great Expectations* (*Dickens*, p. 280).

4. Like most critics, I take *Martin Chuzzlewit* as the novel in which Dickens's characteristic vision is first explicitly developed.

5. This paragraph is based on material from my doctoral dissertation, "Evangelicalism in Dickens," pp. 158–62.

6. *Charles Dickens*, p. 81.

7. Forster I, v, 76; 6 October 1859 to Collins (N III, 124–25); for both passages see ch. 1, the textual references for n. 5 and n. 7. The phrase about divine justice is from the letter to Bulwer-Lytton quoted in part in ch. 4 under "Allegory," footnote reference 27.

8. *GE* 29; another such impression strikes Pip a few moments later. Other such moments occur in chs. 32 and 33.

9. *Charles Dickens*, p. 81. I do not find this quality nearly so evident in *Our Mutual Friend*. This seems to me consistent with Angus Wilson's view that Dickens's style there, "a new and brilliant short-hand" devised for this "entirely modern novel—the only novel he wrote of society as it was in the mid-Victorian world," does not entirely suc-ceed, "because its very brilliance, inclining always to the high comedy of, say, Oscar Wilde, suppresses the delicate psychological nuances of relationship which are new to Dickens, yet which he rightly saw were the only sudden illuminating realities in such a sham world" (*Dickens*, pp. 280–81).

10. "A Preliminary Word," *Household Words*, 30 March 1850, p. 1.

11. Frederick P. W. McDowell uses Forster's own phrase nearly to this effect to title the chapter on *A Passage to India* in his admirable study of Forster in this series (New York: Twayne, 1969). According to P. N. Furbank, Forster himself remarked that the *Times* reviewer of Santha Rama Rau's play based on his novel "was absurd to say . . . that [Forster] was writing about the incompatibility of East and West. He was really concerned with the difficulty of living in the universe" (*E. M. Forster: A Life* [New York: Harcourt Brace Jovanovich, 1978], II, 308; Furbank dates the remark 19 January 1960).

12. The next four paragraphs are based on my dissertation, "Evangelicalism in Dickens," pp. 191–94.

13. *Bleak House* 16, 47; *Little Dorrit* I, 12; *Our Mutual Friend* III, 8.

14. "Self-Help and the Helpless in *Bleak House*," in *From Jane Austen to Joseph Conrad*, ed. Robert C. Rathburn and Martin Steinmann, Jr. (Minneapolis: University of Minnesota, 1958), pp. 93–95.

15. As in Betty Higden, the indomitable old laundress of *Our Mutual Friend*, whom Dickens probably modeled on a street character he read about in Mayhew: "Dickens cut away everything about [the Mayhew character] irrelevant or damaging to [his] theme . . ." (see my article "Dickens's *Our Mutual Friend* and Henry Mayhew's *London Labour and the London Poor*," *Nineteenth-Century Fiction* 20 [1965]: 217).

16. See ch. 5, n. 58 above. Some human hearts indeed are un-swervingly evil: the smiling French landlady of The Break of Day knows some people "have no good in them—none ... people who must be dealt with as enemies of the human race" (LD I, 11; the reader will apply her words to Monsieur Rigaud, there present).

17. Cited from a review of *The Inimitable Dickens* (New York: St. Martin's Press, 1970) by Bert G. Hornback, *Dickens Studies News-letter* 1 (Dec. 1970): 13.

18. "Evangelicalism in Dickens," pp. 195–96.

19. 6 January 1856 to Wills (N II, 722); "On Strike" (*HW* 11 February 1854; printed in Ford and Monod's Norton Critical Edition of *Hard Times*, pp. 286–99. The quotation is on p. 289, from the author's conversation with a fellow passenger aboard a train to Preston, called by the author "Mr. Snapper"—a relative, from his opinions, of Mr. Podsnap).

20. Speech to the Administrative Reform Association (27 June 1855), in *Speeches*, p. 203.

21. 30 January 1855 to Charles Knight (N II, 620). Dickens's at-tack on Sir Peter Laurie in his 1850 preface to *Oliver Twist* also shows this "Swiftian parodic logic" (Sylvia Bank Manning, *Dickens as Satirist* [New Haven: Yale University Press, 1971], p. 24. — Clay-borough, however, thinks that Dickens's satire is "altogether less savage than that of Swift" (*The Grotesque*, p. 247).

22. *Charles Dickens: Radical Moralist*, pp. x–xi.

23. *Dickens the Novelist*, pp. 227–28.

24. *Symbol and Image in William Blake*, corrected ed. (Oxford: Clarendon, 1967), pp. 44, 53.

25. Manning, *Dickens as Satirist*, p. 229 (citing Harry Stone's dis-sertation, "Dickens' Reading" [UCLA, 1955], p. 546).

26. For a more comprehensive summary of Dickens's reading and interests than I have given here, see Johnson, pp. 1126–33. The scholarship devoted to Dickens's sources and successors is formidable. Deborah Allen Thomas summarizes a 1971 Modern Language Associa-tion seminar on "Dickens and the Romantic Tradition" in *Dickens Studies Newsletter* 3 (1972): 4–6. In Forster's *Life* see I, i. On Dickens and Hogarth see Q. D. Leavis's chapter "The Dickens Illustra-tions: Their Function," in *Dickens the Novelist*; Harvey, *Victorian Novelists and Their Illustrators*, ch. 3; and Steig, *Dickens and Phiz*, passim. Steven Marcus's first chapter devotes some space to Dickens's childhood reading and other influences on his early career (*Pickwick to Dombey*, pp. 20–30). The two most thorough surveys, of course, are in Nisbet's and Collins's essays: Nisbet's section "Precursors and

Imitators," pp. 106–16, and Collins's "Literary Predecessors, Contemporaries, and Successors," pp. 81–84.

27. *Dickens*, p. 281. Wilson credits Alice Meynell with pointing out that Gibbon's style "had by Victoria's reign become the small change of journalism or public speech." Her essay, "Charles Dickens as a Man of Letters" (*Atlantic Monthly* 91 [1903]: 52–59), is reprinted in *The Dickens Critics*, ed. George H. Ford and Lauriat Lane (Ithaca: Cornell University Press, 1961).

28. Robert Newsom provides a suggestive discussion of sources for things in *Bleak House* in his *Dickens on the Romantic Side of Familiar Things*, pp. 94–97. Butt and Tillotson's chapter "The Topicality of *Bleak House*," which Newsom mentions, is an early study, and one of the best, and Trevor Blount published nearly a dozen articles on topical aspects of *Bleak House* in the 1960s (see Collins's bibliographical essay, pp. 96–97).

29. See ch. 10, "The Collins Myth," in Earle Davis, *The Flint and the Flame: The Artistry of Charles Dickens* (Columbia: University of Missouri Press, 1963), and my article "Dickens' Plots: 'The Ways of Providence' or the Influence of Collins?" *Victorian Newsletter*, No. 19 (Spring 1961), 11–14.

30. "Dickens in the 1960s," *Dickensian* 66 (1970): 176.

31. *Critical Heritage*, p. 570.

32. *Dickens and Education*, p. 210. Two dissenting critics from that period, George Gissing and G. K. Chesterton, still make good though somewhat dated reading. See especially Gissing's *Charles Dickens: A Critical Study* (London: Blackie, 1898), and Chesterton's *Charles Dickens: A Critical Study* (London: Methuen, 1906), both of which have been reprinted often. — For the critical orthodoxy see Nisbet's bibliographical essay, pp. 75–76.

33. See Angus Wilson's excellent discussion in his *Dickens*, pp. 179–80.

34. What I have argued in these last two chapters is I hope adequate to refute William Palmer's main thesis (in "Dickens and the Eighteenth Century," *Dickens Studies Annual* 6 [1977]: 15–39). While I agree that "Dickens' early novels . . . are not unregenerately optimistic, and the later novels are hardly as pessimistic as they have been painted" (p. 16) I do not agree that natural benevolence is what informs Dickens's vision of hope for humankind from first to last.

35. Burdett-Coutts (30 October 1852), p. 211.

36. G. M. Young, "Puritans and Victorians," *Victorian Essays*, ed. W. D. Handcock (London: Oxford, 1962), p. 69.

37. *Dickens*, p. 15.

Selected Bibliography

PRIMARY SOURCES

1.   Individual Works

I omit Dickens's plays and poems, and from his periodical writings I include only those he gathered himself for separate publication, under the titles of those collections. Publication dates are for the run in monthly or weekly parts; first publication in volume form came at the end (except *Oliver Twist* and *A Child's History of England*, as noted). Names following the dates are those of Dickens's illustrators. My main source is Forster's appendix on Dickens's writings.

Sketches by Boz. 1836 (1st ser. Feb., 2nd ser. Dec.). George Cruikshank.
Pickwick Papers. 1836–37. Robert Seymour and Hablot Browne (Phiz).
Oliver Twist. 1837–39 (1838). Cruikshank.
Sketches of Young Gentlemen. 1838. Browne.
Nicholas Nickleby. 1838–39. Browne.
Sketches of Young Couples. 1840. Browne.
The Old Curiosity Shop. 25 April 1840–6 February 1841. Browne and George Cattermole.
Barnaby Rudge. 13 February–27 November 1841. Browne and Cattermole.
American Notes. 1842.
A Christmas Carol. 1843. John Leech.
Martin Chuzzlewit. 1843–44. Browne.
The Chimes. 1844. Richard Doyle, Leech, Daniel Maclise, Clarkson Stanfield.
The Cricket on the Hearth. 1845. Doyle, Edwin Landseer, Leech, Maclise, Stanfield.
Pictures from Italy. 1846. Samuel Palmer.
The Battle of Life. 1846. Doyle, Leech, Maclise, Stanfield.
Dombey and Son. 1846–48. Browne.
The Haunted Man. 1848. Leech, Stanfield, Frank Stone, John Tenniel.
David Copperfield. 1849–50. Browne.

A *Child's History of England.* In *HW* irregularly 25 January 1851–10
    December 1853 (1854).
Bleak House. 1852–53. Browne.
Hard Times. In *HW* 1 April–12 August 1854.
Little Dorrit. 1855–57. Browne.
Reprinted Pieces. 1858. (Contributions to *HW*.)
A Tale of Two Cities. In *AYR* 30 April–26 November 1859. Browne
    (for monthly part edition).
The Uncommercial Traveller. 1860. (Contributions to *AYR*; augmented
    in later editions.)
Great Expectations. In *AYR* 1 December 1860–3 August 1861. Marcus
    Stone (1862 edition).
Our Mutual Friend. 1864–65. Stone.
No Thoroughfare. 1867. (With Wilkie Collins.)
The Mystery of Edwin Drood. 1870. Luke Fildes.

2.   Collected Editions

Dickens had a hand in three: the *Cheap Edition,* beginning in 1847
and continuing until 1868; the *Library Edition,* 1857–59; and the
Charles Dickens Edition, 1867–75, which remains significant today
as the text most editions go back to. It has lost its authority, however,
as evidence has piled up that Dickens's revisions and corrections were
minimal, and that it introduced many new inaccuracies. Chapman
and Hall published all three.

Works. Gadshill Edition, with introductions and notes by Andrew Lang.
    34 vols. London: Chapman and Hall, 1897–99.
Works. National Edition, ed. B. W. Matz. 40 vols. London: Chapman
    and Hall. 1906–1908.
    The two best editions before the Nonesuch. Both printed the
    original illustrations. National was first to include Dickens's con-
    tributions to *HW*, as identified in the *HW* Contributors' Book.
The Nonesuch Dickens, ed. Arthur Waugh, Walter Dexter, Thomas
    Hatton, and Hugh Walpole. 23 vols. Bloomsbury: Nonesuch
    Press, 1937–38. The original illustrations. Vols. 10–12 contain
    the best collection of Dickens's letters to that date (see below).
New Oxford Illustrated Dickens. 21 vols. London: Oxford University
    Press, 1951–59. Introductions by various hands. The original
    illustrations. No letters, plays, poems, or *HW* writings identified
    by Matz. Widely available, relatively inexpensive.
The Clarendon Dickens. General editors, Kathleen Tillotson, James
    Kinsley, and John Butt. Oxford: Clarendon Press, 1966–. Titles
    issued to date: *Oliver Twist,* ed. Tillotson (1966); *The Mystery*

of Edwin Drood (Margaret Cardwell, 1972); *Dombey and Son* (Alan Horsman, 1974); *Little Dorrit* (Harvey Peter Sucksmith, 1979); and *David Copperfield* (Nina Burgis, 1980). Number plans, original illustrations, narrative introductions, descriptive lists of editions, appendixes, textual apparatus. Definitive.

3. Noteworthy Single Editions

Hard Times and *Bleak House*, ed. George H. Ford and Sylvère Monod. Norton Critical Editions. New York: W. W. Norton, 1966 and 1977 respectively. Authoritative texts and textual apparatus; useful background and critical material. *Bleak House* includes some of Browne's illustrations. By far the most useful editions of these titles in print. (*Great Expectations*, ed. Edgar Rosenberg, is due next.) Available in paperback.

Penguin English Library editions deserve special mention for generally superior critical introductions, good selection of original illustrations, useful annotation, and relatively modest price. No uniform policy on texts; about half follow the Charles Dickens Edition, but with an eye on earlier ones.

The Speeches of Charles Dickens, ed. K. J. Fielding. Oxford: Clarendon Press, 1960. Supersedes all previous editions; none other is worth using.

Charles Dickens: The Public Readings, ed. Philip Collins. Oxford: Clarendon Press, 1975. 21 items, 17 printed from Dickens's prompt copies as last revised by him. A model of editorial judgment. Annotated; authoritative introduction and headnotes.

Charles Dickens' Uncollected Writings from "Household Words" 1850–1859, ed. with introduction and notes by Harry Stone. 2 vols. Bloomington: Indiana University Press, 1968. Dickens's work identified from such evidence as *HW* Contributors' Book, manuscripts, proofs, letters, and style. Careful and discriminating; illuminating introduction.

4. Letters

The Letters of Charles Dickens, ed. Walter Dexter. 3 vols. (10–12 of *The Nonesuch Dickens*). Bloomsbury: Nonesuch Press, 1938. First important collection, superseding the selective, censored, and jumbled edition by Dickens's daughter Mary and sister-in-law Georgina Hogarth, though not entirely free of its failings.

The Letters of Charles Dickens. General editors, Madeline House, Graham Storey, and Kathleen Tillotson. The Pilgrim Edition. Oxford: Clarendon Press, 1965–. 5 vols. to date, through 1849. Definitive;

planned to include every letter known to exist. Awesome annotation.

Letters from Charles Dickens to Angela Burdett-Coutts 1841–1865, ed. Edgar Johnson. London: Jonathan Cape, 1953. Published in the United States as *The Heart of Charles Dickens, as Revealed in His Letters to Angela Burdett-Coutts*. Boston: Little, Brown, 1952. The most complete selection from this important correspondence; indispensable until superseded by the Pilgrim Edition.

SECONDARY SOURCES

1. Bibliography

Dickensian 66 (1970): 102–82. Four important articles by eminent Dickens scholars: Sylvère Monod, "The Age of Chesterton" (1900–20), Michael Slater, " 'Superior Folk' and Scandalmongers" (1920–40), Philip Collins, "Enter the Professionals" (1940–60), and George H. Ford, "Dickens in the 1960's." A survey of readers' and critics' concerns and attitudes as well as a listing of important studies.

NISBET, ADA. "Charles Dickens." In *Victorian Fiction: A Guide to Research*, edited by Lionel Stevenson. Cambridge: Harvard University Press, 1964, pp. 44–153.

COLLINS, PHILIP. "Charles Dickens." In *Victorian Fiction: A Second Guide to Research*, edited by George H. Ford. New York: Modern Language Association of America, 1978, pp. 34–113. Complementary essays; in line with the planned scope of these volumes, Nisbet covers Dickens studies through 1962, Collins 1963–74. Extremely valuable: categorically arranged, comprehensive, readable. (This bibliography is generally indebted to both.)

GOLD, JOSEPH. *The Stature of Dickens: A Centenary Bibliography*. Toronto: University of Toronto Press, 1971. Covers critical and biographical studies 1870–1968 (with some 1969 items), chronologically listed in four categories: studies of Dickens, studies of individual works, dissertations, and works including significant mention of Dickens or on topics relevant to Dickens studies. Very useful.

Dickensian. Annual selective survey of Dickens studies; reviews and reports on Dickens conferences and exhibitions.

Dickens Studies Newsletter. "The Dickens Checklist" in each number lists current publications of all kinds. (Several reviews in each number.)

PMLA and *Victorian Studies.* Annual bibliographies.

2.   Biography and Criticism: Basic and Seminal Works

Emphatically not to be overlooked in this category: the richly anno-ated Pilgrim letters.

FORSTER, JOHN. *The Life of Charles Dickens.* Rev. ed. 2 vols. London: Chapman and Hall, 1876. (Original edition 3 vols., 1872–74).
JOHNSON, EDGAR. *Charles Dickens: His Tragedy and Triumph.* 2 vols. New York: Simon and Schuster, 1952.
WILSON, ANGUS. *The World of Charles Dickens.* New York: Viking Press, 1970.
  Forster's revised text, organized into twelve books, is the text of all modern editions. Best-known and most frequently cited by scholars and critics (though not generally available): the one edited and annotated by J. W. T. Ley (London: Cecil Palmer and New York: Doubleday, Doran, 1928), with much useful information, but outdated by subsequent biographical discov-eries. Forster's book is indispensable, a heroic effort, now more and more highly regarded; see Davies, in *Dickens Studies Annual* 7 (1978). Johnson's book is just as indispensable, incorporat-ing masses of scholarship into rich and lucid narrative. The 1977 revised and abridged edition (Viking Press) is inferior. Both Forster and Johnson include criticism; Wilson is better than either. His is the best one-volume treatment of Dickens's life and work: informed, sensitive, judicious, eloquent: "a Dickens akin to the common reader's" (Collins).
ORWELL, GEORGE. "Charles Dickens." In *Inside the Whale.* London: Victor Gollancz, 1940, pp. 9–85.
WILSON, EDMUND. "Dickens: The Two Scrooges." In *The Wound and the Bow.* Cambridge, Mass.: Houghton Mifflin, 1941, pp. 1–104.
HOUSE, HUMPHRY. *The Dickens World.* London: Oxford University Press, 1941.
  Three critics who, taking Dickens seriously on this side of the post-Victorian trough of regard, helped set the revival going. Orwell described Dickens's moral vision, getting many details wrong but the large impression right; Wilson saw Dickens's work as generated by his "wounds" and gave strong impetus to the view of Dickens as a symbolist; House studied the refractions of Victorian actualities in Dickens's vision of his age. All still de-cidedly worth reading.
FORD, GEORGE H. *Dickens and His Readers: Aspects of Novel-Criti-cism since 1836.* Princeton: Princeton University Press, 1955.

BUTT, JOHN and TILLOTSON, KATHLEEN. *Dickens at Work*. London: Methuen, 1957.
Ford's study, more of readers than of Dickens, gives excellent perspective on Dickens by examining readers' assumptions and values: a history of critical taste (Nisbet). Butt and Tillotson's pivotal work turned attention to Dickens's workshop, demolishing the idea of him as improvisor and opportunist. The debt of my study is obvious.

3. General Studies, Special Topics, Background

My criterion here is usefulness for the general reader. I regret many omissions; my defense is lack of space.

ALTICK, RICHARD D. *Victorian People and Ideas*. New York: W. W. Norton, 1973. Compact, readable, sound; things modern readers of Victorian literature need to know about the period.

BARNARD, ROBERT. *Imagery and Theme in the Novels of Dickens*. Bergen, 1971; rpt. Oslo: Universitetsforlaget, 1974. Perceptive and lucid; good discussion also for other structural elements.

CLAYBOROUGH, ARTHUR. *The Grotesque in English Literature*. Oxford: Clarendon Press, 1965. Approaches concept of grotesque through psychology; good Dickens chapter ranges well beyond grotesquery.

COLLINS, PHILIP. *Dickens and Crime*. London, 1962; rpt. Bloomington: Indiana University Press, 1968.

———. *Dickens and Education*. London: Macmillan, 1963.
Highly informative about their respective topics in the Victorian period as well as about Dickens. Both richly documented, with extensive bibliographies.

———, ed. *Dickens: The Critical Heritage*. London: Routledge and Kegan Paul, 1971. Contemporary reviews and critiques, extensive introduction, headnotes, appendix on Dickens's sales (by Robert Patten, a preliminary sketch of his detailed record in appendixes to *Charles Dickens and His Publishers*).

COOLIDGE, ARCHIBALD C., JR. *Charles Dickens as Serial Novelist*. Ames: Iowa State University Press, 1967. First major work on this topic, mapping its dimensions, discussing broad considerations, categorizing and tabulating narrative materials.

DABNEY, ROSS H. *Love and Property in the Novels of Dickens*. Berkeley: University of California Press, 1967. Traces Dickens's developing conception of mercenary marriage through the major novels. Concise, readable, perceptive.

DYOS, H. J., and WOLFF, MICHAEL, eds. *The Victorian City: Images and Realities.* 2 vols. London: Routledge and Kegan Paul, 1973. 38 essays, one by Collins on Dickens and London, many others on topics relevant to Dickens. Profusely illustrated.

FIELDING, K. J. *Charles Dickens: A Critical Introduction.* 2nd (enl.) ed. London: Longmans, 1965. (First pub. 1958.) The best short account of Dickens's life and works, according to both Nisbet and Collins.

————. "The Critical Autonomy of 'Great Expectations,'" *Review of English Literature* 2, no. 3 (July 1961):75–88. Excellent for perspective on various critical approaches to Dickens.

GARIS, ROBERT. *The Dickens Theatre.* Oxford: Clarendon Press, 1965. About theatricality in Dickens, and narratorial rhetoric; latter part ranges more widely. Provocative.

GILL, STEPHEN C. "Allusion in Bleak House: A Narrative Device." *Nineteenth-Century Fiction* 22 (1967):145–54. Perceptive analysis of how allusions to Bible and Book of Common Prayer inform Dickens's style.

LEAVIS, F. R. and Q. D. *Dickens the Novelist.* London: Chatto and Windus, 1970. Dickens from *Dombey* through *Great Expectations* (omitting *A Tale of Two Cities*), plus a chapter on the illustrations. Superior criticism alloyed with critical warfare.

MANNING, SYLVIA BANK. *Dickens as Satirist.* New Haven: Yale University Press, 1971. Dickens's mixed mode of fiction, the rhetorical strain directed to satire and the dramatic to novelistic realism, with *Hard Times* the first novel to fuse the two strains. Astute and lucid; valuable also on Dickens's women.

MARCUS, STEVEN. *Dickens: From Pickwick to Dombey.* New York: Basic Books, 1965. The early Dickens, in a good context of Victorian intellectual and cultural history.

NELSON, HARLAND S. "Staggs's Gardens: The Railway through Dickens' World." *Dickens Studies Annual* 3 (1974):41–53. Dickens's complex attitude toward modern industrialism, seen mainly in *Dombey and Son*, with correspondences in *Hard Times* and others.

NISBET, ADA B. *Dickens and Ellen Ternan.* Berkeley: University of California Press, 1952. The basic account of a relationship now generally accepted as fact (but still highly controversial in 1952).

PARTLOW, ROBERT B., JR., ed. *Dickens the Craftsman: Strategies of Presentation.* Carbondale: Southern Illinois University Press, 1970. Centennial collection of essays from various critical angles, all by well-known Dickens scholars and critics; title indicates the common assumptions and concerns. Cf. Slater.

POPE, NORRIS. *Dickens and Charity.* London: Macmillan, 1978. Charitable activities Dickens took interest in. Well grounded in primary sources; importance of evangelicalism documented throughout. Extensive bibliography.

SLATER, MICHAEL. *Dickens 1970*. London: Chapman and Hall, 1970. Centennial collection of essays, all by English critics, not all Dickens specialists. Topics of somewhat more general interest than in Partlow.

STANGE, G. ROBERT. "Expectations Well Lost: Dickens' Fable for His Time." *College English* 16 (1954):9–17. Concise and incisive explication and thematic analysis, incidentally setting *Great Expectations* in perspective of French nineteenth-century novels of education.

STEIG, MICHAEL. *Dickens and Phiz*. Bloomington: Indiana University Press, 1978. Detailed analysis of Browne-Dickens collaboration; argues Browne contributed more to it than generally believed. Informative; cf. Leavis.

STONE, HARRY. "Fairy Tales and Ogres: Dickens' Imagination and *David Copperfield*." *Criticism* 6 (1964):324–30. The fearsome old man David sells his jacket to on his way to Dover: Dickens's method of embodying fairy tale themes in his fiction. (One of several such essays by Stone.)

————. "The Genesis of a Novel: *Great Expectations*." In *Charles Dickens 1812–1870*, ed. E. W. F. Tomlin. New York: Simon and Schuster, 1969. Explores with tact and judgment the sources in Dickens's experience.

SUTHERLAND, J. A. *Victorian Novelists and Publishers*. Chicago: University of Chicago Press, 1976. Good overview, with examples of particular novelists and novels (chapter on Dickens as publisher of other novelists in *AYR*).

THALE, JEROME. "The Imagination of Charles Dickens: Some Preliminary Discriminations." *Nineteenth-Century Fiction* 22 (1967): 127–44. Enumerates modes of description in Dickens and the uses made of description, particularly symbolism; good illustrations, illuminating general observations.

WELSH, ALEXANDER. *The City of Dickens*. Oxford: Clarendon Press, 1971. About London in Dickens, but also about "values and purposes expressed by the English novel" (Welsh); uses the tradition of the earthly and the celestial cities to develop thoughtful and provocative analysis of Dickens.

WILLIAMS, RAYMOND. "Social Criticism in Dickens: Some Problems of Method and Approach." *Critical Quarterly* 6 (1964):214–27. Centrally important premises about how Dickens's social criticism is to be understood.

Index